ACCLAIM FOR *HOUSE OF LIES*

"Simultaneously hilarious and frightening . . . an insider's view of the burgeoning world of corporate consulting."

—*Fort Worth Star-Telegram*

"How candid and merciless Martin Kihn is about big-time management consulting! Such a funny and disturbing cautionary tale! And how fortunate that all new MBAs can now read HOUSE OF LIES and prophylactically disillusion themselves before they charge out into this particular circle of corporate hell."

—**KURT ANDERSEN, creator of *Spy* magazine and host of NPR's *Studio 360***

"His reconstructed dialogue from within his (unnamed) firm and from his time serving clients is alone worth the price of admission, as is his relentless taunting (by name) of McKinsey, Deloitte & Touche, and others."

—*Publishers Weekly*

"At the end of the day, it's hard to figure out who the bigger suckers are: the fresh young MBAs . . . or the corporate clients. With HOUSE OF LIES, we can rest assured that there are guys like Martin Kihn out there to pull off the emperor's clothes."

—**JOHN ROLFE, coauthor of *Monkey Business***

"No activity avoids Kihn's scathing pen, including his highly critical analysis of business books."

—*Booklist*

"*Dilbert*-philes everywhere will hail HOUSE OF LIES as a revolutionary screed. Kihn uses his MBA-honed skills of analysis to dissect the very industry that purports to do it best . . . all with devastating wit and clearheaded insight into the secrets 'they' don't want you to know."

—**TAD LOW, creator of *Pop-up Video***

HOUSE OF LIES

How Management Consultants Steal Your Watch and Then Tell You the Time

Martin Kihn

WARNER
BUSINESS
BOOKS™

NEW YORK   BOSTON

Grateful acknowledgment is given for permission to reprint front the following: *Leadership in Administration: A Sociological Interpretation* by Philip Selznick, copyright © 1957 by Philip Selznick, published by University of California Press, Berkeley, CA; and *Competing by Design: The Power of Organizational Architecture* by David Nadler, Michael Tushman, and Mark Nadler copyright 1997, published by Oxford University Press, Inc., New York, NY.

Warner Business Books
Warner Books

Time Warner Book Group
1271 Avenue of the Americas, New York, NY 10020
Visit our Web site at www.twbookmarkmark.com.

The Warner Business Books logo is a trademark of Warner Books.

Printed in the United States of America

Originally published in hardcover by Warner Books

First Trade Edition: March 2006
10 9 8 7 6 5 4 3 2 1

The Library of Congress has cataloged the hardcover as follows:

Kihn, Martin.
  House of lies : how management consultants steal your watch and then tell you the time : a true story / by Martin Kihn.
      p. cm.
    ISBN 0-446-57656-5
  1. Business consultants. I. Title.
  HD69.C6K515 2005
  658.4'6—dc22

                                                              2004009523

Cover design by Diane Luger
Cover photo by John Lamb/Getty Images
Book design by Giorgetta Bell McRee

ISBN: 0-446-69638-2
ISBN-13: 978-0-446-69638-8

for Julia

Author's Note

House of Lies is not a lie. I only wish that it were. Management consulting is a notoriously secretive industry, for reasons both good (protecting clients) and bad (avoiding blame)—and it is not without its vindictive revenge monkeys. So I have changed every name, disguised every client, created composites of individuals, and guarded sensitive information.

—M. K.

When Thales was asked what was difficult, he said, "To know one's self." And what was easy, "To advise another."

—DIOGENES LAERTIUS, *Thales*

❑

Management Consultants: They waste time, cost money, demoralize and distract your best people, and don't solve problems. They are people who borrow your watch to tell you what time it is and then walk off with it.

—ROBERT TOWNSEND, *Up the Organization*

Prologue

My Story: Your Story:
Her Story: History

I will not use that pronoun again. If you have ever been in group therapy, you will know why. "Own the feeling," they say, and "Don't say *you*." Using *you* is a way to distance oneself from the first person—from oneself, in fact. After you have spent two years and more in consulting, that is exactly what you want to do.

So here you are, avoiding the truth. Every word that follows is the truth, by the way, though in the manner of good truth it will seem preposterous. You hope it seems preposterous, since that is much more entertaining than the alternative.

Now, let us start with a little story. This is not a *Liar's Poker* for consulting; this is a little story about consulting. Think of it like that.

Here is the story: It starts in a meeting.

"One hundred thousand . . . one hundred ten . . ."

You are sitting across a table from two of the more powerful people—for the moment—in nonnetwork television.[1] You know they are two of the more powerful people—for the moment—in nonnetwork television because, well, because they told you that they were. Plus, you have worked for them for

---

[1] I.e., cable, pay-per-view, local TV—everything that isn't ABC, CBS, NBC, Fox, UPN, the WB, or PAX (if any/all of them still exist as you read this).

more than two years now and have become used to that phenomenon known as the show-business ego. In truth, you have
developed a bit of one yourself.

Which brings you to this conversation.

"One hundred fifteen . . . eighteen . . ."

You are sitting at Twenty-ninth Street and Broadway in
Manhattan, close enough to Madison Square Garden to be
afraid of it. Nine floors down, past the bubbling piranha-filled
fish tank, the Internet porn empire on the eighth floor complete with working first-aid station, the sad-looking family
watchmaking company with its superannuated helpmeets, the
absent-present doorman and his wrestling magazines—nine
floors down is a store with a block-letter sign saying: NOT OPEN
TO THE PUBLIC. DEALERS ONLY. This store sells the world's
cheapest tuxedo shirts and gaudy pimp costumes and socks
and underwear. You are not a dealer. You shop there all the
time.

One of the two more powerful people on Twenty-ninth
Street looks up from his calculator. (He has been tapping for
a while now.)

"One hundred nineteen . . . one-twenty . . ."

This is your boss, the man who hired you. He was two years
behind you at Yale, yet he is much more famous, powerful,
and outgoing than you. Let's call him Nosering. His success
does not really bother you, however, because he is a cable ad-
dict and a mess and has been fired from every job he has ever
had. He has a kind of nasty habit of hitting on female superiors and then getting sued for harassment. And anyway, you
really like him.

Next to him is his partner, Cereal Boy, so named because
he appeared on a box of cereal as a kid (great smile, golden
curls) and still looks as he did then.

Nosering looks up from his frantic calculations, gives a
freighted nod to CB, then says, "We can offer you one-
twenty . . . one-thirty . . . if you stay."

What he appears to be saying—$125,000, on average, per

year, plus the same benefits—would double your current salary as head writer on the program Nosering dreamed up two years ago in a methadone stupor. the program you and your staff of four have written since the beginning: the program that more than tripled the (admittedly pathetic) ratings of its predecessor and was called "beguiling" by the *New York Times*, "addictive" by the *New York Post*, and "snarky" by the *New Yorker*. It got you personally onto the *Today* show, which your mother watches, and she has treated you differently ever since.

You have no intention of staying. "What would that—what would I have to do?" you ask.

"Just what you're doing now—"

"And," adds Cereal Boy in his disconcertingly boyish voice, "you'd have to help out with *Pop Quiz*."

"What's that?"

"*Pop Quiz*," says Nosering, "is a show; this pilot we did, just got picked up by VH1. We have a one-season commitment from them."

"Starting when?"

"Starting last week."

"Do you have a staff? Have you hired anybody?"

"We're trying to hire you."

You are no math genius, but you've always been facile with numbers. So you calculate . . . one season, which is thirteen episodes, 22 minutes each, say 260 or so minutes of original material in maybe three months . . . something isn't working here . . .

"How big is the budget? For writers?"

"Don't worry about that," says Cereal, who actually never seemed to like or appreciate you. (He went to Colgate.)

"What I'm saying is—would I have to do this show *alone*?"

"Uh, yeah. But you can do it."

"What's the concept?"

This is where Nosering really excels: the pitch. He jumps forward, feeling you slip away, knowing, in fact, you have already slipped. You slipped six months ago when you asked him to write you a recommendation for business school; you slipped when he did it. He lays out the concept with an enthusiasm for the truly mediocre that fills you with a kind of awe. His continuous torrent of hideous, unthinkable ideas— a show where nuns are hooked up to lie detector machines and asked if they're attracted to pro wrestlers, a show where a real small town is filled with hidden cameras and a fake gang of terrorists pretends to take it over—is either pure genius or, perhaps, something else.

Nosering's pitch doesn't really make any sense: None of them do. His point is that, somehow, it will be easier to write *Pop Quiz* than it is to write your current show (which you will continue running, by the way). You know something he doesn't. You know that he thinks *Pop Quiz* will be easier to write than your current show not because it *will* be easier to write than your current show, but because Nosering is like all powerful people in this industry in having very little firsthand knowledge of, and almost no respect for, writing.

You wait a moment, looking at the walls covered with eight-by-tens of pop culture icons from the 1970s and 1980s. Mr. T. Angie Dickinson. Flock of Seagulls. The Fix. Tattoo. Ed Asner. Pamela Sue Martin. They were not hung in irony. This is the late 1990s, and irony has been dead since 1991.[2]

Without irony, you say, "What you're asking is impossible."

"One hundred thirty, Marty," says Nosering, already saying good-bye. "What else do you need?"

"If this were ten years ago, it'd be different. But now I'm"— here you state your age. "I want to go to business school."

"But *why?*"

"I'm interested in business."

"You can do business here. We do a lot of business. You can help Bob with the books."

---

[2] The official end date of the Age of Irony was August 1989, when now-defunct *Spy* magazine ran a cover story with Chevy Chase asking rhetorically "Isn't It 'Ironic'?"

"I don't want to be an accountant."

"Do you even *know*," asks Cereal with some belligerence, "what you want to do?"

You've thought of this, of course. You are getting way too old to be working for guys like this. You don't take drugs, are married, live in Queens. You are tired of being broke, of working with kids who want to go to L.A. and think your show is stupid and beneath them, kids with no discernible talent whatsoever whose every single word has to be rewritten late, late at night and yet who somehow from the depths of their pot-fueled pea brains find a method *to look down upon you.*

You say, "I want to be a management consultant."

Cereal looks like you stole his favorite bowl.

Nosering just exhales and stands.

"What the *hell*," he asks, "is that?"

Part I

Top-Tier
Management Consulting
for Absolute Blithering Idiots

Part I opens the kimono with a hairy entrée into the global megaverse of top-tier management consulting, with these observations:

1. *A bloodcurdling litany of **betrayal** and **alcoholism***

2. *Behind-the-scenes truth about a very powerful, very **short man***

3. *A lighthearted look at global consulting behemoth **McKinsey** and its resemblance to a certain Renaissance warmonger*

4. *Why your child will never go to **Harvard Business School***

5. *A consulting hymnal and songbook*[3]

---

[3]Omitted due to lack of content.

1

The Rainmaker &
the Perfect Storm

No storm is *perfect,* of course—but the Rainmaker tries to brew one. He leaves in his wake such a tsunami of chaos and pillage that the total bill, in dollars and careers, will still be soughing through the eternal adding machine for years and years to come. The Rainmaker tears the heart out of your firm and crushes and pulverizes its testicles at a time when it has left itself for dead. But the wicked always make their way when business is gang-raping the good; this is how they prosper.

Here is the story of a nasty little man and how he rips the soul from his department, pulls its lungs out at the roots, and leaves behind a legacy of victims so vast it is as though a mini-junta storms the halls and opens its grab bag of tricks—people with lives to lead . . . people with *children,* for God's sake, with *babies* . . . are tossed into the street—your *mentor* is tossed into the street—your *mentor's mentor is hurled onto a rotting pile of ex-consultants . . .*

But let's not exaggerate. Let's stick to the truth.

This is the story of the Rainmaker and how he almost—but not quite—destroys your firm.

You took a personality inventory in the tenth grade and it turned out the career you are most suited for is maître d'.

So it is always with some envy that you follow the maître d'
at an exceedingly lavish restaurant—such as this one, in the
Roosevelt Hotel on Fifty-fourth Street near Madison
Avenue—to your table, where the Rainmaker sits in a small
booth at the back with a nervous-looking man with a tan. The
tanned man stands immediately to make way for you. It's all a
bit confusing.

"Marty," says the Rainmaker, not rising. "This is"—he says
his name, which you forget before he's finished—"he used to
work at the firm." He's an older man, so he must be toiling as
they say "in industry."[4]

There is some shuffling as you negotiate one another and
the greetings and the seats. Then you settle and the perfect
service descends with an exquisite cup of coffee. The
Rainmaker's coffee cup is turned upside down.

"None for you, sir?"

"I don't drink coffee."

He is famous for this: not drinking coffee.

"So"—he turns to you—"I've been hearing good things
about you. Very good. How are you liking it here? Oh, excuse
me a second—*Tina!*—"

Suddenly, he's gone from the booth and projectiled across
the precious ivory Aubusson to a slightly frightened-looking
woman who just walked in. They shake hands, briefly, nodding—is it Tina Brown?

Now, the Rainmaker is an important man and, like most
important men in New York City, quite short. You tower over
him, and you have never been accused of gigantism. He has
absolutely no hair and always smiles and dresses impeccably
in Thomas Pink shirts and the subtlest of suspenders, but,
because of a certain schlubbiness of build, despite fastidious
behaviors and careful courtesy, he always seems a bit rum-
pled up. He looks up at people but he doesn't look *up*—

---

[4]"Industry" refers to any company that is not a professional services firm, e.g., Time
Warner, Microsoft, and GM.

rather, *in* . . . deep *in* . . . like the world's most oily general practitioner with the vaguest sense of space. Squinting and smiling, underwhelming at first, and at second and third, but so so powerful you cannot imagine how he got that way—but there he is: a powerful, powerful man with a heart like a cuff link.

You liked him immediately. He is the reason that you joined the firm. It is he who is King of All Media (Consulting Division), the best-known media consultant in the world and perhaps—not perhaps, *definitely*—the best-known *consultant* consultant in the city of New York. No consultant is truly famous, of course, but the Rainmaker tries . . . oh, how he tries.

He was profiled in the *New York Times Magazine,* of all places; he was profiled in *GQ.* He is quoted all the time, and he wrote a book. There you were, working at your cable TV show, so miserable you couldn't sleep at night, and you picked up a book on the New Releases table at the Sixteenth Street bookstore and read the inside jacket copy:

> [The Rainmaker] is a co-founder of Consultants Against Poverty and is one of the best-known growth gurus in the entire media universe. In the 1970s he single-handedly started up and led the Media and Entertainment Group at [your top-tier firm]. Under his visionary guidance, this group became the undisputed thought leaders in the business of entertainment. Reporting to the man they affectionately call "Mr. Media" is an international team of more than two hundred professionals based in the cities of New York, Los Angeles, Chicago, Mexico City, Singapore, and Rome. A graduate of West Point, [he] lives with his family in Greenwich, Connecticut, and Palm Beach, Florida.

Oh, to be one of those two hundred consultants! To travel to Shanghai and scurry around doing—well, you weren't quite sure what, exactly, but how hard could it be? It's media and entertainment, industries erected upon a pile of steaming crap. It seemed a dream come true, but did you have what it took, did you really have it?

It turned out, yes, you did.

It also turned out, no, the jacket copy wasn't purely accurate. In the old British parlance, it was a "tissue of lies." Seventy-five words—how much is creative writing? When you first read them, you were not in a position to know. Now, you are. Let's take another look:

> "[The Rainmaker] is a co-founder of Consultants Against Poverty and is one of the best-known growth gurus(a) in the entire media universe(b). In the 1970s he single-handedly started up(c) and led the Media and Entertainment Group(d) at [your top-tier firm]. Under his visionary guidance, this group became the undisputed thought leaders in the business of entertainment(e). Reporting(f) to the man they affectionately call "Mr. Media" is an international team of more than two hundred professionals(g) based in the cities of New York, Los Angeles(h), Chicago, Mexico City, Singapore, and Rome. A graduate of West Point(i), [he] lives with his family in Greenwich, Connecticut, and Palm Beach, Florida(j)."

a. Probably true.
b. Of the six major global media companies, he had been hired by only two.
c. There was another cofounder, who was forced out of the firm under mysterious circumstances a few years earlier.
d. There was no Media and Entertainment Group— the division was called Communications, Media & Technology (CMT), and Communications (mostly Telecom clients) was the largest category.

e. Probably true, if you don't count financial consultants (e.g., Allen & Co.) and technology consultants (e.g., Accenture).
f. The other twenty-five global partners in the division would not appreciate his taking ownership of their entire staff.
g. The biggest whopper of the bunch—at its peak, in late 1999, his retinue comprised three partners, three principals, four senior associates, about eight associates, and three consultants. Since senior associates, associates, and consultants were in the "general pool" and weren't allowed to align to any one practice, he shouldn't really count them as his. And since all partners are part owners of the firm, they don't work for anyone, no matter how short. So instead of two hundred, there were more like three people working directly for him.
h. A tiny office dedicated almost entirely to aerospace, not media.
i. Unlike every one of his colleagues, the Rainmaker does not have an MBA; his degree from West Point is a BS.
j. True.

The results can be summarized as follows:

❏	Number of words:	75
❏	Number of statements of fact:	18
❏	Percent that are probably true:	28
❏	Percent that are partially true:	11
❏	Percent of whoppers.	61

This is not encouraging.

And there appears to be one even bigger stretch lurking here. It turns out that the book that bears his name and his alone, the one with the dubious jacket copy—well, he didn't even write it. You know this because you met the guy who did. A popular twenty-eight-year-old Latin American fast riser, he was known around the firm as a total media junkie and introduced to one and all as "the guy who actually wrote" the Rainmaker's book. This was not a secret at all. And why should it be? The Rainmaker, after all, should spend his time doing what he does best: making Rain. Chores like banging on a keypad, looking up old articles, researching, writing, and consulting—those were for, as Leona Helmsley used to say, "the little people."

You bought the book, that day on Sixteenth Street. You read it on the train to Queens, where you had been exiled by the necrotic gentrification of the entire island of Manhattan, which daily seemed to become more and more a theme park where the theme was no and the price of entry was a sweet trust fund. You read the book and wondered how a book so simply written could be sold in the grown-ups' section; it seemed to be for curious fourteen-year-olds. But you were to be forgiven. After all, it was your first business book.

Since it changed your life, this book "written by" the Rainmaker, you dwelled on it far longer than it warranted. You wrote a little summary, for future reference. You never know, you thought, someday you might actually have, say, breakfast, with the Rainmaker . . . at the Roosevelt Hotel in midtown, say . . . and is that Tina Brown? No . . . no, after all, it isn't Tina, but a larger woman with a remarkably similar honker.

"I just had to say hello," squeaks the Rainmaker, rising onto the balls of his feet.

"Of course, of course—"

"Have you seen any of Tommy lately?" Tommy . . . Tommy . . . Motolla? Middelhoff? Both were . . . *extremely impressive* references . . .

Faux-Tina shakes her head and glances over at you.

"What about Heinz? Klaus? I had Klaus in last week for a—

oh my gosh, I'm keeping you from your breakfast? You want to join us—I'm with—no, okay, okay . . . I just wanted to say hello . . ."

"See you soon, Monty"—and she's ushered off.

You think: *Monty*? Is this a trick of acoustics, a simple misinformation of the sound waves? The Rainmaker's first name is not Monty. Not even close. Hmmmm . . .

As he sits across from you, missing not a beat, not a snippet of a beat, eating nothing at all while you dip into your ill-chosen waffles and links, you think—not for the last time—*What balls.* Tina-esque didn't even know him.

"That was [her name]," he says softly. "She's the new head of strategic planning at Bertelsmann." So it was Middelhoff, after all.

"Have you guys worked together?"

"Of course. I've known her for years. Tommy and I flew to Germany together recently—it's amazing what he's doing to that company. You know, he has that European charm. They live on a farm in the middle of nowhere."

Tommy Middelhoff took over a family business, European publishing and music giant Bertelsmann, which started out as a printer of Bibles and hymnals, in 1998. A fortuitous (or brilliant) investment in AOL at a strategic moment gave him so much money he (and others) began to think of Mr. Tommy as something of a seer and a visionary, or at least a very rich man with cash to burn on the Internet.

"Are you working with them now?" you ask.

The Rainmaker has that irritating Hollywood habit of looking over your shoulder while he is supposedly in conversation with you—looking around, like a vigilant dog, always surveying—this is a working breakfast, it turns out, and the work is not with you. He's up again—"Excuse me . . ."—and he's gone.

The waffles are really quite delicious, now that you have time to spend with them.

Complete Summary of [Book Title]
"written by" the Rainmaker

❑   People want to have fun.
❑   Products and stores need to make themselves fun.
❑   There are a lot of products out there.
❑   People like big stars.
❑   Hire a big star to push your product.
❑   Businesses need hit products.
❑   How do you get these? Have hit ideas.
❑   Also, it helps if a group of "cool" people love your product.
❑   Then you have a hit!

Your host is behind a pillar now, up and down on the balls of his feet, buttonholing a man who looks vaguely but not entirely like Harvey Weinstein at Miramax. He is a very ugly man, whoever he is. The waffles have a kind of silk butter texture, and they slide across the palate like vanilla pudding. You love vanilla pudding. Your watch tells you that twenty minutes have gone by—67 percent of your allotted time with the little man. He seems in no hurry to cram it full of belated welcome to your new career . . .

To be a management consultant is to be always on the defensive. Clients attack your credentials—*What do you know about my business?* Competitors attack your experience—*They're really just an IT implementation shop.* Colleagues attack your analyses, your logic—*There's no way inventory at the stores can be higher than inventory in the warehouses; check your math.*

But these besiegings are as nothing compared to the utter, irredeemable, unknowing cruelty of one's parents, siblings, and friends when they ask—as they always do—when they ask, quite coolly but not without a certain challenge to their tone: *So what do you actually do?*

This is a wickedly difficult question—one that cannot, in truth, be answered.

We will not try to answer it here, at breakfast, but it is appropriate to point out an odd paradox at the heart of top-tier consulting. A paradox that explains how a man like the Rainmaker can cause so much damage to a seventy-five-year-old firm with ten thousand employees and a global presence.

This paradox consists of two apparently contrary statements of principle:

Principle One: One is promoted from associate to senior associate to principal based *solely upon one's ability to analyze data and present these analyses.*

Principle Two: One is promoted and rewarded thereafter *solely upon the basis of one's ability to sell the firm's services.*

The less-than-subtle transformation these principles imply can be described visually as follows:

1   2   3   4   5   6+
Years with the Firm ---▶

The firm would come to deny it later, but it almost fired the Rainmaker at many points during his struggling early years. He was not a rising star. He was not anyone's idea of a partner. He was tagged and tagged again as a potential counsel out. He was warned—it became an annual ritual, this warning of the Rainmaker. Principle One dictated that he should not have made it past associate. Why? His analytical skills were unimpressive; he never went to business school and didn't particularly care for numbers. Value a company?—hah, he couldn't even find a company's 10-K[5] with an SEC code and a map. It's not that he was dumb; old-timers would tell you he just did not have *It*. *It* was missing. *It* and Rain were unacquainted.

Inertia, some shrewd ass work,[6] a Lady Macbeth in the bedroom back home, and/or some awareness of just how vast these family connections were—something somehow saved him. Reluctantly, far later than his peers, he was promoted to principal by the slimmest of majorities on the principal committee.

The next day he showed up for work, and everything was different. It must have been like flying through the cloud cover into the bright silver sky. He was a principal now—and the rules changed completely, just like that.

Principle One didn't matter anymore *at all*. His progress at the firm would now be determined entirely by Principle Two.

Overnight, the Rainmaker was born.

Within two weeks, he had found his first client—a friend of his mother, who was a disc jockey or a lawyer or an heiress to a radio distribution fortune, it's not clear which. A small job, maybe $500,000, but it got him some notice. The extension, sold the following month, got him more notice. Within six months he had earned the firm maybe $3 million and the partners thought *All rightie then* and invited him into their ranks. No one had ever spent less time as a principal. But it didn't matter—he was selling. He was fulfilling the requirements of the job, and then some. The analytics—well, there were people to do that somewhere. He had other missions to accomplish . . .

Like breakfast. You finish up your waffles, skip the links. No—you have a link. If you have waffles, what's the point of pretending to diet by avoiding actual food? The damage is

---

[5]Annual report filed with the Securities and Exchange Commission (SEC) and required of all publicly held companies; it includes detailed financial and operating information, though never quite the information you're looking for.

[6] I.e., butt kissing.

done. Your time with the great man is done. A shadow approaches from behind, and you turn to see if it's him. No—he's still behind the pillar, shaking hands with pseudo-Harvey. The shadow belongs to an apologetic maître d' trailed by a good-looking young guy in a suit. He seems kind of familiar.

"I'm sorry, sir, are you dining with [the Rainmaker]?" asks the maître d'. It's disconcerting, but his accent is American.

"Yeah."

"I'm afraid this gentleman is his eight-thirty."

"I'm sorry?"

"His eight-thirty. Appointment."

The young guy steps forward. "And you're his eight o'clock?"

"I guess I am. Or I was. Do you want to sit down?"

You get the feeling that they're kind of losing patience with you. You're just not getting it—and then you do.

The Rainmaker has scheduled at least three breakfasts at half-hour intervals, of which you are—were—the second. A rinse of disappointment coats you, makes you cold. You look down where your waffle platter was: It's gone.

"The service is tremendous," you say, making way for Mr. Good-Looking.

"I'm sorry?"

"The waffles . . . are tremendous."

It is your curse in life that nobody ever understands your dry brand of sarcasm, which in fact is simply truth. And the Rainmaker himself appears, unruffled, almost hopped up, actually, by the commotion. Bodies coming and going; acts occurring. This must be his life—how utterly, entirely, completely exhausting.

"Let me know how you're doing," he says to you or to the maître d'. And after all, who are you?

Twelve days after your breakfastlike meeting with the Rainmaker, you find yourself working rather late at the office. The economy is not good at this time, and the consulting

business across the board is showing obvious signs of cyclical-
ity. Where a week before you started work in May 2001 there
had been a client staff of 250 at your firm, there are now
about 200. It is two months later. Were you to annualize such
a rate of shrinkage, the firm would be gone by November.

But it isn't gone, and you are working late. It is midnight
or quarter after, your wife has gone to sleep, most of the other
teams have gone home. You sit in your office, all alone.
Occasionally, one of the doomed summer interns will call you
from the nineteenth floor, and even these calls are not un-
welcome. The summer interns are nice kids; you don't like to
be all alone.

You scroll through your interview notes, wondering. Like
many questions consultants are asked to help answer, the one
perplexing this company—ToyCo, we'll call it—is simple.
One customer accounts for over 90 percent of its revenues. It
is beholden to a fast-food giant. This scares the company,
which is quite profitable but has been forced to give up more
and more margin to its big customer over the years. The customer is hardly stupid and knows exactly how far it can push
ToyCo before it will be forced to pick up its paint kit and exit
the business. For various reasons, the customer does not want
this to happen; maybe it likes the toys. But it faces sharehold-
ers of its own, and cost pressures, and it is not making life easy
for ToyCo one bit.

You need some decaf. The Chicago office has eliminated
its free gourmet coffee caddies from the pantries, but New
York has priorities: Coffee caddies first, jobs second. So the
jobs are gone, but the caddies remain. Right now, you are
glad. You stand and genuflect in the direction of the MetLife
Building, then begin the perc walk.

The halls are quiet, but not utterly so. Only on a Sunday
morning, early, is a consulting firm entirely unoccupied.
Partners are never present late at night, but associates and
summers often are. In professional services, there is a well-

known inverse correlation between length of tenure and time spent in the office.

Which is why it is so surprising to find a partner at the coffee caddy. He pushes the little self-brewing pouch into the slot and closes the door with a *click*, stepping back.

"Hi there," you say.

He gasps—*whaaaha!*—and hikes back.

"God. Sorry," you say.

It is the Rainmaker, of course. He looks at you, not returning your smile.

"What are you doing here?" he asks.

"Working. Late. How about you?"

He doesn't answer. The machine sputters and spits its last, and then he takes the warm cup in silence.

You stand there.

Later, around 2:00 or 2:15, when you're going back for another cup of decaf, you see him again. He's carrying a large box in the direction of the elevator bank. Through the glass doors leading to the elevator lobby, you can see another box. It sits under the call buttons.

The next day, you get in around 8:30. At 9:17 an e-mail is sent firmwide from the New York office's managing partner. It reads:

```
From: "Van der Brink Hymen"
To: NYC User List

Colleagues:

As many of you are already aware, [the
Rainmaker] has resigned his position
within the firm, effective immedi-
ately. The CMT partnership is working
with the firm's global leadership to
ensure that the transition is seam-
less. The commercial assignment com-
```

mittee has scheduled a meeting July 30
to determine permanent leadership re-
sponsibilities within the practice. In
the meantime, Mr. Raymond Faulkes will
be handling ongoing engagement rela-
tionships for the media and entertainment space.

Should you have any questions or con-
cerns, please do not hesitate to reach
out to the CMT partners at any time.

Thank you, Hy

The e-mail fails to mention the most salient point, the one
that transformed the Rainmaker's abrupt departure from a
major blow to a form of ritual humiliation.

He has left to join McKinsey.

2

Consultant,
Heal Thyself

Business books are boring. They are bloated compendiums of half-baked ideas committed in fourth grade prose. Their purpose is to transform a commonsense concept or two into a consulting career through the catalyst of hollow jargon.

By the time you graduate from business school—two years or so after the scene on Twenty-ninth Street with two of the more powerful people in nonnetwork television—you have read dozens of business books and been impressed by only one.[7] The one you were impressed by is not the source of the following quote, which echoes long-established managerial wisdom regarding the mood of an organization in the midst of a necessary layoff:

> For those involved, the transition from the current state to the future state represents a frightening journey from the familiar to the unknown. It's only natural that people will have a host of concerns. . . . All those concerns boil down to the same question, the one that every person worries about as soon as he or she hears of an impending organizational change: "What does this mean for

[7]See Part IV: Analyze This: A Minute History of Classic Consulting Texts.

me?" The longer that question is left unan-
swered—and the less complete the answer—the
greater the stress and the anxiety people will experience. Before long, behavior and job performance start to suffer. . . . *They may engage in
irrational and even self-destructive acts.* More typically,
they find subtle, passive ways to derail the new
processes and procedures.[8] (italics added)

Moreover, the literature is entirely harmonious on one
point of execution: *When you're throwing people out into the
streets, do it quickly.* Do not linger (perhaps to savor the moment?) . . . do not dawdle and hesitate and allow rumor and
fear to rule the day. Make a clean break, suck it up, move on.
This makes common sense; this makes human sense; this
makes sense sense. Everybody with an MBA—everybody in
your top-tier management consulting firm, which you joined
today—knows this. They learned it. They *feel* it. It's the right
thing to do.

But they do not *do* it.

You start work on a Monday, five days after graduating
from Columbia Business School, and three days after your
firm chose to fire *every single consultant on the staff.*

A word of explanation. *Consultants* at your firm are—
were—not what nonconsultants think of as consultants—that
is, people with MBAs and dreams of being partner. Such
MBA-wielding partner-dreamers, such as yourself, are called
associates.[9] Those former souls called consultants were
younger people with degrees from good colleges who typically spent two to four years at the firm and left for business
school; many were sponsored by the firm and returned as as-

[8]David A. Nadler and Michael L. Tushman, *Competing by Design: The Power of
Organizational Architecture* (New York: Oxford University Press, 1997), 186.
[9]The ranks are associate, senior associate, principal, and partner; the entire process takes
six to eight years, with only one in five who enter the pipeline as associates coming out
the other end as partners. Most leave by choice (until recently).

sociates. Because there were fewer of them across the industry, competition was stiffer; they tended to be, though quite
young, very smart, very dedicated, and, at half an associate's
salary, very cost-effective.

You go out to lunch with another associate, an affable guy
who got out of Columbia a year ahead of you. He's purely
media; media consulting is what you want to do, it's why you
joined this firm and only ever wanted to work here. It has the
best media-consulting practice in the world. You go to lunch
at a Japanese restaurant around the corner from your offices
near Grand Central Station, talking small. He's a small fellow,
this associate. His words are small, his feet, his hands—they
punch the air in front of him as though he's making room for
something—and he's bald, much balder than you remember,
and heavier. Everyone is heavier. It's a heavier firm.

"We've been waiting for this—we knew it was going to happen for a couple months now."

"*Months?*"

"Yeah—they didn't tell us anything"—they, in most contexts, is a shortened form of *the partners*—"but we could kind
of tell."

"How so?"

"The deferrals, for one." They'd been deferring new associates since January. The take-it-or-leave-it offer was wait six
months to start work or take $15,000 and say good-bye. The
economy was so dismal now, the alternatives so untasty and in-
frequent, most everyone opted for time off. You weren't deferred because you were the *only person* who volunteered to
start in May, without even a week off after school. You were
the only person, and the HR woman—like most women, actually—liked you and seemed to know you needed money
badly. (Your wife is a musician.)

"What did they say about that?"

"Nothing much. They had a conference call, we all called
in. They said there were some capacity issues in North
America and they were going to make a few adjustments so

they didn't have to do anything later on—anything like lay-offs, they meant."

"They said that?"

"I'm not sure they said it exactly, but it was definitely presented like a onetime thing. That was that—"

"Then they fired all the consultants."

"They fired all the consultants—maybe twenty people. Not so much."

"Is that it then? Now it's over?"

The waiter comes up and you let your friend order for you. You are very bad at Japanese food. Like all recent B-school graduates you revere the Japanese to the point almost of idiocy—but you are very, very bad at Japanese food. Whatever he orders, you are not going to like. Silence follows the waiter's retreat, and that whiff of mild elation, the one that comes with knowing you've got something coming to you.

He says, "I don't think so."

"What?"

"I don't think it's over."

"Why?"

"I heard some things. There's a ton of people on the beach. Louis told me they're something like eighty percent below plan for the year." Louis was a big media partner—an Ohioan with an oddly Southern cadence and a pals-y manner—he was known as *the friendly partner.* There was only one.

"Eighty percent?"

"Or something. It's really bad."

"Maybe the plan's too high."

Your friend lowers his voice, glances around. You would get used to this combination, repeated like a dance: Glance around, lean forward, lower voice, eyes forward. "The number I heard was twenty more," he says. "By June."

"June is like—it's like two weeks away."

"That's right."

"Who told you this?"

"Can't say."

You leave it there—it was probably Louis, which scares you some. Louis is a partner; he would most definitely *know.* Which meant that number twenty was more than Japanese food chitchat and chin music. Which meant the lowest value-add people would be chopped first . . . who adds less value than a guy who just (last week, in fact) graduated from business school?

This line of thought is unproductive. It represents your universe for the next eighteen months.

Two more things: (1) your friend chose wisely, even the little orange gooey thing with the skin on it was quite tasty; and (2) he is right about the month, wrong about the number—it is twenty-four.

He is one of them.

"One thing I need to stress to you—this is a onetime thing . . ."

This is the conference call. You all call in. By now you all know what has happened—have known, in fact, for weeks, largely because of people like Louis who tend to talk too much, or feel too much. And despite the fact that all twenty-four were from the same office on Park Avenue near Grand Central Station in New York City—despite the fact that it's a Friday, and so every single person on the call is probably at this moment within four or five floors of one another in the exact same building[10]—despite this, the partners do not choose to meet downstairs in a private room off the first-floor restaurant called The Club, a room perfect for mass executions. They choose to talk by phone.

"We need to size the professional staff for the business that we actually have, not the business that we want. I need to stress now that this is a—not a sign that we're in trouble. Don't believe what you read on vault.com.[11] Our balance sheet is very strong—we don't have any

---

[10]Consultants generally work at the client site Monday–Thursday and return to their home office on Friday.

[11]Vault.com is a Web site with a little information and a lot of gossip about a host of companies, posted anonymously by employees or opinionated observers.

debt. What we're hearing about our competitors is . . . not good. They're having capital calls on the partners. One of them [he names the firm] had to borrow money at near-junk interest rates. We heard that from the bank because we had to go in to meet some seasonal working capital issues—at our A++ interest rate. Like I said, we have no debt. But again, the business is not where we would like to be. The market is soft right now . . . very soft. Everybody's struggling. Where you go on calls, you used to see one or two competitors—now there're four or five. The whole market's got some capacity issues because of all the over—overexpansion in the dot-com boom. We just went—we went crazy . . ."

Now you recognize the voice. It spoke to you at one of the sixteen gatherings the firm held at Columbia during recruiting season. You kept your name tags, hung them on the wall in your kitchen, out of pride. This voice is the skinny, tall, beautifully dressed partner with the goofy look on his face who does Telecom and, despite being based out of the New York office, lives in Arizona. That explains the conference call.

While he expands, you check out vault.com. As usual, it's rather clearly accurate.

- ❏ Cnsltngsucks: "Twenty-four people got whacked this week. They called them in from the clients & told them."
- ❏ Newsboy2: "I got deferred until January. Did they say anything about us deferrals?"
- ❏ Insider27: "Hah! Hohohohohohoho . . ."
- ❏ Doomsayer: "That firm is going bankrupt. Bain is in trouble too. Their [*sic*] borrowing at junk bonds, or they can't borrow at all."
- ❏ Cnsltngsucks: "Deferred people are getting whacked, probably in August."
- ❏ Newsboy2: "How do you know this?"

Of all the questions dispatched during this difficult, difficult time rife with know-it-alls and real-smelling bullshit, Newsboy2's is the one that never gets answered. Never can get answered. For that is the nature of rumor.

Managing Organizational Change:
Best Practices . . . Managing the Transition

1. Develop and communicate a clear image of the future state
2. Use multiple and consistent leverage points
3. Use transition devices
4. Obtain feedback about the transition state; evaluate success[12]

As the call continues, you come to believe you are not the only one who has lost interest in this particular "clear image of the future state." Your image is pretty clear right now: homeless, friendless, alone. No wife, no job, nothing but a buddy named Jimmy Beam and another named Johnnie Walker.

An MBA used to mean something in this world—when was that?—how little you know, how little. You went through the Columbia brochure with your wife, and she crossed off jobs you weren't allowed to take because they started under six figures. The only options left were investment banking and consulting. You remember T. S. Eliot said the result of all running away was you end up in a shitty room in some stupid town in a gray undershirt, smoking Winstons, a single GE gray lightbulb dangling from a cord over your gaunt and aging frame, and you're singing the song that has no verses, just one endless chorus: "Why . . . why me? . . . why me? . . ."

[12]Nadler and Tushman, *Competing by Design*, 195.

On the other hand, there are advantages to massive layoffs. These can be grouped into two divisions.

<u>Division One</u>—Real estate: You get more space. When you started, four weeks ago, you were put into a room on the twenty-fourth floor the size of your bedroom out in Queens. There were five desks in this room, a monstrous filing cabinet, and four associates. Five desks, four associates—already the benefits were showing, for that fifth person (there had once been a fifth person) was one of the ill-fated consultants. Her name plate made the migration of the departed: It was taken off the door and put on the side of the behemoth filing cabinet. This is an example of "subtle, passive ways to derail the new processes and procedures" (whatever they were).

So for four weeks there are four people, five desks. The desks have massive steel cabinets bolted to them at about eye level. Your colleagues peck at their firm-issued IBM ThinkPad 60s, keeping their heads down as though avoiding ray guns. Maybe it is your background in the arts, but you can't help but notice these big cabinets block all light, sun, *life*, and a breathtaking view of Grand Central and the MetLife Building over it, so you ask Saint, the Caribbean office fellow with the religious medal and the big smile, to remove the bolts, take it away.

The day this happens you feel the brutal slap of "subtle, passive" conformity in the professional services firm. Saint comes in with his team and they unbolt the cabinets. It's a Friday; your three colleagues, unusually, are all at their seats at the same time. The process is loud, but it is not the volume that disturbs them. They look at you—at *you*, not the far more interesting extrication process unfolding in their midst—they look at you as if you had asked Saint to please take a pair of pliers and remove your penis.

"*What* are they doing?"

"They're taking out the cabinets."

"Taking them *out*. You mean taking them *out*?"

"It's going to be great," you tell them. "There's gonna be a lot more light. And it's better feng shui."

"I can't believe you did that," says a guy who, in four weeks, has said nothing else.

"You'll thank me later."

As usual, you feel your essence has been squandered on these clowns. There is scant room for light in the consulting firm in the midst of a massive round of layoffs that manifestly is not—is most definitely, absolutely not—a onetime (two-time, now) thing.

But back to the conference call. It winds down, and you take solace in your lovely, completely unobstructed view of the MetLife Building. There is a highway slanting up that feeds into the building like an IV tube and is always filled with cabs. MetLife is kept alive by a continual infusion of the juice of yellow cabs.

"... *Okay, so what we need you to do now is to put this behind us. We have no debt, we're positioned for growth, we're sized now perfectly for the market that we're in. We have some capacity to meet the turn-around, when it comes—and we already see some signs of that. This is a onetime thing—it's painful, but it's over. We'll work with our new alums to help in their transition. Okay.*" There is a rather long pause. You think you can hear the sound of a wild coyote baying across the Arizona sands.

"... *Now let's get back to work.*"

As the dust settles this morning and the latest victims become known, you learn that the quiet guy—the one who disbelieved your redecoration scheme—is gone.

Division Two: This is obvious, right? It's schadenfreude.

After the conference call, you decide to have lunch with your mentor. At least you think he's your mentor; the firm has restructured so many things so many times over the past two years, the mentorship situation is entirely clear to no one. Since your mentor also isn't sure he is your mentor—he's heard something about *four-man mentor teams* somewhere—he's not sure he has a mentoring lunch budget, so he's not sure he can pay, so you necessarily make your way to someplace cheap. The cheapest decent place happens oddly enough to be the same Japanese restaurant you were taken to your first week.

It is now week five. You may have changed, but the restaurant has not.

You let your mentor order.

Now you make a mistake. A quite conscious mistake.

You say, "You know the last time I was here?"

"Huh . . ."

"I came with"—here you say the name of the little bald fellow, the one who was axed. He was Mr. Media, and your mentor is known as something of a Mr. Media himself. Like all the media specialists at the firm, he knows almost nothing about show business you cannot learn from a 10-K. Your mentor was seen as something of a friend to the bald man; they would stand side by side at recruiting events (they both went to Columbia). This was pretty funny, since your mentor is an enormous man, someone whom people ask quite seriously if he ever played professional football. He always says, "I tried—but they don't take Jews in the NFL."

"Huh . . ."

"Why was he let go? I thought he was great." Indeed, that was the rumor: he was *great.*

"Well, it's complicated . . ."

"I don't understand this. There are a lot of people worse than him."

"Not anymore."

"Sure there are. It seems almost as if they picked people at random."

"Not quite. It was pretty careful."

"That guy was *always* working. He went to every recruiting thing. He helped everyone who asked him. I saw those decks he put together—they looked really good to me. What's the criterion they're using?"

"He was behind on some development needs."

"Which ones?"

"You have to compare him to his peers—it was a ranking order and on some of the dimensions he was coming up a little short."

"How short? Which ones?"

Your mentor seems a bit uneasy; you have been pushing too hard. It occurs to you he might have been in the room when the decision was made. Associates are not allowed in any room when any decision is made, but your mentor is a senior associate on the verge of becoming a principal. He may have been in the room. He may have been in the room and said something like what he says right now, a thing that startles you and grows you up:

"Look, Marty, he was the last one on the list"—so the big guy *was* in the room after all—"it was really close. It isn't easy at all to pick these people, but the partners give us a number, you know, we, we have to honor it." He speaks in a low, slow, almost soothing voice; it starts to rise. "What happened was we had some other people on the list but they had defenders, there was some partner or principal in the room who spoke up for them. We went alphabetically. We got to him and no one spoke. I should have said something but—I don't know. It was hours we'd been in there, I was hungry."

The food arrives. It looks disgusting.

You say, "You guys were best friends."

"Come on, Marty."

"Are they gonna do it again? Next appraisal cycle?"

"I don't think so. This is one time and move on."

You realize that your mentor, who seemed so genuine and *real* when you worked at the firm last summer—the only Mr. Media with these qualities—has changed too. He has been sucked into the House of Lies.

You trust your instincts. Your instincts are good. Every instinct and outstinct you've got is telling you it's *not* over, not over *at all*, not slightly, not hardly, not yet.

Later, you can't believe how naive you were.

Some consulting statistics:[13]

❑ Number of top-tier management consultants in the U.S. in 1990: 22,000
❑ Number in 2000: 61,000
❑ Number at the end of 2002: 49,000
❑ Revenue of the top ten consulting firms in 1990: $5 billion
❑ Revenue in 2000: $14 billion
❑ Revenue in 2002: $10 billion
❑ Average starting salary and bonus for associate at top-tier firm in 2000: $120,000
❑ Average in 2002: $100,000
❑ Average professional staff reduction at top-tier firms, 2001–2003: 25–30 percent
❑ U.S. unemployment rate during the Great Depression: 25–30 percent
❑ Average time laid-off U.S. worker spends looking for new job: 3–4 months
❑ Average time ex-associate spends: 10–12 months
❑ Number of years average U.S. worker stays at same firm: 3.7
❑ Average for management consultant: 1.6
❑ Average for statistician: 3.3

---

[13]U.S. Bureau of Labor Statistics; company reports; author analysis; "top-tier management consultants," in this context, include only those primarily engaged in strategy—as opposed to IT or HR—consulting.

From *Strategic Consulting*[14]

"Top Ten Reasons Companies Give for Hiring Fewer Consultants"

1. Overall economic conditions
2. Mandate to control external costs
3. Professional fees not in line with value received
4. Bad experiences in the past
5. Services not required at the present time
6. Relying more on internal expertise
7. Developing internal strategic capabilities
8. Never used consultants
9. Hiring from the same talent pool
10. Lack of up-to-date industry knowledge

---

[14]*Strategic Consulting* magazine does not yet exist.

The McKinsey Problem—
or, the Mind of Machiavelli

Immediately after starting work at McKinsey, the Rainmaker alters the Web site he created for the purpose of promoting his book. All remotely positive references to your firm are excised or replaced with neutral mentions of a former place of business. The firm itself is named nowhere. Its two-hundred-strong team of loyal consultants are commended nowhere. Aristotle is said to have believed rats could appear spontaneously from within a pile of dirty rags. Overnight, your firm becomes that pile.

At times, indeed, he appears almost ungrateful. His revised "Biography" starts like this:

> Prior to coming to the firm, [the Rainmaker] spent ten years heading the Media and Entertainment Group of a *mid-sized consulting firm.* (italics added)

Two observations come to mind. One notes how the Media and Entertainment Group so proudly described mere months before on his book jacket has magically become the Entertainment, Media and Internet Group—a retrospective rechristening that may not in fact have been wise, given the state of the Internet. But no matter: Internet it is.[15] More insultingly, your firm has been demoted in a way that begs for argument. McKinsey is not in fact "the world's largest consulting firm," unless one is judging size by the inflation of egos within its walls.

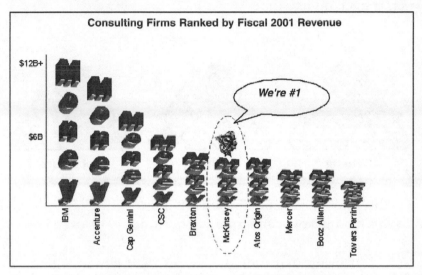

Sources: *Business Week*, July 8, 2001; *Consulting News*, August 2002.

Some might argue that what the Rainmaker *really* meant to say was not that McKinsey was "the world's largest consulting firm" but simply that it was the firm that derived the greatest amount of revenues from *strategy* consulting, as opposed to the more lucrative but plebeian work done by the IBMs of the world, which focus primarily upon information technology and the integration of corporate computer systems. This is a fair point, although even industry-standard sources such as *Consultants News* are unable to come up with consistent estimates of exactly how much any firm makes from pure strategy—as opposed to pure IT—consulting. Estimates for

---

[15]Two years after his departure, the firm still has no Internet Group.

McKinsey range from over 50 percent[16] to less than 40 percent.[17] Such distinctions are never easy to make.

If a certain workhorse company's 2001 revenues *from strategy consulting alone* were bagged up and set beside McKinsey's and those of the formidable number three, Accenture, they would stack up like this:

Deloitte   McKinsey   Accenture

Who is looking distinctly midsize, now?
The Rainmaker's "Biography" continues:

> . . . During that time, he has worked closely with some of the world's biggest companies internationally and *currently oversees more than 200* professional consultants worldwide. (italics added)

There it is again—his staff of two hundred! Did they follow him, every one, to the world's largest consulting firm, there to work upon the Internet? Why, no, they didn't—not a single person. You see them now, dejectedly swinging their résumés around the halls of your firm, by turns falsely optimistic and waiting for the ax drop. No one followed him, yet still he found 200 to command! There is apparently a rule of thumb in the military that war-fighting units under a single field commander cannot be larger than 200, and that 150 is more manageable. Does the Rainmaker know this rule?

[16] *Consultants News,* August 2002.
[17] *Business Week,* July 8, 2002.

... Fortune is a woman, and if you wish to keep her under it is necessary to beat and ill-use her; and it is seen that she allows herself to be mastered by the adventurous rather than by those who go to work more coldly. She is, therefore, always, woman-like, a lover of young men, because they are less cautious, more violent, and with more audacity command her.

—MACHIAVELLI, *The Prince*

It's hard to combine being a consultant with being a mother.

—MCKINSEY MANAGING PARTNER,
RAJAT GUPTA (2002)

You are not a young man when you interview with McKinsey. You are thirty-five, an age when Machiavelli himself was on the verge of leading his own small army on a success-ful campaign into Pisa. Your only armies are the foot soldiers of doubt parading through your brain. You are an artist, not a player; you are entering a world of players. It was always quite clear to you that you would never work at McKinsey. Yet still you endure the ego-deflating gut punch of an interview in their New York offices.

It is a truth universally known that every man and woman of ambition who applies to business school applies to Harvard Business School. Likewise, every MBA candidate of ambition who wants to go into consulting applies to work at McKinsey & Company. Both truths are universally known, but they are never admitted. In a business school environment with mini-mal laws of decorum and scant emotional sense, there exist two inviolable rules:

1. If someone is not attending Harvard, do not ask
   the person if she applied to Harvard.
2. If someone is not working at McKinsey, do not ask
   the person if she interviewed at McKinsey.

These rules stem not from some atypical fear for another person's "feelings," of course. Nobody cares about those. No—these rules are in place for the entirely pragmatic reason that the answers are known a priori.

There is cruel logic at work here. The personalities you meet in the halls of business schools are not racked with self-doubt. These are not people who wonder "Does he really love me?" or "Do I have what it takes?" They have their moments, of course, but those come later; they are hardly concurrent with the business school experience. For two years, B-school bodies are inviolable; while attending, they are transcendent; and when applying, they are superbly confident. Who is Harvard to tell her she is not good enough? Who is McKinsey?

And although business is in many real ways the most democratic of our institutions, at the level of higher education and hiring it is so elitist as to become a parody of old England.

So you apply to Harvard—though you will never admit it—and do not get in. You interview at McKinsey.

Your first encounter with the Machiavelli of consulting firms is in the course of a group "information session" on the second floor of Uris Hall at Columbia Business School. These sessions, much beloved during the dot-com era, are supposed to be a way for students to gain information about the host company from a regular employee or two—sometimes the marketing companies might send an HR rep, but that's why nobody wanted to work at a marketing company. Eight or ten first- or second-year students will sign up and gather in a room with the one or two regular employees and ask questions, the sole purpose of which is to impress. The employees take notes. Even *they* don't listen to their answers. There is

nothing outrageous about a large firm one cannot learn from
a few moments with their annual report, a visit to their Web
site. There is nothing an employee can say that will alter a single student's desire or lack of desire to work there.

No—the unstated but overt purpose of these sessions is to
give you a chance to ask such a *great* question that you are cat-
apulted onto the "closed list,"[18] given an offer and granted
the luxury of refusing it.

McKinsey has always seemed to have a halfhearted attitude
toward your school. Until the dot-com era inaugurated years
of high turnover and a pressing need for fresh blood, some
years they didn't come to campus at all. Columbia students
could get a job there, but McKinsey didn't make it easy. This
year, they're on campus. But barely.

The guy they send—not two employees this time, just
one—is a young person, certainly much younger than you.
Perhaps twenty-five. A new associate, a slick and small person
originally from South Africa. He talks about himself with such
precision you can see right away it is his favorite topic.

"I've been on the beach all week," he says. "I haven't done
anything. So I called down to recruiting and said, 'Hey, put
me on something.' They sent me down here. I've never been
to Columbia before. When I was growing up, I don't think I
ever heard of it. The only school we really heard about down
there was Harvard."

"Where did you go to school?"

"In Cambridge."

"You went to Cambridge?"

"No—*in* Cambridge. Allston."

"You went to Allston?"

"No—*Harvard.*"

---

[18]Large employers interviewing on campus often have both "closed" and "open" interview lists—the former by invitation only (based on résumés and contacts), the latter
open for bidding, with each student allotted a quota of points to bid across all companies interviewing during a given season. The point-bidding system allows companies to
gauge a student's relative level of interest in working there. Virtually all the eventual
hires at a firm are derived from candidates on closed lists, however.

"Oh. Undergrad or business school?"

This is a moment he *loves*. He pauses—to savor it—then inhales just a wisp, just a sip of this glorious earth. "Both—actually."

"I went to Yale," you say.

"I hear their business school is improving."

Harvard Boy doesn't bother to take notes; you feel that for a kid who's been asleep all week, he surely seems tired. He tells you about his own experience interviewing with McKinsey.

"I just looked at this partner who's across from me and I said, 'This is what I want to do. If you gave me an offer right now I'd take and run with it.' There's no reason for me to mess around. I—I want to do this thing, and if you're going to do something you should start at the top. McKinsey is an international brand. It's the best way for me to see what I have to do to get where I wanna go. I don't know if I'm gonna stay in consulting forever . . . who does? What I do know is wherever I'm going the only path I can see to get there—the only way there is through, through here . . ."

Even he loses interest in what he's saying. He turns to the most attractive women in the group. "So—what's your background?"

His business card is strange. There is a standard business card size, and it's widely accepted throughout the United States, Europe, and Asia. It fits in a wallet. This size is apparently not useful to McKinsey: The card this kid tosses your way while he's getting the attractive girl's phone number (for "follow-up questions") is quite long, and quite narrow. It's plain and black and white and won't fit in any wallet.

McKinsey & Company, it says. And: *Throw me away.*

Your next encounter with the firm is at their official presentation to the student body. Again, there is a distinctly secondary flavor to it: as though they left their *real* presentation somewhere else. Most firms trot out the most senior management they can find who attended your school, and these men

and women scroll through a prewrapped PowerPoint slide
show assembled by somebody else, somebody they barely
know—you can tell this by the twitch of pain that crosses their
faces as they parrot out what's on the screen. *Putting people
first . . . Diversity is our priority . . . We challenge you to challenge
yourself . . . Hiring the best to be the best . . .*

You will learn much later that presentations put together
by consultants, as opposed to people in MBA-recruiting de-
partments, do not read like this. For one thing, there would
be numbers on each page; there would be lots of numbers,
and a graph. These placid bullet points do not inspire.

Presenting for McKinsey is a ruffled European with a brush
of five o'clock shadow. From yesterday at five o'clock. He's
wearing a gray outfit that needs a breath freshener and his
hair is steely and vivid, as though startled from a nap. He did
not attend Columbia Business School—he does not say where
he went to business school. He does not need to say.

And from the beginning, there is something very wrong.

"Thank you for coming tonight," he whispers. "My name is
Steffan Ribbletropp [or something like this, he's slurring].
I'm an engagement manager with McKinsey and Company
based in New York. I work mainly in financial services, though
I have . . ." [*four-second pause*] ". . . done work in other areas. I
was originally based out of . . ." [*three seconds*] ". . . Munich,
Ch-Ch-Chermany. I transferred to the States last year and . . ."
[*five seconds*] ". . . have been here since. My background before that . . . I was a banker. I have, we, I think we have
some . . ." [*four seconds*] ". . . slides. For you."

He indicates to dim the lights. They do not dim. For a moment, there is awkwardness in every corner of the room, but
not from Steffan Ribbletropp. He's utterly still, in a cone of
silent beauty. He stares at the presentation room door, on the
fifteenth floor of the tallest building at Columbia University,
the School of International and Public Affairs. You wish he
would exit through it.

"We'll try to put this th-thing together," he seems to say. His lips move, but he's still very, very quiet.

It's almost disappointing when he gets the slide show going. The slides are not important; you have seen them before. Everyone in the room—everyone has seen them before. The drama is in Ribbletropp.

"We put people first . . . at McKinsey," he says. "I'm not sure what that means. Let's hope it is a good thing, eh?"

He's getting giddy. You wonder if you have ever seen anyone so tired. He's so tired, Mr. Ribbletropp, that's he's shot out the other side of tiredness into a land of strange objects. Like slides.

"We hire the best at McKinsey . . . like me. That was a joke." [*five seconds*] "We . . . we hire the best and we expect the best from them. There is an 'up or out policy,' and it is enforced. There is no . . . what you would call here 'wiggle room.' You understand what I am saying? But it's a very coll-ee-gee-uhl culture. We get along ferry well." [*three seconds*] "My colleagues are ferry impressive pee-pull. They are—we are by far the least impressive people you will find among of them."

There are perhaps two hundred people in this room. Every single member of your class who wants to go into consulting is there. The other big-money option—investment banking—draws larger crowds: This *is* New York. But no consulting presentation draws as many hopefuls as McKinsey's.

You turn to your friend and say, "I have to go."

"Not yet."

"I have to get out of here."

"But you haven't seen The Slide yet."

"I don't want to see it. I don't care about it."

"You," he says, "don't know what you're saying. Sit down."

Ten minutes later, Steffan puts up [their growth Slide]. There is collective relief, a dissipation of a fume. For once The Slide goes up, the presentation's winding down. There's not much one can say beyond The Slide. Like the mandala, it is an end within itself; an end, and the beginning of the end.

"Now this slide shows . . . quite fifidly, I think . . ." [*three seconds*] ". . . it shows we have been growing quite a lot in the past few years. And we expect to keep this up for quite a while. There is a shtrong market for the kind of work we do . . . and this is due to fundamental . . ." [*cough*] ". . . changes in the structure of managerial practice. You can see here . . ."

The Slide is deceptively simple. You and your classmates have something of a McKinsey fetish, and you are expecting it.

". . . you can see here the extra-ordinary growth we have been acheeffing over the past five years. Both in terms of billings and the number of professional client staff we have been . . ." [*four seconds*] ". . . been. On staff."

The Slide is simply a curve showing 20 percent annual growth. That's 20 percent compound annual growth over the past decade in both revenues and in the size of McKinsey's staff. What people do not understand is just how astronomically high 20 percent compound annual growth is. If you made $1.00 last year, you made $1.20 this year. Next year you will make $1.44 . . . then $1.73 . . . then $2.08. You'll note that the dollar growth each year is getting bigger, from 20¢ to 24¢ to 29¢ to 35¢, as growth rates apply to previous growth. Compounding is not unlike magic. And since consulting professional staff size is highly correlated with revenues, for reasons discussed later, this means the staff has also been growing at about 20 percent per year. If last year there were 100 McKinsey consultants, this year there are 120; next year there will be 144, then 173, then 208, and so on. You have more than doubled your staff in four years. Not only is the real number of McKinsey consultants getting larger each year, it's getting larger *at a faster and faster rate.*

You know enough calculus at this point to get scared. With such a high first derivative, or rate of change, the implications are alarming.

To put it bluntly, The Slide implies that *McKinsey is on a path toward total world domination.*

This is not a figurative statement. It is quite literal. (See the figure below.)

Steffan has admitted more than he meant to. A secret has emerged from the House of Lies. "We expect to keep this up for quite a while . . ." Do you see? He admits what so many have tried so hard to conceal: At 20 percent growth per year, starting at its current base of about ten thousand consultants, McKinsey will employ every single man, woman, and child in America as soon as May 2060. Fifteen years later, the firm will have to look to other planets for its customers, for every person on Earth will be a McKinseyite.

If you don't get a job with them this time around, you can always wait. You'll be very old in May 2060—but it won't really matter. They'll have to hire you. (See below.)

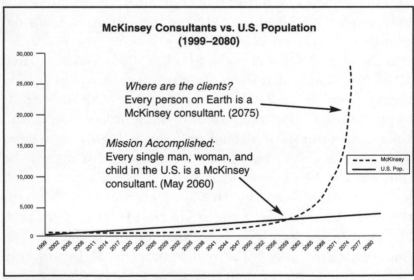

Source: McKinsey & Co. Author analysis

Is there another option to this scenario? In the dot-com years, there didn't seem to be. Twenty percent growth was kind of lame, to tell the truth; business plans were regularly predicting 50 or 60 percent. People who went into consulting were pitied by many. They would never make *real* money.

It turns out, of course, there is an alternative to 20 percent compound annual growth. It looks like this:

- ❏ Number of McKinsey consultants in 1999: 10,000
- ❏ Number in 2000:   12,000
- ❏ Number in 2001:   7,200[19]

We had no professional layoffs other than our traditional "up-or-out" stuff.

—MCKINSEY MANAGING PARTNER RAJAT GUPTA
(2002)[20]

Your firm is less traditional, unfortunately. Within six months of the Rainmaker's departure, as the long cold winter of 2001 approaches, the winds of optimism have fled. Where you started in May with 250 colleagues, reduced to 200 by July, as your annual Seasonal Affective Disorder sets in during early September you'll see the ranks of your workmates cut again. You can hardly work for all the chainsawing going on around you; you can hardly work, because there is no work.

You're very busy, of course. It's just that the work isn't *billable*. From the firm's point of view, work that isn't billable is like money set on fire. More charitably, it's an investment in human capital and knowledge building, a time for promising and experienced staffers to hone their skills and lay the groundwork for big sales to come. But work that is *unbillable* is literally work for which the firm cannot submit a bill. No one has hired you. You are working, and drawing a paycheck from the firm; but the firm isn't drawing a paycheck for you.

Consulting firms always operate at less than 100 percent

[19]Vault, Inc. Employer Profile: McKinsey & Co., 3
[20]*Business Week*, July 8, 2002.

Consulting firms always operate at less than 100 percent billability,[22] even during good times. Projects start and stop frequently and there is always some downtime between assignments. There are proposals to be written "on spec," and assignments that require more work and more people than the client agreed to pay for. There are always some people not billing. It's just that, during the lean years of 2001 and 2002, not billing became for a time more common than billing. Even at McKinsey. In June 2002, McKinsey's utilization was about 50 percent—meaning half of its dwindling supply of consultants were working for free. This was the lowest level of busy-ness in thirty-two years.

At your firm, the number is closer to 30 percent. It is an odd time, that winter of 2001. A time of great rumor.

"They're cutting muscle now," you hear.

"We're looking for a merger—maybe with BCG," they say.

"Bain is going bankrupt."

"There's a capital call at McKinsey."

"AT Kearney's going bankrupt."

"Arthur D. Little's going out of business."

"They're talking about 'resizing the New York office.'"

"How can they resize it any more?"

"Make it more like Cleveland." The Cleveland office, you know, has thirty people.

It's a time of great rumors—some of which may even be true. But you're very, very busy.

The reason, oddly enough, is September 11.

Following that date, consulting firms are asked by a nonprofit development group called the New York City Partnership if they wouldn't mind donating some time and expertise to productive work—the only kind they can really contribute. Namely, research and speculation. The result is a massive multifirm effort to analyze in rather minute detail the effects of the attacks on the economy of greater New York. It is also thought

---

[22]Firms prefer to call this "utilization," which seems less greedy.

itself more quickly. Seven major consulting firms agree to do-
nate their staff and resources, and each is assigned a particular
area of the economy to examine: real estate, insurance, financial services, health care, media, and so on. The output of the
effort is to be a report presented directly to people in a position
to act, like the deputy mayor and Senator Hillary Clinton.
Mayor Rudy Giuliani is reported to be all ears.

The firm selected to head up this effort is, of course,
McKinsey.

You are assigned to a subteam examining retailing. It's a
pretty good assignment, actually, and for six weeks you experience the placid flow of a life where you don't mind getting
up in the morning. You do your light treatment for Seasonal
Affective Disorder, go to the gym, feel like a man. Your wife
loves you. You're not so very old, not really. You still have most
of your hair, and your subscription to the New York City
Ballet. Life is good.

Or it would be—if not for McKinsey.

They run the model. In any consulting engagement, the
model—pronounced The Model—is the nexus of power. It is
an Excel workbook, or multiple workbooks, that is built carefully over a period of weeks with an elaborate cross-mesh of
references and formulas so complex it is only really understood by its maker, and often not even by her. The model is a
holy thing, like Nomad in *Star Trek*. It accepts your offerings
and issues its cryptic response, which is never questioned,
only puzzled over.

McKinsey is the maker, and it is never happy.

The model is a mathematical re-creation of the New York
City economy, specifically its overall gross city product. The
inputs demanded from each subteam are employment numbers and total output, or value-add.[22] These inputs are demanded weekly, sometimes biweekly, in little groups or big

---

[22]This is the sector equivalent of GDP, or the sum of total "value added" by a segment of
the city economy; in reality, because there is little manufacture anymore in NYC, it's
wages paid plus firm pretax profits.

groups by month and then by year, according to a complicated schedule McKinsey claims it disseminated early on but
no one seems to be able to find.

You talk to the McKinsey guy quite often. The conversations go like this:

MCKINSEY: When are you going to send the template?
              [*It requires submissions using McKinsey-
              standard templates, which look funny.*]
YOU: Oh—was it due today? Which template?
MCKINSEY (*being patient*): The one with today's date on it.
              It's in the file name. Today's date. Can you
              see it?
YOU: Did we get that one?
MCKINSEY: Do you need another copy of the stuff we
              sent last week? It's the same thing I sent you
              Monday? And yesterday?
YOU: I got it. It's kind of hard to read.
MCKINSEY: Is English your first language? I'm kid-
              ding—listen, why don't you look it over and
              get back to me.
YOU: When do you need it by?
MCKINSEY: We kind of need it by ten minutes ago. But I
              can give you guys longer. I usually do, right?
YOU: Are we holding you up?
MCKINSEY (*veneer dropping*): It's just . . . we prefer to work
              internally.

Four weeks of this makes you feel really stupid. You begin
to believe you don't deserve to work with McKinsey. You really
don't have what it takes, and this is a depressing and liberating
thought. You have found your people: the truly second-rate.

You believe this until you see the final presentation and
read the final report.

McKinseyites dress in black. They wear black suits and crisp
white shirts and thin black ties and walk together like the men

in *Reservoir Dogs*. They are the Men in Black. Long after others abandoned jackets and ties, they persist. BCG, Bain, Booz Allen Hamilton—the three B's they consider their closest competitors—all three have built B-business-casual workplaces. But not McKinsey. They are taller, smarter, better looking, and better dressed.

But are they really *better*?

Their work is certainly *simpler* than your firm's. Despite being the only management consultancy with a full-time graphics "guru" on staff, McKinsey churns out presentations as plain as any on the planet. There are few words on the page, in large fonts. There are graphs and boxes here and there with straight lines and a minimal use of color. Clip art is vanquished. Curved arrows and "starburst" patterns so beloved of cubicle jockeys are avoided. Every inch of every slide says "We are strategic thinkers. We are the avatars of Truth. We are the Oracle. These are our words."

Less is most definitely more, you believe. You have gotten so sick of words you barely talk at all anymore. People don't shut up. We live in a country of yappers and it's getting worse. You love ballet—you love how no one *talks*. "Words," said Lenny Bruce, "are all lies." And so they are.

So you are predisposed to the McKinsey approach. Or you would be if it were in service of the truth. In the case of the New York City Partnership, however, it appears to be employed in the service of saving McKinsey time. For simpler slides, true or not, have the advantage of being much easier to create. The clean boxes and fourteen-word messages seem to say "We leave all the really complicated hard work we did off the slide, because you couldn't understand it. Here's the *bottom line*."

Other firms, much less secure, tend to put all the complicated hard work on the page, where the client can actually see it. Maybe this is a mistake.

A typical McKinsey slide might look something like this:

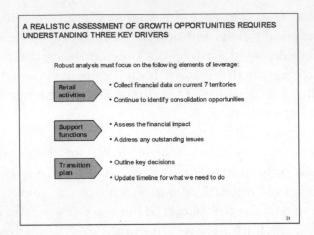

Whereas a typical slide produced by your firm would look more like this:

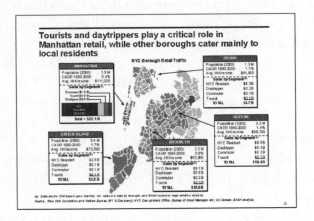

Which is better? It depends on the content, of course; McKinsey's aura allows it to get away with a lot less content. Doubtless the firm has done brilliant work for its storied clients—for United Airlines and Kmart and Enron and DaimlerChrysler, for General Motors and the city of New York, and so on. But top-tier consulting is a secret industry, conducted in the dark, and you have not been allowed to see this brilliant work. All you have seen is the work McKinsey did for the New York City Partnership.

In the end, McKinsey enrages all six other firms by entirely rewriting the final presentation the night before it is to be delivered to ex-President Bill Clinton, among others. "We're consulting our graphics expert," they say. The final result has almost no graphics.

Afterward, your principal says, "My key take-away from this project is we're better than we think we are."

It's sad, how bad you think you are. There is an element of self-loathing in all consultants.

One Anand Raghuraman, a leader of the AT Kearney team participating in the project, was quoted in the *New York Times* in late November: "My wife is an elementary-school teacher, and when I talk to friends I always used to say, 'at least one of us does something good for society.' Here, for the first time, I could say I was actually doing something for society."[23]

The New York City Partnership consulting coalition's findings were ignored by the city, and not a single one of its recommendations was adopted.[24]

By December, your firm's New York office approaches half its former size. Two of its five floors are leased back to the building's landlord. Your office, once home to five busy media strategy consultants, holds only you for the duration of the NYCP job. And then you are demoted two floors, as the twenty-fourth floor is abandoned forever.

The Rainmaker's old office is gutted by the next tenant, a Scottish bank.

It is the coldest day in the warmest winter in human history when you show up at McKinsey for your interview. A first-year business school student, you have had exactly three months of schooling in the ways of industry. You feel as though you know next to nothing, and you are about to be proved right.

McKinsey's New York offices are in midtown on the East Side, not far from the United Nations. It is a deceptively un-

---

[23]*New York Times*, November 21, 2001.
[24]The final report is posted on the partnership's Web site at www.nycp.org.

decorated suite in an indifferent silver-toned building. You
think of the CIA, how it hides in dull quarters and sits behind
nondescript doorways making trouble.

You wait with the other potentials, not making small talk.
You look each other over openly. There is a table, and a very
beautiful HR woman with hair as red as Dana Scully's gives
you a name tag. You smile at her and she looks sick. You take
coffee and stand, waiting your turn. The room smells like a
doughnut, but there are no snacks whatsoever. Your hands
are still cold. And you are terrified.

Consulting interviews are unique in the world of interviews
for one reason: the case.

Throughout the fall, you have been preparing for this. You
know it's out there—you all do. How many times have you
been told by second-years,[25] "Relax—just be yourself" and
"They only want to see how you think"? That last one especially is repeated so often by recruiters and second-years as to
become a kind of mantra: *They just want to see how you think . . .*

That, you think, is the problem.

A typical case goes like this: After the cursory slam through
the résumé, your top-tier interviewer will say, "Okay, would
you like to do a case?"

And you say, "Absolutely not."

In your mind, that is—in the room itself, you say, "But of
course."

"Are you familiar with the [insert interviewer's favorite industry here] business?"

"Some . . ."

"Well, I was at a client in [this godforsaken industry] last
year and they had a problem. It went like—"

"Do you mind if I take notes?"

---

[25]In the U.S., an MBA is generally obtained in two years; the summer between years one
and two is often spent doing a ten- or twelve-week paid internship with a prospective employer; and about 50 percent of students get a full-time offer from their summer employer and enter their second year of B-school with a good job in their pocket.

"Please." [*waits*] "Okay—so I was at this client and she said . . ."

That's another thing—right after they say, "They only want to see how you think," those second-years always offer, "Ask permission to take notes."

Now, this exchange has become a kind of leaden scripture and an inside joke among interviewers. Every single consulting case begins with this same ridiculous exchange—"Do you mind if I take notes?" "Please"—passed along from generation to generation like a predisposition to madness . . .

It turns out there are two very distinct versions of the case: (1) the one you read about in the Columbia Business School *Management Consulting Association's Case Interview Guide* and similar books from Wharton and the Vault, and (2) the one you actually get. Case 1 is terrifyingly complex, involves graphs and charts and hard math on the fly while you figure out distribution patterns for, say, bicycle wheels in war zones around the world—all leading to a moment, within the twenty-minute time limit, of pure and crystalline epiphany when you sob out, "Aha—I've *cracked the case!*" . . . and you deliver an answer ("You should consolidate all your manufacturing in Thailand") so simple it has the ring of the oracular.

Case 2 is so simple you think you heard it wrong. Then you ask a lot of leading questions to try to make it more complex. Then you think: *This is easy.* And the pain begins . . .

The classic version of Case 2 is this: "Your school cafeteria workers all decide to go on strike, leaving hoards of hungry MBA students with nowhere on campus to eat. The Hamilton Deli is across the street, and its workers are not on strike. The deli is a pretty good size and offers a full selection of sandwiches, drinks, doughnuts, and coffee. During the strike, the owner's really excited and expects a windfall. And for the two weeks the cafeteria workers are out, there are lines literally down the street outside the deli. Business is booming. But at the end of the month, when the owner does the final tally of his receipts, he sees his profits are only up about 10 percent. What went wrong?"

There is a classic version of Case 1 but you don't understand it. Something about leasing time on communications satellites . . . it's a McKinsey case.

"You"—you hear it, like a whisper in a dream, and then it's louder— *"You!"* A wonderful smell, like a lavender bath; a gentle tap, a dog's nose on your left shoulder . . .

"YOU!"

And YOU! are startled awake—you have been daydreaming—and it's Dana Scully leading you to the office where you are to have the first of your two scheduled forty-five-minute interviews at McKinsey.

Like many women, Dana is much better looking sitting down. Her body's kind of lumpy. For this, you are thankful.

The man who greets you is younger than you. McKinsey, it seems, is younger than you. You have not seen an old McKinseyite. It's like Harvard Business School, which hardly enrolls a single person over thirty: Seasoning is not the taste of choice. So the young man squeezes your hand and asks you to sit. He's got short, tight curls on his head and a big, fat pen in his left hand. This he bangs and bangs and *bangs* on his right palm for forty-five straight minutes, once per second, bang bang bang.

"You know," he starts, "who is buying all these apartments?"

"I'm sorry?"

"You figure—look, say I'm making one-twenty, one-twenty-five, right? I've got to be in the top one percent of earners in the country, right? If the median is something like—let's make it thirty thousand. One-twenty-five plus the bonus—but they're selling apartments in this city that are barely livable for like *half a million dollars*. Who's buying these apartments? Do you know?"

"People who can afford them."

"Obviously. I mean—if I can't get a one-bedroom on the Upper East Side, then I'm wondering what's going on? Am I right here? What do you think?"

What you think is: *Is this the case?*

"Well . . ." you start—

"But never mind. Where do you live?"

"Queens."

"I'm sorry. Okay—" he glances down at a piece of paper on his desk, a résumé—"How's Wharton?"

Wharton? "I think . . . it's a good school . . . ?"

"Yeah—gotta hate those winters though, huh? Now listen—I see from this you have a kind of an unusual background for consulting, right? I had a background too—I was, I had been what you call unusual before I went to HBS."[26]

"What did you do?"

"I carried a bag for P and G—I was a salesman in the Northeast. I handled detergent products—Tide, you know?"

"Sure—"

"So tell me, how did you like the Peace Corps?"

You have never been in the Peace Corps. You wonder if this is some sort of extreme interview tactic.

"*¿Habla Español?*" he prompts.

"Not really—"

He shakes his head, with pity. "Then you shouldn't put it on your résumé."

"I didn't."

You look at the piece of paper upside down on the desk in front of him. It is, of course, the wrong résumé. He doesn't seem too fazed when you point this out to him; in fact, it's almost as though he thinks you're lying. Like you really *are* the guy who said he could speak Spanish after his years in the Peace Corps.

"Look," he says, "we don't have much time here—let's do a case, okay?"

"Okay."

"How many restaurants are there in New York City?"

---

[26]Students and alumni of Harvard Business School never refer to it by its full name, or call it Harvard; they invariably use this acronym, presumably to soften the blow to the egos around them.

You think: *You are ready for this.* You have practiced with your classmates, read all the books, studied up on McKinsey to anticipate its style of case—it likes quantification, estimation—and written issue diagrams in your head while you slept. But first—

"Do you mind if I take notes?" you ask.

"On what?"

"The case."

"You want to take notes?"

"Is it okay? I don't have to."

He nods.

He seems sad, suddenly, as though informed of the grizzly death of a fish.

There are long moments of utter silence as you wait for the case to begin, pencil poised.

He breaks it. "Are you going to write something?"

"As soon as we start."

"It's done."

"What's done?"

"The case. I just gave it to you."

You think: *What kind of mind game is he playing?*

And then you remember—what was it? He said *something* a minute ago—something you thought he was just saying, like to pass the time, but maybe . . . maybe he was *saying* saying it. Maybe that was the case.

But what did he say? Something about food . . . now you're hungry.

There are no snacks at McKinsey. There is a pool table in the hallway and a minibar stocked with the cleanest empty glasses you have ever seen.

There are no snacks . . . no snacks . . . God, you should have slept last night.

"Do you want me to repeat it?"

"I'm sorry. Yes."

"How many restaurants are there in New York City?"

You wait for more.

You say, "And . . . ?"

"That's it."

"That's the case?"

"Are you going to try it . . . ?"

Of course—of course you try it. You start drawing a map.

During your anxious preparations for this moment of high farce, you purchased the classic book on structured problem solving for business people, *The Pyramid Principle*. In this clearly written, highly structured book, author Barbara Minto lays out her five basic rules for solving a problem—any problem.[27] These rules can be summarized as follows:

1. Visualize the difference between the result you get now and the result you want
2. Visualize the "structure elements" of the current situation
3. Analyze each element to see if it's the problem
4. Figure out what to change
5. Say how to change it

You have never found this approach to be remotely useful in any situation. It is particularly unhelpful right at this moment, when you're frantically trying to figure out the answer to a question that could easily be cleared up with a quick trip to the Yellow Pages. Now you're pondering your map . . .

"I'd start by segmenting the population."

"What population?"

"The population of people who eat in restaurants in Manhattan."

"This wouldn't just include residents."

"I know that. There are commuters—there are—there are visitors, people visiting, tourists—"

---

[27]Barbara Minto, *The Pyramid Principle: Logic in Writing and Thinking* (Englewood Cliffs, NJ: Prentice-Hall, 1987), 185; Minto herself graduated from Harvard Business School in 1963 and joined McKinsey's Cleveland office as the first female consultant; her book is widely thought of as a primer on "the McKinsey Mind."

"How many tourists?"

"I don't know."

"How could you find out?"

"Count them—"

This is fast becoming absurd. It has crossed the threshold of absurd and become absurdist.

"How would you do that?" he says.

You breathe in—and you survive the interview. You survive the next one, with a very scary straw-haired woman whose sister you knew back in high school (by coincidence) and whose roots are so deeply black they look dead. She laughs a lot—an awful lot for someone who is so obviously a miserable wreck. But then who are you—?

That evening the phone rings in Queens. Your wife answers. It's for you: McKinsey.

You don't get the job.

4

An Analytical Digression: "On the Means by Which the Prince Maintains His Power"

People do not understand how hardwired McKinsey is into the power grid of American business, nor how annexed it is to the Harvard Business School. It sounds hyperbolic to say Harvard and McKinsey own the U.S. economy, and it is not true. Harvard and McKinsey together do not own, run, or manage the U.S. economy. This may have been true in the 1960s and the 1970s, when McKinsey alumni were running American Express and micromanaging General Electric and HBS professors consulted to the White House.

No—by now they own, run, or manage the entire world.

Is this statement a steroidal stab at sensation? Let's consider . . .

When Michael Eisner was chosen to lead Disney in the 1980s, he observed, "The Disney board didn't look at me and say, 'Now here is a business guru, a **Harvard MBA**.' [emphasis added] They were much more interested in whether I could recognize a good script."[28] (Eisner was a theater studies major at Denison.) Unfortunately, most other corporate boards are not so theatrical.

[28]"Magic Needed: Perennial Powerhouse Disney Is Struggling, and Many Blame Eisner," Bloomberg News, August 31, 2002.

Let's imagine you live in Chicago—because, well, because it's a helluva town, right? So you're in Chicago, in business. Your activities are overseen by the competent counsel of the Chicago Board of Trade, whose chairman worked at **McKinsey** and whose president is a **Harvard MBA.**

It's morning now; you just got up. One of the pleasures of the day is shaving with the ultrasmooth Mach 3 razor made by the company with a virtual monopoly on shaving tackle in the U.S., Gillette. Speaking of corporate boards, Gillette's happens to be headed by a former professor at **HBS** who was also a partner at **McKinsey.** Now you step into the shower and lather up some Ivory soap, cleanse your scalp with the magical Head & Shoulders, towel down and slap on some Old Spice aftershave—all products from the consumer products powerhouse Procter & Gamble, whose president is a **Harvard MBA.**

It's a Sunday, thank God, a day you sometimes get off. You celebrate by popping a Vioxx (for arthritis), a Prinivil (for hypertension), and a couple Pepcid ACs—all courtesy of druggernaut Merck, whose CEO is a **Harvard MBA.** You throw on some Hanes underwear and a pair of Levi's, whose chairman is ex-**McKinsey**, and then head into the kitchen for your favorite breakfast: Sara Lee Chocolate-Dipped Original Cheesecake Bites™—dee-licious. Both Hanes and Sara Lee, it turns out, are owned by the same company, whose president and CEO is a **Harvard MBA** who worked at **McKinsey.** Oh, and then you remember to turn on the overhead light, courtesy of the most successful company in the world, General Electric, whose CEO is a **Harvard MBA.**

Into the home office, a sanctuary of GE light and truth. You power up your Dell, whose U.S. head is a **Harvard MBA,** and notice the sticker reassuring you that inside there is Intel, whose directors include a **Harvard MBA** and an ex-**McKinseyite.** You're not exactly proud of the fact, but like most Americans who access the Internet, you have an account with AOL, which is owned of course by Time Warner, whose fifteen-person strategy group is sometimes referred to as "the **McKinsey** finishing school." While online you quickly check up on the status of your auction (some bootleg Elvis Costello LPs) on eBay, whose well-known president, Meg Whitman, is a **Harvard MBA**. Reassured, you type your name into Google, which is co-run by a **Harvard MBA** who worked at **McKinsey**. As usual, a 1980s one-hit wonder New Wave singer with a name similar to yours is all over the Internet—and you are nowhere.

Dismayed, you power down the Dell and decide to do something *real*: work on your music. So you bang out a couple love ballads on your Baldwin piano, then work out some changes on your Gibson guitar (the CEO of both Baldwin and Gibson is a **Harvard MBA**). Mellow now, you decide to unwind in front of the TV. So you trot into the den in your Levi's and flip on Home Shopping Network, whose president is a **Harvard MBA**, then switch to your favorite station, CNBC, which is co-run by an irritatingly successful woman named Pamela Thomas-Graham, who is not only a **Harvard MBA** and ex-**McKinsey** partner but also a published mystery novelist. Not to mention younger than you . . .

The business news is all about the troubles of Martha Stewart, who has appointed as her company's CEO a woman she met while climbing Kilimanjaro in Tanzania; the woman is a **Harvard MBA** who worked at **McKinsey**. You pick up a magazine from the table and start idly paging through it, looking for the articles. Okay, it's *Playboy*, whose president is a **Harvard MBA**. By coincidence, you're looking at a full-page ad for Miller Beer at the same time a spot comes on TV for Miller Beer. Both ads were created by advertising behemoth Young & Rubicam, whose CEO is a **Harvard MBA** and whose branding strategy was heavily influenced by a large-scale study done by Miller's consultant of choice, **McKinsey**. All this talk of amber pleasure juice makes you wonder if you have any more of your favorite poison, Heineken, whose CEO is a **Harvard MBA**.

But enough lazing around consuming media, thinking about beer. You have some errands to run—so you hop out to the garage. Should you take the car made by the world's number one automaker, General Motors—whose president is a math adept and **Harvard MBA**—or the more refined Jaguar, made by Ford's Premium Auto Group, also headed by a **Harvard MBA**?

You opt for the Jag, throw down the top, and head out onto the open road. Naturally, you turn on the radio, rejecting station after station, both AM and FM, owned by airwave megalith Clear Channel, which controls over half the popular stations in the U.S. and whose CEO is a **Harvard MBA**.

First stop, Starbucks—whose strategy team is headed by a thirty-five-year-old ex-**McKinseyite**—and on to Citibank, whose executive committee is led by Robert Rubin, Bill Clinton's economic policy adviser and a **Harvard MBA**. Irksomely, you have to stop by and pick up a package at UPS, whose board features both **Harvard MBA**s and ex-**McKinseyites**. Then . . . on to the strip mall, where you pass a Toys "R" Us, whose chairman is a **Harvard MBA** and whose consultant is **McKinsey**; past a Circuit City, whose senior vice president is ex-**McKinsey**; finally wheeling the Jag into a tight spot in front of your second-favorite retailer, the phenomenal Home Depot. As a businessman, you can only marvel at the store's logistics, and it turns out the Sr. VP of Logistics is a **Harvard MBA**. Home Depot's consultant is **McKinsey**.

Feeling a tad overwhelmed by the **Harvard-McKinsey** duopoly, you wonder—*Is there any escape?* Not in the United States, for sure, but what about other countries? On a whim, you decide to tool out to O'Hare. Two hours later, you're standing in line at the Delta counter when you happen to read in *Business Week* that the airline's CEO is a **Harvard MBA** and former **McKinsey** partner who recently hired **McKinsey** to help restructure the airline. Peevishly, you decide instead to fly United, not knowing its consultant of choice is, of course, **McKinsey**.

United isn't going your way, so you get back into the Jag and head home. Your feeling at this moment is not unlike that shared by many consultants from non-**McKinsey** firms—you feel as though the battle has already been lost. Seeking solace, you do what you usually do when life seems gray, or blue: go to Wal-Mart.

Why do you like Wal-Mart so much? The great prices, yes, but also something deeper—something most shoppers don't know or vaguely care about. Wal-Mart is certainly the most successful retailer on the planet, probably the greatest success story in the history of American-style capitalism. And of the many, many men and women who run this great company *not one has a **Harvard MBA** and not one ever worked at **McKinsey**.* You shop at Wal-Mart as often as you can.

You are a practical woman. You realize the limits of your own personal power don't extend much beyond the walls of your one-bedroom apartment out in Queens. You have read up to here . . . you have been a fool perhaps . . . but now—*now* you see the way the world works. Say you were to have a child. You don't like children much; you're not perhaps so young as you could be. But still—you could bow to pressure or some atavistic urge and bear a child.

Wouldn't you want her to have all the benefits of employment at McHarvard & Company?

Put another way: Is it reasonable to expect you can change the machinery of mastery, built up over decades of private meetings and secret snacks, and find for your offspring some *back door to greatness?* Of course not.

So you think . . . what will it take to get my kid into McHarvard? Into the smoke-filled rooms making large decisions with the big boys?

What will it take to make my kid a McSuccess?

These are reasonable questions, and ones bearing consideration.

To begin, your child has already beaten the odds simply by

being born. It is estimated that of all pregnancies that occur
in the U.S., only about three in five will result in a healthy
birth—the rest being lost to miscarriage, abortion, or still-
birth. So assuming your kid is born—and born healthy—we
start on a high note.

And it gets better. We have been reluctant to admit this so
far but, well, you are white. There it is. Whitey. A honky. The
man. For the present purposes, however, this is an advantage:
Your kid is white. Eighty percent of those accepted in
McHarvard are white, and you want to give your kid the best
shot she can get. Of the 140 million babies born worldwide
each year, about 8 percent are Caucasian. So she's already
beating the odds—and she's only one minute old.

And it gets even better. Although some have raised questions, Queens is technically in the United States, so your baby
is an American—a considerable asset. For this scheme to
work, she would have to be born in the United States,
Canada, or Europe. Although McHarvard claims to be a
global conspiracy with offices around the world, it is over-
whelmingly U.S.- and Eurocentric, and Canadians have always
been able (nefariously) to pass as Minnesotans without too
much trouble. So again, for present purposes, we need her to
be in this geographic group—and she is. The odds of a baby
being born in North America or Europe are about 18 to 1.

Running total so far: just over 1 in 500

Happy birthday, baby!

Unfortunately, she's going to have to get to work now. The
coasting is over. She's got to start setting her sights on college.
You might do the practical thing and send your kid through
the public school system you're subsidizing out in Queens;
after all, you believe in public education, and you're happy to
support it in any way you can. In theory. But let's not delude
ourselves—suddenly, we're talking about greatness in a
bassinet, your baby's future, McHarvard for God's sake.
Public schooling isn't going to get her there. Statistics aren't
advertised, but informal polling indicates no more than 40

percent of McHarvard's constituents soldiered their way through the U.S. public school system with their flak jackets and tutors.

So you know where this is going—private kindergarten, private elementary school, private middle and high school—and, finally, a reward for all your hard work as a parent . . . but let's not get ahead of ourselves.

We'll start in kindergarten. There are some private kindergartens out in Queens, and you look at them and get depressed. They seem like parking lots for abandoned buggies. No—you're going to need a really *good* kindergarten, one with heft. A launching pad. In Manhattan, there's no dearth of such platforms, and they'll cost you about $15,000 each year. But never mind—odds of getting into private kindergarten in Manhattan: 1 in 6.

At the high school level, options open up somewhat. Where there were only about twenty quality private elementary schools in your city, when you look into high schools you find about forty that will fit your purpose. Never mind the annual bill's going to run you $25,000 and more—you trot her past all the right admissions committees and stand up to scrutiny, bravely answering skeptical questions about your ability to pay. You're a good actor, a great liar, and they let you apply. Odds of getting little Hera into a private high school: 5 to 1.

Odds of scoring 1500+ on the SAT: 50 to 1

Odds of being admitted to an Ivy League college: 5 to 1

Odds so far: 3.8 million to 1

Now we enter a dangerous time. The Buddha said, "We are furthest away from our goal when it is almost within our sight."[29] Hera is in many ways a dream come true, but she is not a universe apart. She is twenty-two. Strong forces attack from within and without. Older people often forget what a tragic, vexed decade is the twenties. Things happen with ur-

[29]This quote is apocryphal.

gency and supernatural strength. We are torn apart by voices. Specifically, people in their twenties are more likely than others to (1) die at the hands of another or in an untimely accident; (2) commit suicide; (3) become schizophrenic; (4) commit a felony; or (5) decide to be an actor.

Hera is not immune to dark forces. She is living on her own, after all, on St. Mark's Place in the East Village, in a noisy apartment across from Kim's Video.

Odds of a twenty-year-old's being murdered: 1 in 50

Odds of dying in an untimely accident: 1 in 25

Odds of committing suicide: 1 in 80

Odds of becoming schizophrenic: 1 in 350

Odds of committing a felony: 1 in 50

And, perhaps most alarming of all . . . odds of deciding to become an actor: 1 in 100

Combined odds so far: 4.1 million to 1

Now, the first step in any B-school application, of course, is to take the Graduate Management Admissions Test (GMAT), a computer-based, multiple-choice test of basic verbal and math skills. The math it tests is high school level, and the verbal skills it probes are mainly usage and reading comprehension. You're not too worried for her, but she still needs a good score. Say, over 700 out of 800.

Odds of scoring 700+ on the GMAT: 14 to 1

Harvard Business School (hereafter HBS) is well known for disdaining the GMAT. For years, it was the only top-tier business school not to require its students to take the test. It is now required and, though HBS denies it, quite important. Not as important as the LSAT is to a law school admissions committee, perhaps, but still critical. Hera also needs three strong letters of recommendation, preferably from HBS alumni or vice presidents of the United States. She doesn't know any alumni or vice presidents, sadly, but you're hoping her stellar undergraduate performance sees her through.

Odds of an applicant being admitted to HBS: 6 to 1

She's in! You couldn't be prouder. She has to graduate, of

course, but that's a simple matter. Most HBS entrants are serious enough to graduate.

Odds of her graduating: 48 out of 50

Now she's ready—to succeed, or McSucceed. So much
work for this moment. The point upon which all your doughnut glaze–glazed eyes have been fixated for lo these many
decades. The McKinsey interview. You look in the mirror and
scream, and your husband is dead in a tie-selling accident—
but it's been worth it, to see Hera smile! To know she's prac-
ticing the case, polishing her Blahniks, about to enter . . . but
wait. Before she can start her career at McKinsey she has to
land an interview with them. They're known for ignoring all
the résumés they're sent and paging through the HBS "résumé book" looking for interesting candidates. How could
Hera not catch their eye? What are the odds of that?

Odds of a top-tier applicant getting on McKinsey's "closed
list": 3 to 1

Odds of an interviewee getting a job offer from McKinsey:
5 to 1

Now it seems almost cruel to tell Hera that the *real* hazing
has only just begun.

Odds of a McKinsey associate making it past year one: 1.5
to 1

Odds of making it past year two: 3 to 1

Odds of making it to partner: 20 to 1

**Cumulative odds of reaching the summit of Mount
McHarvard: 488 billion to 1**

Anything worthwhile is difficult. Success is never easy, no
matter what you do, and just when it's cradled in your arms it
slips through like an angry ferret. Still, you didn't quite realize how *special* the denizens of Mount McHarvard really are.
They have beat some pretty long odds in their journey of self-
perfection.

How long?

We have seen how the transit from fetus to McKinsey partner is a one-in-*almost-half-a-trillion* event. You're no statistician; are those incredible odds? Let's compare . . .

Odds of various very rare events occurring within our lifetime:

Baby becoming a McKinsey partner	488 billion to 1
You winning an Oscar	3 million to 1
Extraterrestrial invasion before 2097	500,000 to 1
Meteor hitting the earth	10,000 to 1
You ending up in an insane asylum	2,000 to 1
Airline losing your luggage	175 to 1
You having 0 friends	10 to 1
You having a below-average IQ	2 to 1

This entire analysis is, of course, false. It has no statistical validity. It commits the errors known as autocorrelation and heteroskedasticity.[30] However, the observation remains: It is very, very difficult to get to the top of this mountain.

History is made by those who beat the odds, and the Rainmaker is certainly making history. He may not have an MBA, or have graduated with honors, or have taken the GMAT, or been an economics major—but he's not a functionary within the walls of McHarvard. Like all those men with real success, he found a backdoor to someplace special.

You mention the Rainmaker again because he turns up—we are not quite rid of him yet.

He turns up, of all places, at a party hosted by your top-tier firm for its media alumni. Consulting firms are most unlike other organizations in the way they treat departed colleagues. People who quit, people who get fired—everyone is greeted with a warm bear hug and a grin. Consulting may be the only

---

[30]To be statistically valid, each filter in the weeding-out process would have to be independent of the others—that is, getting into Dalton would not affect the odds of getting into Harvard, which, of course, it does. There are other problems with the analysis, but this is the main one.

industry in the world where people are actually *paid* to quit. This is called "repositioning." The amounts ebb and flow with the seasons, and right now are most definitely ebbing, but consultants at top-tier firms are generally paid some substantial amount of severance to ease their transition into a new position, even if they storm out of the firm in a rage. After giving notice, consultants may finish out their current engagement in a few weeks and then continue to receive full salary for a while—a month, maybe two, depending on tenure— *even after they start their new job.*

This puts them in the most happy position of being paid twice to work once.

And it extends beyond "repositioning"—far beyond that. Quitters are routinely invited back to speak at firm events, particularly recruiting events. This seems strange to you the first time you encounter it: someone who *left* a firm being trotted out as a spokesperson for *joining* that very same firm. If it's so great, you wonder, why did you leave?

To think thus is to miss the point entirely.

Consulting is dominated by two overwhelming realities. Reality 1 is that it is a locus of transients, bedouins, nomads, people just passin' though. Nobody stays. Two years and out—that's the rule of thumb. It's like a medical residency; a way station, not an end point. (Because business is easier than medicine, it doesn't take five years to complete.) Ask any and all partners and they'll tell you the same: "I planned to stay only two years. Every two years I said to myself, 'This year I'm going to get out.'" They hate the travel; they hate the lack of security. But they stay, despite themselves. You can go into a consulting interview and say, "You know, I'm not really sure I want to stay in consulting forever—I think I'll reevaluate in two years or so"—and that's the *right answer!* It's honest . . .

Consulting is a profession peopled by clock-watchers; but the clock measures years, and not hours.

Reality 2 is that a large proportion of any top-tier firm's client base consists of that firm's alumni. Ex-consultants tend to hire their own former firms as consultants. They like using consultants, in fact. It allows them to take revenge.

The net effect of these two realities is to make consulting firms somewhat like those girls in high school who have no self-esteem. They're mistreated, insulted, abandoned—but they're still available. Still nice.

You know all this, by now. You've been with the firm seven months; you've made it to the holidays. No snow is on the ground, as global warming hits Manhattan. But you remember snow. There's snow in your mind. Along with the snow, all Christmas parties have been annihilated. There are none this year; it would be unseemly, what with all the floors being shut down and the blood on the walls. There are no Christmas parties, but the firm honors its alumni so much it has decided to sponsor a Media Alumni Holiday Party.[31] It is held two blocks from the office, in the basement of a Japanese steak house on Third Avenue.

You don't want to go. Through some misguided principle of loyalty to the dear departed, you have opted out of corporate merrymaking entirely this year. Informal drinks with partners, dinner with despondent principals at their place— everything is a pass, as you wait for the season to die. But then, as you shut down a workbook and close out Excel in your cubicle, the most attractive female associate in the firm appears and says, "Are you going to this drinks thing?"

"You mean the media alumni thing?"

"Uh-huh?"

You look at her. She is married; and you are, of course, married. But you are far from dead.

"Let's go," you say.

And you go.

Now, if she were to ask you who is the last person in the world you would expect to be standing at the foot of the basement staircase as you wend your way down them, turn left,

---

[31]Cash bar.

and appear in the Japanese basement with the top-tier media alumni—who is the very *last* person on earth who would be standing there, like a tiny maître d', soft hand extended, hair most definitely in place, eyes aglow with deals going down, you would have to respond "the Rainmaker."

You don't see him at first—you're looking over his head, at the walking wounded. All the fired people, the carcasses of ex–media consultants, hanging out by the cash bar in the dark.

But you stumble into something, as your eyes adjust, something squishy and vile—and it's him.

"Hey," he says, stepping back, "glad you could make it."

You take his hand; it's been called fishlike, but that's not quite correct. It's not like a fish. It's warm-blooded, and furry.

He looks at your companion, whom he doesn't know. "Hello," he says. "I'm [the Rainmaker]."

You are pushed along by someone and he's moved to the next hello.

"Wasn't that . . . ?" asks your beautiful friend, and you nod. "Yep."

You order a *mojito* and it turns out the cash bar is not a cash bar after all—why, the Rainmaker himself has decided to pick up the tab. Why not? He can certainly afford a few *mojitos* to dull the pain of all the lives he has shattered by destroying a practice and taking not a single person with him to his reward.

As you drink and talk, you count. There are maybe a dozen people in this room with the Rainmaker's fingerprints clearly visible on the shaft of the knife in their backs. He makes his way to every one, talking quietly, sincerely, eye to eye. He looks up—in some cases *way up*—at them, nodding thoughtfully. You overhear some of these words exchanged in confidence.

"Of course," he muses. "That sounds like a great opportunity. Good luck to you." And always, in closing: "Let me know if I can do anything for you—anything at all. Seriously, call me. Great to see you again . . ."

"It's pathetic," you say to Beauty.

"What?"

"These people are all so nice to him."

"Why wouldn't they be nice to him? He paid for the drinks."

"He lost them their jobs."

"It's only consulting, for God's sakes," she says.

And she's right: It's consulting. It's not serious. Somehow, it's just not serious. Nothing about top-tier management consulting seems remotely like life or death or even close. It's an industry built on frivolity. Realizing this, you feel better.

Some combination of the gratis *mojitos* and the pulchritudinous company makes you bolder than, in retrospect, you might have been. You don't make a pass at Beauty—no, that is not in your nature.

But you do make another pass—one perhaps more ill-advised and dangerous. You make a kind of pass at the Rainmaker.

At some point you edge your way through the room full of sycophants and pull him aside.

He indulges you, kindly.

"You know," you say, "I really enjoyed working with you. And maybe . . . maybe we can work together again someday?"

He looks at you as though you're standing on his shoes—which, in fact, you are.

"*That*," he says, "is very unlikely."

Part II

Consulting Craft Skills for a Well-Stocked Tool Kit

Part II presents, in a single handy package, a grounding in those craft skills necessary to become a top-tier management consultant. These are the basic craft skills required, in order of importance:

1. *Ability to give—and, more important, to receive—erroneous **feedback** from colleagues and partners*

2. *Ability to **speak with authority** about topics of which you are ignorant*

3. *Intimate knowledge of the **consultant's "lingo"***

4. *Knowledge of **basic mathematics**, specifically:*
   a. *Subtraction*
   b. *Addition*
   c. *Multiplication*
   d. *Nonlinear multivariate logistic regression[32]*

---

[32]Optional.

5

The Gentle Art of Feeding Back— or, a New Way to Grow & Hate Yourself

It's very difficult to tell if you're serious or not," says the woman, feeding back.

"I'm always serious," you say.

"See what I mean?"

After a year you are sent to Feedback Camp. It is in the woods in New Jersey and, like most woods in New Jersey, right next to a large highway. Cars hurtle past your talk circles; they infiltrate the corners of your bed. The purpose of Feedback Camp is never quite clear, but you suspect it has something to do with teaching you to work well with other people. It is a mandatory week in the woods for all (surviving) associates . . . and it is by far your worst week with the firm.

By far.

"My name is important to me," says the man in the military reserves, suppressing a quiet rage.

"Of course it is, Jim."

"My name is Jason."

The title of this week is "Consulting Team Skills," and you were supposed to have taken it shortly after joining the firm. In fact, it's supposed to be completed within six months of your start date, but things occurred. For instance, half the firm was fired. And all training programs were suspended. Morale among the lower ranks inexplicably began to plummet and so the partners decided to do what they presumed everybody did in moments of self-doubt: They hired a consultant. That consultant haunted the halls for a few weeks talking to the war-wounded and the battle-weary . . . and she reported back that what everybody needed was not an end to the madness, no, what they all needed was a week in the woods of New Jersey with their top-tier colleagues from around the world telling one another in excruciating detail just exactly what it is about them that makes them so difficult to work with.

What they needed was Feedback Camp.

"What I wish," says the woman who talks too much, "is that you would talk more."

"About what?"

"I just want to let you know that I'm feeling that you're not exactly *hearing* what I'm saying."

"I'm hearing you."

"What I'm feeling is I doubt it."

"Can I give you some feedback now?"

"It's not your turn."

"Well one of my feedbacks is you're hung up on whose turn it is—"

"Guys," says the moderator, a Mormon who makes you want to avoid Salt Lake City, "take a step back. Breathe. Center."

There's a moment—just a moment—when nobody talks. Ah . . .

It's inculcated in the business school–bound that industry is all about "team work." In fact, it's so often used it's elevated to a single word: *teamwork*. You've got to work as a team. It's all about the team. You're only as good as your team. The team is more important than the individual. What's your role in the team? Which team are you on? You've got to report to the team; check in with the team; have team dinner, team lunch, team debriefing in the airport lounge.

It sounds strange to you, the first time you hear it: "We."

A partner said it in a meeting your first or second week at the firm. He was walking past the team room, on his way to a different team meeting, and he steps in and gets to asking what your team is up to; so your team leader briefs him, and the partner asks a question about the client, which goes something like, "Do we have any capacity in Asia . . . ?"

We?

He means, of course, we, the client, the company that hired us. We are *we*. It's routine by now—this convenient linguistic fiction that we are actually employees of the companies we serve. There is no us and them; there's only us and us. The team. So ingrained is this usage, top-tier consultants even slip into it with the client.

"What *we* need to focus on," your principal says to a client in Dearborn one time, "is getting more value-added content onto the handsets."

The VP looks unmoved. "*I'll* focus on that," she says. "Why don't *you* focus on getting the numbers right."

We are amused.

So it is to build the narrative *we* that you are put into a cluster at Columbia Business School, and broken down into an independent project team, with a specific team role. It is in service of the *we* that you are on a home team at your top-tier firm, and a mentoring team, not to mention your actual work teams and subteams. When you see your friends from business school, always on a Friday night, you all refer to it as "team dinner." For that's what you are now—a team player.

The problem is—it's all a lie.

There are no teams. Teams accomplish nothing. Good work is done in a cone of real quiet. Truth comes from the silence alone. Is this true? *We* don't know.

All we know is—right now—we hate other people.

They're all so *critical.*

Feedback Camp starts with an online questionnaire. It asks you to rate yourself along a number of dimensions supposedly correlated with the skills you are thought to need to do your job well, and it's sent to a dozen or so people who have worked with you. Your co-workers are asked the same questions, and they can jot down anonymous comments about what they like and don't like about your unruly personality. Most team members wisely choose to comment very little, but those that do give themselves away immediately. It is amazing how few words it takes to ferret out a voice.

"Marty has a magnetic, disarming personality," one says, and you immediately picture the job manager on the secret government project[33] down in Baltimore. It is the word *disarming*, a favorite of his in many contexts, most of them not related to the U.S. military.

"Marty needs to make sure he takes team members to meetings with the senior staff"—you know this guy at once, the reedy, picky fellow in Stamford who was obsessed with his free box of pears at the Hyatt. He walked past a room once when you were in there with the senior team members talking about what you should think about ordering for dinner, and the look on his face betrayed *such* abandonment . . .

The single biggest problem with Feedback Camp is that it used to take place in Brazil. There was training in the morning and beaches and Brazilians in the afternoon, and from what you hear the training was optional. They are becoming almost unbelievable—these stories of the past. There was a cruise the firm sponsored every year in August for the summer associates; an entire Carnival cruise liner was rented for a week so the kids and their spouses could spend tropical time with the partners in an informal setting of heaving waves and salt spray. Abruptly canceled last year, of course, these cruises have gained in debauched reputation since. An associate passed out in a stairwell. An associate threw up on a partner. An associate hosted a "train" in her cabin. There were castles rented in Scotland for the operations practice annual dinner,

[33]Betrayed in Part III: "In the Client's Own Godforsaken Town."

and there were strippers and worse charged to American Express with a wink. These stories of the "go-go '90s" always reminded you of something, and then you realized what it was. The "go-go '80s."

You'd like to go-go home right now.

You're sitting around a conference room table in a windowless hutch in New Jersey, hearing what people think of you. There are four of you, including the Mormon moderator. You have spent a week together already and there are strong opinions in the room. The comments are supposed to be structured as one good thing (capability area), one bad thing (room for improvement), but it all sounds the same. Very bad.

"The thing I like about you," says the woman with the troubled teeth, "is . . . oh God, I knew I wrote this down somewhere." She fumbles with her index cards. "I'm sorry," she says at last, "I have to pass."

"Can—can you paraphrase what you were going to say?" prompts the Mormon.

"I just can't remember."

The first day you were handed back the results of the online survey, including the anonymous responses of your coworkers and your own self-ratings. Your self-ratings were consistently lower than those of the others, and this depressed you.

You're supposed to go through the prefeedback, looking for patterns, then come up with a goal for the week around repairing your most glaring capability gap. Fixing what's most obviously wrong.

Once you've decided what your goal is, you gather in the windowless conference room that is to be your home with your three core team members and the moderator, and you do what hordes of businesspeople have done for decades in Basking Ridge, New Jersey—namely, you *share*. You tell these previous strangers your major fault and what you're going to do about it.

When you realize what you're going to have to tell them, you want to cry. It's just too perfect, as if you made it up. It turns this week in the woods into a magnificent postmodern business experiment.

Can you guess what your major fault turns out to be? Can you even imagine?

It's this: *You don't like feedback.*

Well.

Think about the irony of it—the sublime ridiculousness. The firm's considered feedback to you is you need to go to a camp to get feedback about yourself, and that feedback is: You don't want any feedback.

There's a lot of feedback in here.

Your wife is, sadly, a musician; to her this word has other connotations. To her this word is repellent.

"Okay," says the Mormon, considering. "So what's your goal going to be for the week?"

"I'm going to ask for feedback."

"Solicit it."

"Yeah—solicit feedback. All week."

"And on the job?"

"I'm going to ask for feedback from my co-workers. And my team leaders."

"And?"

"And what?"

"Anything else?"

You think about it. "Not really."

"What are you going to do with the feedback?"

Ah—that is the real question, isn't it? What are you going to *do* with the feedback. You suspect the truth—ignore it—is not, in the circumstances, acceptable.

"Listen to it."

"And?"

"Take it in."

"And?"

"Really listen."

"*Hear* it."

"Yes—hear it."

"*Hear* the feedback and *act on* the feedback, right? And how are you going to do that—"

"Can I say something," interrupts the woman who talks too much, the one with the eating disorder and the terrible skin. She has been wanting to talk this whole time, and now she is going to talk.

You all turn to her.

"I feel that Marty is mocking us."

Beginning consultants are always afraid of confronting this scene: The grizzled old VP of sales puts down his 7-Eleven carafe and hooks his thumbs into the ring of blubber at his belt. "Now what," he spits out, "do you know about my business? I've been forty years selling tires and you think you can come in here and tell me how to sell tires? How old are you, anyway? I've got shirts that're older than you, boy!"

Trouble is, that scene never happens. It's more common, as we have said, to have friends and parents question exactly what it is that you know about selling tires and how old are you, anyway? This kind of second-guessing of skill levels never happens for the simple reason that the clients know the answer. You're probably not that old, and you probably don't know that much about their business. You're a *consultant,* for God's sake. You don't work anywhere for forty years.

Consultants are not hired as experts. This is a misconception common among nonconsultants: that they are hired for their *knowledge.* They are not. They are hired to accomplish in very rapid order a daunting, discreet piece of fact-finding and analysis that they are then required to present in exceedingly clear and convincing form to their client. There may or may not be an element of strategic thinking in the presentation; there may or may not be a series of recommendations. These recommendations might seem to an outsider suspiciously like *telling the old guy how to sell tires*—but they are not. The recommendations are there, in the end, to make the consultant feel more like a manager and less like the hired help, but they are generally entirely ignored. The client knows where they came from, after all.

So consultants are not hired as experts, but they can never appear to be anything less than expertlike. The critical part of that word is *-like*. It's an act, a charade, a delightful pas de deux. But it is absolutely essential.

Your fourth or fifth month with the firm, you find yourself in a position that would be terrifying were it not so dirt common. You are working for a happy client, a beer and hard liquor manfacturer in the midst of trying to restructure the way it deals with its distributors. As you have heard, alcohol is a great business to be in; since the days of moonshine, it has a large and avid customer base that will risk something like death to be served. And it has evolved over the years since Prohibition into a bewildering web of factors and third parties and state rent-a-cops that do nothing but sit and watch the cash wash in. It's extraordinary—the amount of money these people soak up for nothing.

Your particular client contact is a woman you've been warned about—a rather squat little person with a puzzled look who is draped in gray sweaters. It is the middle of summer. Her name is Cate, with a *C.* She's young, too, maybe twenty-eight or twenty-nine, and makes two times your salary for no reason at all. She used to work at McKinsey, but they fired her. Now she's head of something to do with realigning the organization or whatever.

And she always says, "Uh-huh . . ." She nods and says, "Uh-huh . . ." Hers is speech minus content; she's a human agreement machine.

So you are rather alarmed when, on the morning of your second day at the client site, she waddles up and says, "What are you doing right now?"

"I was—"

"Can you come to a meeting?"

The rule in these situations is to say: *Yes*. Whatever the client asks, you say: *Yes*. This much you know.

"Yes."

As you enter the meeting room, she hands you a stack of pages not stapled together. They feel kind of wet, like a runner had strapped them to her body. They're out of order—you try to order them, absently, as you sit. Then it's quiet, and you notice something . . .

Everyone is looking at you. And there are a lot of them—maybe fifteen or eighteen. Some of them you recognize from yesterday, the get-acquainted meeting. These are senior people; actually, now that you reminisce, rather *senior* senior people. There's a tanned Welshman who is president of something. There's the client himself, the VP of sales. The HR woman, who has a distinctly VP-like aura and a colorful scarf. They're *senior* senior people and you're fumbling with a wet stack of pages and you're in the middle of the room and suddenly, suddenly it hits you—

You are alone.

There are no other consultants in the room. Where are they? You turn to the woman who led you in, but she's talking.

"Do you all know Marty?" she asks.

"We met yesterday," says the Welshman, and the bright light flashes off his teeth.

"He's with [your top-tier firm], as you know," she continues. "I thought I'd ask him to take us through some pages."

Everyone is sitting. She turns to you and smiles.

There is silence. Extended.

You start to talk—then stop. The pages are upside down; they're upside down and in a foreign language. No—it's English after all. They make no sense. You see a word there, an anchor. The word is *distribution*. And again, you start to talk.

"The purpose of today's meeting is to make sure we're all aligned on the distribution piece going forward—"

"Sales and distribution," interrupts the Welshman, who bears a disarming resemblance to the actor Tim Curry.

"Right—because what's the point of distribution if the product's going to sit there, right?"

"Uh-huh . . . ?"

"Now—Cate asked me to take you through a few pages here. . . ." You look around the room and notice—nobody has any pages to look at. This would not be the case if you were leading them through some pages—"At some point—once we're all on the same page, so to speak. About the distribution. And sales."

You look desperately at Cate; she's checking e-mail on her Blackberry. Outside would be a magnificent view of the city of Stamford, Connecticut, if the blinds weren't all drawn. You could be in any ecru box in any faux city in the world.

You might as well try.

"There has been a lot of work around distribution that's been done recently, over the past few—well, decades really. As you know, the tendency as transportation networks improve and information transfers happen instantly is—it's to try to streamline distribution to the point where all unnecessary middle steps are gone. What's not necessary—idle time spent sitting in warehouses. That's inventory, which is an element of working capital, it's equivalent to frozen assets. More than frozen, they're actually diminishing in value. So the work we've been doing—most of the work—has been around this issue of trying to eliminate the transfer costs and inventory costs in distribution."

Is anybody buying this? Maybe you should move on to the liquor business . . .

"Now—the business we're in has an unusual structure—as, as you know. There are, for regulatory reasons, and other reasons, there are strong distributors between the manufacturer—us—and the outlets. There are requirements against direct distribution, which would be the way most industries

are going. The issue is these distributors are getting a lot
of . . . well, power—"

"We know all this," says the Welshman not unkindly.

"What's important," says the woman with the scarf, "is what
the new structure's going to be."

It occurs to you this could be an elaborate put-on. That
Cate and the others are subjecting you to some kind of elaborate high-level new-consultant hazing ritual and in a moment they're all going to start laughing and spray champagne
in your face. But no.

"What we'd like to know," you say carefully, "is what you're
feeling about that."

"About what?"

"The new distribution structure. What would you do?"

"Well—I . . ."

She doesn't have any more of an idea than you do about it,
of course. None of them do. That's why you're sitting in this
blacked-out room in the middle of nowhere like a bunch of
goats. The distribution works fine; it doesn't matter.
Everybody's getting rich. People are drinking themselves stupid and always will. You're filling up your day, and so are they.

You remember a partner said once there are two fallback
techniques to use in a desperate situation.

Consultant's Panic Buttons
  1. Flatter the clients
  2. Ask for their opinion

You decide to hit both buttons.

"Listen—you guys are the experts," you say with some passion. "You've lived with this business a lot longer than most of
us have. We could talk about our opinions all day but ultimately you're the ones—you're going to know if it will actually work."

Button 1—check.

"So let me turn it around for a second, if it's okay. We'd really like to know—just in a kind of background, basic way—what you think would work in a situation like this."

Button 2—check.

"Well," says the woman with the scarf, "I don't think we should—"

"You know what we need," pipes a high voice from the end of the table—a guy you've never seen before in your life. He's wearing a blue blazer that seems to swallow him up. "What we need is a state-by-state discussion."

"Start in California," says the Welshman, liking this idea. You know he's spent time in the sun—just look at his leather skin replacement. "In some ways they're the most likely to let us go direct."

"I know that," says Blazer Boy. "But the dedicated resourcing we're talking about is already there in a lot of places."

"Not in the North, with Alhambra and Giacometti . . ."

And they're off.

Ask any consultant—he'll tell you. There is a moment in most client meetings when the client team starts to argue with itself, and those are the moments you dream about. You can check out and look concerned. The pressure is off. Now's the client's time to show her ignorance.

When you were a summer associate, ten months after you had entered business school and eleven months after you left your job on the television show, your job manager came into your cubicle and said, "We have a call right now."

And you said, "Okay."

And she said, "It's right now."

"Do you want to do it here?"

"Do you know what it's about?"

"You're telling me about it."

"I don't know. Did you schedule it?"

"I don't know anything about it."

"Who scheduled it? Where's Ken?"

Ken was the principal. He was in the air right now between LGA and LAX. He was totally unreachable and it occurred to you that he was the person who scheduled the call.

"He's traveling," you said.

"Oh shit."

"Who's it with?"

"Some guy named Jason."

"When is it?"

"Two minutes ago."

"Do you have the number?"

"Yes I have the number—how can we call without the number? All I have is the number."

She was getting hysterical, which seemed like an overreaction.

"What do we know about Jason?" you asked her in what you hoped was a calming tone.

"Fuck all. Nothing. We know his name is Jason and here's his number and we're calling him."

You looked at the printed out e-mail with this information. It was from Ken.

"Can we reschedule?" you asked.

"We have to call him." She was dialing, stabbing at the digits on your phone. The area code and prefix meant he was in the client's headquarters building in L.A. *Who was he?*

"Jason here," he answered.

Your job manager had put him on speakerphone.

"Hi, Jason, this is Lisa Han from [your top-tier firm], we had a call right now."

"That's right."

"Sorry we're late. I'm here with my colleague Marty [your last name]. Is it okay to use the speaker?"

"Okay."

There was a silence. Unfortunately, he didn't sound very friendly, and he seemed to be waiting for you to pick up the ball.

"Are you familiar with what we're up to, Jason?" you asked tentatively.

"*Very* familiar."

"Have you seen the—the July eleventh update?"

"Have it right here."

"Great. Then we won't need to—to walk you through that deck."

"No you won't."

This was very bad—you couldn't ask him who he was without sounding incompetent, and you couldn't really talk to him without knowing who he was. In the back of both your minds was the terrible feeling he was somebody very important. There are a handful of people on the client team who have the power to snap their fingers and make consultants vanish *just like that.* Was he one of these?

You hadn't yet learned the two consultant's panic buttons, which might not have worked with this Jason character anyway. But Lisa, bless her, got an idea.

"We were wondering, Jason—we don't want to take a lot of your time. But we've been working various angles of the problem trying to figure out how to put together a solution with you guys. And we wanted to—basically, to get your reaction to the way this thing is going."

"My reaction?"

"Yeah—we wanted to know what your thoughts were—if you took a step back for a second—what you thought about the overall direction we're headed in and if you had any ideas—any *tweaks*—for something different?"

He waited. Maybe we had lost him . . .

But no: "You're asking for feedback?"

"Uh-huh. On the overall direction."

"Oh," he said, much less belligerent. "I can do that all right—"

Another irony of feedback is that, while to receive feedback requires good listening skills, the feedback itself is often about the quality of one's listening skills. Like tax breaks and complimentary beverage service, those who need it the most are the least likely to get it. Everybody knows that to talk is easy; to listen is not. There is a universal impulse to write, but not to read. We explode with life, burst with community; implode into silence. To listen is to question oneself, and this is terrifying.

Obscure Minnesota writing teacher and memoirist Brenda Ueland put it this way, once: "The true listener is much more beloved, magnetic than the talker, and he is more effective and learns more and does more good."[34]

What a nice woman.

The second day of Feedback Camp you take a multiple-choice test of listening "styles" called the "Listening Styles Inventory." It is one of those entirely transparent personality tests wherein questions are repeated at the end to see if you're paying attention. The questions are vaguely Jungian, like all personality test questions written since the days of Jung. Circle to what extent you agree with the following statements: "When someone is speaking in an angry tone I feel threatened . . ." "I usually take notes when I am attending a lecture . . ." "I am not afraid of speaking in public . . ." "When I am alone, I sometimes talk to myself . . ."

You try to answer in the way that will make you seem the most extroverted. This is the way of the introvert in business.

Your favorite question in this brief inventory is the second to last: "I seek out feedback on my work performance . . ."

Highly disagree.

The Mormon collects your questionnaires to return them after a ten-minute break, which is lethal. Breaks are to be dreaded in these off-site training sessions. The simple reason is that there are entirely too many snacks. Since the cutbacks, all so-called training is held in a series of identical conference

---

[34]Brenda Ueland. "The Art of Listening," *Strength to Your Sword Arm: Selected Writings by Brenda Ueland* (Duluth, MN: Holy Cow! Press, 1993), 42.

centers in the same ten-mile-square region of New Jersey near Basking Ridge, Bridgewater, and Morristown. This is ConferenceLand. Every conference center on the East Coast is here, and the only difference among them is whether they are ten or twenty yards from I-287. The rooms are equipped with fax machines that never receive a fax and cable boxes that never receive the Sci-Fi Channel or Comedy Central. Acres of landings extrude onto empty pre-entries to vacant meeting rooms with labels in the door pockets with the black name of some pharmaceutical company's "Sales Training B."

And in your oasis of hallway, outside the room where the Mormon silently assesses your ability to listen, are cartloads and bongloads of snacks: doughnuts and bear claws and fudge cookies in the morning, dextrously replaced by M&M's and Klondike bars and fudge brownies in the forenoon, relieved by slabs of chocolate cake and mounds of raw brown ice cream after an engorging lunch of cruel roast beef and Mounds. It is as though you are being tended by some force that wants to see you break—you will not leave here looking good.

It is the revenge of New Jersey upon its consultants.

As so often happens, your colleagues from around the world all turn out to be from Chicago. You don't know what is happening in Chicago, but it appears to be something. People are there.

It is easy to strike up a conversation in such a setting—same firm, same generation, same J. Crew wardrobe—but who really wants to?

Nonetheless, you're reaching for a Fast Break when this very thin woman bumps up against you and apologizes. It would have been okay but she bounced off some fat in your side and you suddenly feel grotesque. Once, you were as thin as she is—

"Those are great," she says.

"What are?"

"Fast Break—those are new products, right? Reese's?"

You put it back in the bowl and look at her; she is smiling. Her hair is long and black and she dresses like a J. Crew boy, and she appears to be from India.

"I need to cut down."

"Me too."

There's a pause, as you decide you like one another. Those are good pauses.

"How's the feedback?" she asks.

"It's okay, I don't know—how's yours?"

"My problem is I'm not serious enough when I give the feedback."

"Who said that?"

"The group said that—I'm not serious enough. But you know, it seems kind of silly to me that we're giving feedback to people we don't even know."

This—you could not agree with more. This woman really is not like the others.

"What's your problem?" she probes.

"I'm not good at feedback."

"Like how?"

"I don't like to give it very much, and I don't really want to get it."

She assesses you, thinking. "You know what—I don't think that's right."

"It came out of that team. They made that assessment."

"It's not right—you proved it wasn't right when you told me you don't like to get feedback. See, that itself is feedback and you have no problem with it—so I don't think the problem is you don't want to get feedback at all. That's like a—a smoke screen. I think you're very clever, and you managed to construct this thing—this false problem."

She's right of course, completely right.

"Why would I do that?"

"Probably to show your contempt for this week. This whole camp thing."

You can't say anything. You have nothing to say to this.

"Anyway," she whispers, "nobody likes to get feedback. And *nobody* likes to give it."

"My group does."

"No," she says gently, "they don't."

The military guy appears and pushes past you to get a Fast Break, not really making eye contact.

"My name is Shelagh," she says to you. "I'm from Dallas."

The Mormon reappears and calls you back for your listening styles assessment.

Back in the little room, he goes around the room, starting with Military Boy. The short form of his feedback on the test instrument is this:

❑   Military Boy—High in Analytical Listening, Low in Empathetic Listening
❑   Troubled Teeth Woman—High in Analytical Listening, Low in Empathetic Listening
❑   Talky Girl—Low in Analytical Listening, High in Empathetic Listening
❑   You—High in Analytical Listening, Low in Empathetic Listening

Question: Can you spot the nonconsultant in this group?

That's correct—it is Talky Girl, who is actually an HR person who has come up from your firm's headquarters and is auditing the Feedback Camp for the purpose of being able, at some point in the future, to be a group session facilitator. In other words, she's in training to be a trainer, like the Mormon.

"What we have found," says the Mormon anticlimactically, "is that there's remarkable consistency across the classes, over the years. The listening styles for people drawn into consulting are pretty much consistent."

He puts up a graph that entirely backs up his point; so much so it looks like false data. Analytical listening is an average of nine out of ten over the thousands of associates who have cycled through this camp—and empathetic listening comes in around a three. There is another slide, this one charting the results of partners who have taken the assessment. Strangely, they are a bit more empathetic.

"We're not sure what this means," says the Mormon.

"Maybe they're more relaxed," says Talky Girl, betraying her superior empathy skills—which, quite frankly, you had not observed. But then, you're probably too analytical to notice.

This feedback was a good learning for you, it turns out. You realize you are in an environment where nobody has any feelings.

Including you.

Feelings almost appear the next day, after you cross the Acid River and hurtle yourself through the Web of Pain.

The acid river is not, of course, a real river—it is a metaphor created by consultants hired by your consulting firm to train consultants in how to give feedback, this time in an outdoor setting. The metaphor-creating consultants are not like you: They wear khaki shorts and sport mustaches and tans. They are handsome men and quite flirtatious with the few ladies, including, you notice, Shelagh.

"What we need you to do," explains one of the handsome men in khaki, entirely at ease under a large shade tree, "is to get across that river." He points to an expanse of threadbare lawn within yards of the superhighway. Two long orange ropes mark the banks of the river, and on the far bank there is a pile of wooden boards. The river itself has "rocks" in it: irregularly spaced gray cinder blocks. It seems you will have to cross the river on the boards, supported by the cinder blocks, with a twist:

"The whole team has to get over to the other side. All of the boards have to get over to the other side. And none of the boards can touch any part of the river, just the cinder blocks."

It is an exercise in geometry, as well as balancing on narrow boards holding hands with a person from Chicago you don't know. You saw it in business school as well—people appear, usually men, usually in their late- or even mid-twenties, usually shorter than average—people appear and decide they are in charge and yap and yak and push people here and there like sheep in the meadow. Then, after a few minutes of futility, another person appears, this one usually a woman, also young, perhaps average height—a woman appears, and figures out the answer.

"Put one board across the cinder blocks. Then put another board on that board and a cinder block."

At the time, in context, this is a brilliant observation.

She doesn't help with the web of pain, but that is not a brain puzzle. It is an exercise in lifting people up and putting them down. They're lifted by the team, stiffen their bodies, keep their hair pinned down, and are passed through a web that looks like an acrobat's net turned vertically. There are dire consequences for touching the plastic mesh on the way through the web.

For the debrief, you retire to a porch next to the tennis courts as the sun goes down over ConferenceLand and you assemble fold-up chairs into a time-honored circle of truth.

The head khaki man is glowing with health, while the rest of you are itchy and smell. The highway gets louder. You could really use a Fast Break.

After a moment to respect the moment, the khaki man says, "What did we learn from the web of pain and the acid river?"

The correct answer is: *Nothing.*

Nobody says it. And you are astonished, but nobody tries to be funny. They are surpassingly serious, this new class of drones.

"We learned that it's really important to work as a team."

"And . . . ?"

"And that's all."

"What did you learn about working as a team?"

"That it's really important."

"Besides that?"

Blank looks—when you start this far from the truth, it is almost impossible to leave the realm of cliché. Debriefing phoniness requires phoniness in return.

And as you pack up the boards and disassemble the web of pain, you find yourself working beside the junior khaki man, the one with the mustache, and you venture: "So . . . what were we supposed to learn from this?"

It was now a pile of aluminum poles and a mess of mesh in the dirt.

"I don't know," he says not thoughtfully. "I think you're supposed to tell us."

Every year, either in March or in September depending upon when they started work, the members of your firm are appraised using a method called "360 Degrees." This refers not to the temperature of the appraisee but to a concept of fairness wherein all those *around* the victim are contacted to deliver their feedback: underlings, peers, superiors, and the superiors of superiors who may have something to say. This feedback is delivered anonymously to an appraiser who, by definition, does not know the victim or, if she knows him, has not worked with him. Thus, the appraiser is free to form a negative impression of the victim based not upon personal loathing but upon off-the-record insults delivered by those in a better position to be unimpressed. Once all "360 Degrees" of co-workers have been interviewed, the appraiser completes a six-page appraisal feedback form, which attempts to inject objectivity into what is essentially a binary process—she is/is not good—by forcing observations into various matrices and "skill areas" supposedly useful for executing the job. Strengths are called "core competencies." Weaknesses are called "development areas."

Once complete, the appraisal document is discussed in the course of a two-day set of meetings. Only staffers of a higher rank than the appraisee are welcome—no peers. The appraisee/victim herself is not invited. A verdict is reached, often within minutes. The next victim's appraiser appears.

Some weeks later—and, at times, not at all—those victims not immediately relieved of their livelihoods will sit down with the appraiser and receive the "feedback," with particular emphasis upon the development opportunities identified. It is made clear that, if these development opportunities are not addressed, there will be no more appraisals.

Now, some at the firm like this "360 Degree"/anonymous system and believe it is "as fair as it can be."

You would disagree, based upon two facts:

Fact 1: The appraisal interviews are conducted off a list drawn up by the victim herself. The only people contacted to provide feedback are those the victim has named, giving appraisees some real discretion in weeding out sources of trouble. Few of us are universally loathed; there are usually only pockets of antipathy. A job manager cannot be excluded, of course, without the appraiser getting wise. But job managers are rarely the problem. The problem is peers—all those mini-Machiavellis gaming the system by doing body slams on as many hapless peers as they can. Or perhaps peers who have seen through you to the inept depths below the glib surface. Whoever—these can be neutralized via a carefully honed list.

Fact 2: The appraisal is a charade.

Fact 2 may require some explanation. You are too angry to explain the obvious, that the appraisal process provides an arbitrary Potemkin façade to an equal-opportunity maw of destruction.

You are angry because you learned something, about four weeks after Feedback Camp ended, from which the only things you took away were eight pounds of ugly fat plastered to your sides and a bad case of low self-esteem.

You learned that, after her appraisal, they fired Shelagh.

Her feedback was she didn't "know how to listen."

6

The Complete
Consultant's Dictionary

Imagine you are listening.

It gets worse—now, imagine you are listening to a consultant.

She is dressed in the McKinsey uniform of black outside, white inside, and she is standing on a slightly raised dais in a cavernous hall with some company's logo woven into banners draped across walls in the darkness. An audience surrounds her; some sit behind her at a long table the length of a darkened stage, populated by clean water pitchers and august old men and women at rest. You are in a large and hugely silent group of, say, three hundred people in stadium seats facing her. She is pretty and for that and other reasons you find yourself interested in what she has to say.

Looking down at some notes on the dais, she takes a sip of water from a glass and replaces it.

Then she begins to speak.

She says this:

> Thank you for coming. Today I'd like to socialize
> our sanity check and robustify the straw man we set
> up to drive your strong-form learnings going for-
> ward. As you know, when we ramped up the pod

and began to iterate on the so-what's, we archi-
tected a baseline without boiling the ocean or rein-
venting the wheel. At the end of the day—net
net—our key take-away was that the environmen-
tals in this space are target-rich, and with the right
learnings we could chunk out a deck that laid out
the red light/green light to top-line growth. We
knew this gap analysis was far short of a grand uni-
fying theory, but we liaised with the stakeholders
and put a chinning bar up. After a few revs, we got
some reasonable pushback that—while our hy-
potheses were sufficiently outside the box—they
were also sporty, and perhaps even off the reserva-
tion. Our worry bead at that point was that we were
populating a deliverable, but we were not far
enough along the curve—and may even, frankly,
have been building a mag-a-logue that couldn't
pass the red-face test. Off the record, it was largely
PIOUTA and FHA.

[*long pause for laughter*]

So we did a process check—and a bio break or
two [*more laughter*]—and we decided our journeyline was suboptimal. We got no sat from the client
team. A realization came that we were noodling
around in la-la mode while we were in reality
being incentivized to plug in our skillsets and
knowledgeware to drive step change. We were vi-
sioning the incrementals, though we had been
tasked to blue-sky rich change and drill down to
the bogey of really opening the kimono. Once we
understood the disconnect, we had a food fight
with the summers on the farmer's math [*tit-
ters*] . . . and we did what we had to. The stake-

holders threw up on the process deck, and we were on receive. We needed to vision this wasn't the moral equivalent of being the stuckee on a cactus job in a pre-*Excellence* ecosystem. No—we needed to make a five-forty to keep our cadence true north.

[*pause for water and approbation*]

The pod remained convinced there was a burning platform, but didn't have the bandwidth to go into a black factory and blow up the paradigms with a white paper. Ultimately, we fell back on our core competency—we did a bounceback into crunch mode, and reached for your internal capital to take on a brain dump and data dump. With all the air cover we called in, the engagement became a kind of deathmarch into la-la land. But we didn't want to end up as new alums.

[*she chuckles, alone*]

Our journeyline took on a lot more granularity. We got better visibility into the real drivers of our exposure, and decided it was game over if we didn't change the optics. So we did that, and some client education. We knew this particular knowledgeware could have knock-on effects—and could even hockeystick into an advance, or some afterwork. It was determined by the SAs to pro-act and risk the pain zone. They pinged the practice area internal thought leaders and got some key parachutage into the critical path. After that, we were able to avoid a showstopper by assembling a series of work streams to craft a deliverable with a true end state vision.

[she looks directly at the audience, pausing for effect]

What we need now is your buy-in for the warm
handoff and a warm fuzzy—not to mention the
call up for afterwork!

With a triumphant flip of her mane—it's a magnificent
golden umber—she steps back to greet the applause.

And it comes . . . slowly at first, then with more vigor as the
old men and women at the long table begin to bang their raw
claws together like carpet beaters and—yes!—it is a triumph . . . a speech for the ages . . . and you join them—how
could you not?—as the approval rolls over the crowd like a
wave of despair. . . .

The one question you would have is: *What did she say?*

You look at the program. It says that her name is Meredith,
she went to HBS and works at McKinsey for the Rainmaker.
She studied speechwriting with Barbara Minto in England. She
is more intelligent than you; that much is clear. And popular,
to judge from the calls for an *encore!* rampaging through the
room.

What do these people know that you do not? For to you—
to you, her speech was indecipherable. Words and phrases
held together, but only for a moment, and the moment's
gone.

Much later, when a sympathetic partner takes pity on you,
you will learn that the only difference between these enthusi-
astic speech lovers and yourself is a slim pamphlet entitled
*The Complete Consultant's Dictionary: Words & Phrases You Need
to Know to Talk Like a Top-Tier Management Consultant.* The
pamphlet contains fewer than two hundred critical words and
phrases and their English translations—words and phrases all
consultants know, and use to distance themselves from the
truth. Each profession has its jargon, of course; it's a mechanism for inclusion and, more important, exclusion. Private

languages are used by gangs, by married couples with their
baby talk and cooing, by pediatricians and bartenders and
venture capitalists. *"Ce sera notre probleme,"* says theorist
Jacques Lacan, *"quand nous aborderons la fonction du transfert, de
saisir comment le transfert peut nous conduire au coeur de la répéti-
tion."*[35]

Consultants are no different. No, actually, they are—for
their jargon must exclude without being unapproachable. It
must function along very slender dimensions, creating a
patina of authority and internal wisdom while also seeming
quite clearly to say *something* to the listener, the industrialist,
who has his own language of choice.

If you'd had your dictionary with you that day, you would
have been able to translate Meredith's speech into English. It
would have read something like this:

> Thank you for coming. Today I'd like to tell you
> what we have been doing. When we got here, we
> believed you were in a troubled industry and we
> could probably figure out some way to help. But
> we showed you a few ideas, and you didn't like
> them.
>
> [*long pause for laughter*]
>
> So we did some soul-searching and decided to try
> again.
>
> [*pause for water and approbation*]
>
> We still felt like you were in trouble. To cover our
> asses, we called in some additional partners, even
> though we knew this probably meant more work

[35]You don't speak French and have no idea what this means.

for us. We also did some actual research—we
didn't want to get fired.

[*she chuckles, alone*]

We figured out you weren't happy with the $1,500
team dinners, so we cut down and scheduled many
pointless meetings with you to make you like us.
Also, we found someone in our firm who knew
something. After that, we put together a slide show
we hope you'll like better.

[*she looks directly at the audience, pausing for effect*]

What we need now is your agreement that we can
stay!

You see—entirely clear. Well-structured, even.
Encore.

SELECTIONS FROM *THE COMPLETE CONSULTANT'S DICTIONARY*[36]

Words & Phrases You Need to Know to Talk Like a Top-Tier Management Consultant

Consulting Word/Phrase	*p.o.s.*	Definition / Used in a Sentence . . .
afterwork	*n*	work done after the original **engagement** ends, for an additional fee; the ultimate goal of all consulting, really
bake off	*n*	process whereby a sadistic client auditions a number of different top-tier consulting firms for the same **engagement**, only to hire none of them
beachage, beach time	*n*	time between **engagements**; usu. spent pretending to optimize your **knowledgeware**
bio break	*n*	an extended **process check**, to allow for #2; usu. can only be called by partners over fifty
black factory	*n*	where consultants go when they're doing an open-ended "study" no one will ever read
boil the ocean	*v phr*	what associates do, when they are not **reinventing the wheel**
brain dump	*n*	process of a person who actually knows something imparting information to a consultant
counsel out	*vt*	ax; terminate; fire

[36]The complete dictionary can be found at the end of the book, as Appendix A.

Consulting Word/Phrase	*p.o.s.*	Definition / Used in a Sentence . . .
data dump	*n*	same as a **brain dump**, only more numerical
deathmarch	*n*	an **engagement** that rarely ventures out of the **pain zone**
dentists	*n*	investors
farmer's math	*n*	flawed, quick, in-the-ballpark calculation; usu. accepted as the answer because it is done in public by a partner
FHA	*adj*	made up; comes from, "from Henry's ass," although Henry remains unidentified
five-forty	*n*	changing your mind, changing it back, then changing it again; a combination of doing a **three-sixty** and a **one-eighty**
la-la land	*n*	**la-la mode** that extends beyond six hours . . . to a few months
la-la mode	*n*	state of doing nothing, usually waiting for a **data dump** from the client
new alums	*n*	recently fired employees
pain zone	*n*	the product of (a) the number of partners involved in an **engagement** and (b) the inverse of the time until the first **deliverable**

Consulting Word/Phrase	p.o.s.	Definition / Used in a Sentence . . .
PIOUTA ("pee-yáh-tuh")	*adj*	acronym for "pulled it out of thin air," e.g., "Tomorrow's presentation is gonna be strictly a **PIOUTA** strategy"
pod	*n*	work team
process check	*n*	coffee break, urinary break, or both; not appropriate for defecation
puke/ throw up on	*vt*	react negatively, e.g., "Marianne really **threw up on** your deck at the **pulse check** yesterday."
reinvent the wheel	*v phr*	*see* **boil the ocean**
rolling off	*vi*	leaving an **engagement**, probably to go **on the beach** and then get **counseled out** due to low **billability**
suboptimal	*adj*	loathsome
swag	*n*	a **wag**, only a *s*mart one
wag	*n*	a *w*ild-*a*ssed *g*uess

Employing *The Complete Consultant's Dictionary* early and often can get you a long way toward developing that faux expert-in-everything glow of the successful top-tier consultant. But it is not enough—there is another critical speech element you will need to master. It may seem simple, but it's absolutely essential to fitting in within your pod.

The origins of this mode of speech are obscure, but it is common to all top-tier firms in English-speaking countries. Rather than come right out and say what it is, you will try an experiment. You are writing this at work.[37] As usual, you are camped in a tiny windowless room with four other youngish men and two of them are having a loud work discussion, disrupting the thought flows of your other cell mate, assembling a bar graph in PowerPoint, and yourself, writing this.

You transcribe their discussion verbatim:

"Tom's going to Claudia, I want her to know where it's coming out, right?"

"Right—is she gonna present to Claudia?"

"Right."

"If she's supportive of this I kind of want her to present, right? We kind of want that."

"She's in training, she can't help us at all, right? We positioned—we're positioning this as—it's just an update—"

"Essentially what we're saying is your first pass has larger ramifications than—"

"Right—"

"—than what you were planning for, right?"

"Right—"

"So we're gonna drive that home to them and hope she—she doesn't have something off the top of her head like she does sometimes."

"Like the sales of Wal-Mart channel, or whatever, they're like . . . blah blah blah, right?"

"Okay. Right."

A funny person might enjoy writing dialogue for a couple of consultants driving somewhere and giving one another directions like, "It's left, right?"

"Right."

"You said left."

"Right."

---

[37]Don't inform the client, please.

"Right or left?"

"Left, right?"

"Right—"

But a funny person would not be in a car with a couple of consultants driving somewhere, right?

7

The Good Partner

The Good Partner knows all the words—in fact, he invented a few of them.[38] He never interviewed at McKinsey and did not attend HBS. At the time he joined your firm, ten years ago, he was a professor of economics at a small Midwestern university. He ran eight miles a day, drank filtered water, loved his wife and Lhasa apso. He's an ordinary-looking man—neither tall nor short, fat nor thin, bald nor not so bald. And he's the most successful, joyful consultant you know, right?

You pause in the course of this litany of atrocity to ask a simple question: *What makes the Good Partner good?*

You are no expert in the art of leadership; most of your life has prepared you simply to be an expert in followership. You have followed many and have followed well. You have won prizes for your ability to follow and have been praised in year-end job reviews at length for your remarkable acquiescence to authority. There have been some very difficult bosses who have been utterly grateful for your ability to suppress your own personality to the realization of their greater vision. Your secret is, of course, that you have very little to suppress and no appetite for responsibility. The sheep is your favorite animal.

It has sometimes puzzled you that so much attention has

[38]See *warm fuzzy, GUT,* and *farmer's math*—although *farmer's math* is also claimed by a partner based in Amsterdam—in Appendix A.

been paid to leadership. There are leadership seminars and books—encyclopedias—on leadership. Learned articles are written in the *Harvard Business Review* and *strategy + business* on the seven or eight or twenty principles of first-rate leadership. Courses abound at HBS and lesser schools on the characteristics of the great and important leader. *Business Week* and *Forbes* weekly and biweekly, respectively, profile leaders, lionize leaders, scrutinize and itemize and systematize the observed minutiae of the leadership class.

But when it comes to *followers . . . ?* Nothing.

As far as you can tell, not a single article has ever been written in the eighty years of the *HBR* about the secrets of the great follower. Not a single cover of *Business Week* has been given over to this country's Follower of the Year. There are no seminars on following at HBS or other lesser schools on the psychodynamics of following . . . and this, as you say, has sometimes puzzled you.

The reason is that most people will spend their lives as followers, not leaders. The kind of leaders who are studied by the business scribes and academics—people like the great Jack Welch of General Electric, the great Lou Gerstner of IBM, the great Attila the Hun, Elizabeth I, and Jesus[39]—these leaders are extremely rare. You could enter a business career assuming you will *never* be a leader of that rarefied caliber and you would almost certainly be right. Why waste time obsessing over Jack's criteria for divesting underperforming units, or Attila's predilection for attacking enemies from the rear? Almost none of you will ever single-handedly get to divest a unit—underperforming or otherwise—or attack an enemy from any direction whatsoever.

There is no shame in this. Following is essential. It is one of the core values of the U.S. Navy: "Obey Orders." Without good following, there is no point to leadership. It is essentially

[39]See Wes Roberts, *Leadership Secrets of Attila the Hun* (New York: Warner Books, 1990); Alan Axelrod, *Elizabeth I, CEO* (New York: Prentice Hall Press, 2000); and Laurie Beth Jones, *Jesus, Entrepreneur* (New York: Three Rivers Press, 2002).

vacuumed, like two actors doing *Zoo Story* in their apartment for their cats.

In his 1960 classic *The Human Side of Enterprise*, Douglas McGregor outlined two well-known models of worker motivation, which he called Theories X and Y. The former assumes "that the average human has an inherent dislike of work and will avoid it if he can." The latter, on the contrary, assumes "that the expenditure of physical and mental effort in work is as natural as in play or rest." Moreover, goes McGregor's Theory Y, a lot of people—maybe even *most* people, maybe even *you*—have within them "the capacity to exercise a relatively high degree of imagination, ingenuity, and creativity."[40]

This Theory Y was considered something quite unusual in an era when the Dow Jones Industrial Average was composed of companies such as International Nickel, Corn Products Refining, National Steel, and American Smelting. Theory Y is, however, true. People do like to work—provided they are in the right job.

Or provided they need the job they're in.

You are in one of these two categories yourself, and that is why you appreciate the Good Partner. For to this day managers adhere to Theory X or to Theory Y, and no others. There is a quick and flawless test of whether people are true Republicans. Ask them, "Do you believe people with money generally deserve it?" If they say yes—Republican. If they say, "It depends on how they got it"—Democrat. In the same way, you can tell bad partners from good partners by the answer to a simple question: "What do you think associates do when you're not looking?" If they say, "Precious little"—well, they're bad.

The Good Partner is a Theory Y person, though he doesn't make it obvious. Subtlety, too, is a hallmark of good management.

*   *   *

[40]Douglas McGregor, *The Human Side of Enterprise* (1960; reprint, New York: McGraw-Hill/Irwin, 1985), 419.

Philip Selznick wrote a 1957 book called *Leadership in Administration*, unearthed by McHarvardites Thomas J. Peters and Robert H. Waterman Jr. in their best-selling *In Search of Excellence*. You think it may help answer this question about what makes the Good Partner good. There is something about Selznick's style that is impenetrable—almost poetic. So you decide to present his prose in the form of a distinctly postmodern tone poem:

> The art of the creative leader
> Is the art of
> Institution building
>
> The reworking of human and technological
> Materials to fashion
> An organism
> That embodies new and enduring values
>
> . . . .
>
> To institutionalize is to *infuse with value*
> Beyond the technical requirements
> Of the task at hand.
>
> The prizing of social machinery
> Beyond its technical role
> Is largely
> A reflection of the unique way it fulfills
> Personal or group needs.
>
> Whenever individuals become attached
> To an organization or a way
> Of doing things as persons
> Rather than as technicians
>
> The result is a prizing of the device
> For its own sake . . .

The institutional leader, then,
Is primarily an expert

In the promotion and protection of values.

So there it is: the Answer! Great leaders are . . . are . . .
What?

Or, as Peters and Waterman themselves comment, in a rare moment of levity: "We should pause briefly here, as we exalt values, to ask what values?"[41]

The Ten Most Overused Words in Business

1. Leverage
2. Grow (*vt*)
3. Going forward
4. Skillset
5. Drive (*vt*)
6. Pushback
7. At the end of the day
8. Buy-in
9. Incentivize
10. Core value

Price is what you pay. Value is what you get.

—WARREN BUFFETT

---

[41]Thomas J. Peters and Robert H. Waterman Jr., *In Search of Excellence* (New York: Warner Books, 1982), 85.

Defending the core value of the company that is different from the competitor [*sic*] during difficult times is the quintessence of the search for the truth north.

ORIT GADIESH, president, Bain & Co.

In every culture there is a central core of religious convictions and moral values which constitutes, as it were, its soul.

So greatness in leadership may be related to values. You've heard this word a lot since leaving show business behind: *Values.* Core values. They are supposed to be the bedrock upon which any successful enterprise rests, right? Right?

What exactly are core values? You begin to wonder what one might look like. Like the Ten Commandments? Those are commandments, not values. Those are things you have to do or you will be punished, whereas values would seem—from their name—to be more like things that come from inside and aren't punishment-related. They're an aspect of goodness.

And as you ponder values, you begin to wonder—as you so often do—about McKinsey. Does it have core values? Come to think of it, do you? You remember something from your new-hire orientation in New Jersey—some partner with glasses saying something about the permanent values or core values of your firm. *What were they?*

You have no idea.

You decide it would be a good idea to find out. Surely any good partner is only as good as the values she embraces, embodies, and lives. Surely these values are a part of her secret.

You turn to the colleague toiling next to you in your windowless, airless death pit in New Jersey. Trying to sound matter-of-fact, you say, "So, what are our core values?"

"What?"

"[Your top-tier firm's name.] Our values. Our core values—what are they?"

"Do we have some?"

"Of course we do. Everybody does. They're our soul."

"I don't think we have any."

"So you don't know."

"I'm saying I don't think we have any."

Undaunted, you ask a few other people on the team. They do not think it a strange question; they haven't slept in three weeks; any oddity is ingested quite calmly.

"We used to have them," says a new associate, a woman who lives not far away in Montclair, New Jersey, and so is better rested. "They decided they didn't apply anymore."

"What do you mean, anymore?"

"They changed them and then they went away."

"Are there any left?"

"There might be one or two. Just the good ones."

"Which ones?"

"I think like . . . I don't know."

"Why did they shorten the list? What was wrong with the long list?"

"People were getting confused."

You feel she's nervous and committing the sin of many new associates: acting like an expert. But what she says can't be right—are values really so powerful they can *actively hurt* a company?

You ask your team leader, a partner who—while not qualifying for the title of good partner—is nonetheless not exactly bad either.

"I don't remember," he says, over $450 worth of team sushi in the conference at 10:30 p.m. that night. This is a man who joined the firm out of Kellogg at twenty-five, half his life ago. "Check the Web site."

You check the Web site—and there they are! The core values. Rather a lot of them, in fact. Your firm appears to have a number of cores—multitudes of souls Ping-ponging around through cyberspace shoring up the commitment, character, and aspirations of your cohorts, entirely unbeknownst to them. It is dismaying, in a way, just how *many* core values you have.

There are ten. In the manner of David Letterman,[42] you list them backward:

10. Trust
 9. Respect
 8. Integrity
 7. Fairness
 6. Professionalism
 5. Teamwork
 4. Entrepreneurship
 3. Diversity
 2. Excellence

And the number one core value of your top-tier management consulting firm is . . .

 1. Client Service

[42]The most admired celebrity in your age group (thirty-two to thirty-nine), according to a recent poll in *US Weekly*.

There it is. The "soul"—as Pope John Paul II called it in a speech at the University of Havana—of your firm. The "true north" toward which your compass points in the turbulent seas of commerce and dismemberment. The rigid spine around which the magical character of your treasured Good Partner is wrapped.

Why do you feel so empty inside?

Is it that these words are like the current president—they sound like something but mean a little less? It's not that they're impeachable—of course not. Who could argue that "trust" is entirely toothless in life, or that "teamwork" is trivial in a business where people work together all day in teams? Who could call "diversity" a bad thing or summon the troops together to argue that never—under *any circumstances*—is anyone in this building to strive for anything remotely resembling "excellence"? One you might quibble with is "entrepreneurship"—what does *that* mean? Should you start your own Web site on the side, perhaps selling client company secrets to the highest bidder? That jibes with the "entrepreneurship" value, but it would seem to conflict directly with the value about "client service," unless kickbacks are involved. And those kickbacks would have to be fairly distributed ("fairness") among *all* the client team members ("diversity").

This is troubling. You had expected more, somehow. Your firm is best-in-class in its ability to disappoint. You've found yet another region where you're falling behind the competition. Or are you? What about all the other top-tier management consulting firms? What are their core values? What drives them to be great? What sets their compass, points their sled dogs, blows their forecastle? You decide this is worth finding out.

Bain & Co.: You locate an undated white paper called "Winning in Turbulence," written by Bain's Darrell Rigby. In it, Mr. Rigby echoes his boss Orit Gadiesh: "The best compass in turbulent times is a strong set of core values that consistently guides choices among tradeoffs." There is that *compass* again, presumably pointing toward you-know-where. A very nautical firm, Bain. It turns out that the compass may be encountering some turbulence of its own. For Bain's core values do not appear to be consistent; Gadiesh, in her frequent speeches, alludes to them and at times enumerates them, but her own personal lists do not agree with those put out by the company itself.

Gadiesh's core values are: passion, teamwork, responsibility, and fun.[43]

Elsewhere, Bain recites its core values as follows: ownership, communication, collaboration, teamwork, and value creation. The value creation core value has some subcore values of its own, namely, client service, analytics, and collaboration. Note that the last core value there—collaboration—appears on both lists, perhaps indicating a lack of collaboration among those dreaming up Bain's lists and sublists of core values.

If your firm was guilty of core value inflation, Bain & Co. has fallen victim to a fritzy guidance system.

Boston Consulting Group: So you turn to BCG—a truly impressive firm. Not full of egregious pricks like the McKinsey crowd, BCG is the regular guy's top-tier consulting firm (provided that regular guy was Phi Beta Kappa and went to Wharton). Perhaps a bit too regular—they don't have *any* core values. That is, they don't have a list of traits they explicitly label "core values." They do, however, have a mission that reads a lot like a set of core values. "We see the essence of our work as a virtuous circle of insight, impact, and trust," declares BCG, naming what could easily be construed to be its top three values. Other values cited by BCG in its corporate and recruiting literature include diversity, personal growth, and passion.

---

[43]Orit Gadiesh, "Protect Your Core Difficult As This May Be" [*sic*], *Maeil Business Newspaper*, October 17, 2002.

Not really passion so much as: "A passion for going beyond the obvious."

Though not, apparently, in its core values.

You look at other firms—AT Kearney, BearingPoint, Accenture—and notice *not a single point of agreement* among them, valuewise. The only plaintive note is sung by Cap Gemini Ernst & Young (CGEY): its Web page takes a postliterate approach to the whole core values ad hocracy by citing honesty, boldness (!), trust, freedon [*sic*], teamwork, modesty (!), and fun (solo fun: "the feeling *one* gets when *one* is happy to work, feels good in the team to which *one* belongs, is proud of what *one* does and achieves *one*'s objective in the never-ending search for top quality and the greatest possible effectiveness"). (italics added)

And CGEY has summed it up best in a recent corporate statement: "Under pinning [*sic*] our values is a common aspiration on [*sic*] all of us—'We say what we do and we do what we say.'"[44]

One agrees.

McKinsey & Co.: McKinsey weighs in with *two* missions ("Help clients make lasting improvements" and "Attract and develop exceptional people") and *four* so-called aspirations ("Service clients," "Deliver the best," "Environment for superior talent," and "Values-driven governance"). Moreover, not to disappoint seekers such as yourself, they close out this impressive run with *four* actual, official "core values."

McKinsey's four core values, paraphrased:

1. Impact
2. Being the Best
3. Meritocracy
4. Self-governance

[44]Available for admiration at http://www.uk.cgey.com/careers/transition/our_-people.shtml.

While your firm had ten values and can't spell any of them, McKinsey has just four and lives at least a few. It occurs to you that maybe there is a key lesson in here—that having *fewer* val ues is better than having *more* values, because people have bad memories.

As it happens, you're pondering this shortly after *Fortune* magazine issues its annual list of the Most Admired Companies in America.[45] Because it is what consultants do, you decide to perform a quick analysis. You take a sample of companies from the top and the bottom of the list—the most-admired and the least-admired, as it were—and compare their core values, looking for patterns. Among the most-admired, you pick the top five: Wal-Mart, Southwest Airlines, Berkshire Hathaway, Dell, and General Electric. Among the least-admired, you go for Tyco, Waste Management, and— everybody's favorite disaster story of the new millennium— Enron. You throw in a few wild cards such as Comedy Central, which sometimes makes you laugh; the U.S. Navy, inventor of core values; the CIA, inventor of fear; Wrigley, because you like gum; the Dollywood theme park; the Catholic Church; and the Buddha.

It turns out *they're all the same*. That is, the twenty-five enti-ties in your sample cite fifty-two different core values. Of these, twenty-two (42 percent) are mentioned only once. Fully 65 percent are mentioned only once or twice; these cats and dogs include such values as **modesty, honor, freedom, family**, and **heartfelt emotions**. On the other hand, ten values are mentioned by five or more of the survey sample and an additional three are cited by four or more. These are the top ten core values of the survey population, in order from least-to most-mentioned:

10. Fun
 9. Honesty

---

[45]See the *Fortune* cover story "America's Most Admired Companies," March 3, 2003.

8. Trust
7. Diversity
6. Responsibility
5. Teamwork
4. Excellence
3. Respect
2. Integrity

And the number one core value of your survey sample is . . .

1. Client Service

You are about to give up on this core values idea completely when you run across a little company that reaffirms your faith in the basics. We should not allow the Enrons of the world to corrupt our belief in the Judeo-Christian ideal of first principles. Maybe the pope was right. Maybe a company's soul can be scrawled onto parchment and embodied wholly within word and deed. The company in question is Dollywood, a theme park in Tennessee founded by country superstar Dolly Parton. With a tip of the briar to Lacan and Derrida, the wits at Dollywood decided that their core value was simply this: **value**. So obvious it's brilliant. Moreover, they take the next step right away and turn this **value** value into a series of *actions*. No vague chitchat. No running around stewarding the environment. No, at Dollywood they deliver value through their key principles. These include "special kid's [*sic*] meals at 10 different restaurants" and "reduced admissions for seniors and children."

With value like that, who needs values?

Dollywood aside, you begin to suspect that, like the war on terror, this core values idea is a lie developed to serve the master race. That is, until you happen to run across a copy of the *Pfizer Annual Report 2001*. Pfizer is one of the most successful companies on the planet, making over $10 billion every year *in profits* selling drugs like Viagra and Zoloft. It also turns out to be one of the most honest. In bold yellow text on a deep blue background on the cover of its annual report sits this sentence:

> "Our mission is to become the world's
> most valued company."

That's a step in the right direction you think.

It reminds you of a corporate finance class in business school where the professor posed a profound question on the last day before spring break. "What," he asked, "is the ultimate goal of all corporate finance?" Kids shouted out nonsense like "To keep companies in business" . . . "To make the markets more efficient" . . . "To fund important projects" . . .

"No," he said, "it's more practical than that. It's to *maximize shareholder value.*"

You didn't know it at the time, but that phrase—"maximize shareholder value"—is a business cliché, a commercial mantra as overworked as "core value" and perhaps even more so. But it occurs to you both phrases have the word *value* in them . . . and that leads you to think maybe you have been approaching this question from the wrong angle. You have assumed the values in core values are something eternal and vaguely spiritual, like religious or ethical laws or the works of Tony Robbins. Perhaps they aren't. Value has another meaning, after all—the one called forth by Pfizer and your professor:

> Value = Money

That's an honest-to-God core value.

*   *   *

You shoehorn the Good Partner in here—in a not entirely convincing way—because you have taken some of your feedback to heart. Talky Girl's words— *"It's very difficult to tell if you're serious or not"*—didn't bother you; you have heard that before. Sometimes, when you look back, it seems you have heard nothing *but* that before. No—it is something the Mormon says, on your last day at camp. On that day, after you have circled the room giving your feedback to the other members of the team, he pauses a moment and then says:

"Okay—now, I think it's only fair right now. To ask. Do any of you have any feedback for me?"

There is a rather long silence, as everyone waits for someone else to say something.

You hear "Not really . . . no . . . uh-uh" from the others—and think: *Cowards!* And then a subtle shift in focus . . . away from the Mormon . . . around the room and up and toward the door—please let us leave—and then settling upon . . . *you.* Why you? This was inevitable: You are the one with the feedback development need. You are the one who supposedly has a problem with feedback, and here it is—a perfect opportunity, just handed to you, to do some work on your development need. That's what they're all thinking.

As it happens, you don't like the Mormon. It's much easier giving feedback to a person you don't like.

"All right," you say, "I have something."

"Yes?" he asks, gently.

"I think sometimes you—you try to use humor as a way to get people to like you, or something. Not to get people to like you—more like, to, to avoid an unpleasant moment, or something that might be uncomfortable."

"Yes?"

"Like yesterday, in the big plenary in the room. You were setting up that slide show about how we all want to be chiefs but we have to be Indians—"

"Yes?"

"That slide show—you started off with a joke, and, and,

and . . . I just think sometimes it's okay if you're—if you want
to be, I mean, it's okay to be—it's just that, that . . . it doesn't
have to be, you don't have to. Setting things up, okay, I see
maybe—what I mean is, you don't have to."

"Say again?"

"All I mean is, it's okay to be serious sometimes. Totally serious."

He pauses to think, perhaps, or to make you suffer in the
toxic afterglow of some seriously inarticulate feedback.

"Thank you for that," he says, leaning forward. "I have a
question, though."

"Yes?"

"Whether or not my jokes are funny—well, that's not really
important, at the end of the day. Right? What's important is,
it seems to me, whether I'm communicating what I need to
say. Right?"

"Uh-huh."

"Now *you* have this really dry sense of humor, almost British
in a way. It's so dry it's really difficult to tell when you're jok-
ing and when you're not. I feel like that's almost worse than
if you were making bad jokes, or whatever. Do you get my
point?"

"Well . . ."

"That's right," pipes up Talky Girl, of course. "My feedback
would be your style is *more* confusing than his. Anyway, that
joke was funny yesterday."

"Thank you," says the Mormon.

"Yeah," says Military Guy, who had been slowly peeling the
label off a bottle of something. "Especially in, like, a professional environment. You have got to know where you stand."

"I agree," someone chimes in—and you wonder how this
turned into a feedback session about *you*.

"Do you agree with that?" the Mormon asks you.

"Sure."

"Good luck," he says.

Now—what sticks with you from this exchange is not the

feedback you got from the group. You happen to think British people are funny. What sticks with you is the Mormon's rather defensive inability to accept your feedback graciously—his low-key lashing out. *Good luck!* This, you decide, is very bad listening. It's not analytical, or empathic—it's pathetic.

Feedback Camp was on the right track, after all.

The Good Partner is good because he knows *exactly* how to listen.

8

Basic Math for
Regular Einsteins

Something else the Good Partner does very well is rough, rough math problems *superfast*!

"How much for tires?"

"Um . . . um . . ."—you fumble through your pages and pages of printed out Excel spreadsheets. "Five cents."

"Mileage per year?"

"Um . . . um . . . two hundred fifty or three hundred."

"Let's say two-fifty. Coast to coast?"

"Pretty much."

"Yes or no?"—this is the Danish Partner. His child is not well, pretty seriously not well, in fact. The stress has turned him into a first-class jerk, which nobody holds against him.

"Um . . . yes."

"And full truckloads?"

"Yes."

"What's the price of diesel?"—this is the Good Partner, asking you an obvious and easy question to which, unfortunately, you do not have an answer.

"Right now?"

"Yes, right now."

You make something up. "One-sixty."

"One-sixty?"

"Um . . . yes . . . ?"

"All right."

And they're *off*—three highly paid quite senior members of your firm's partnership, crammed into a conference room sixty stories above the city of Cleveland, scratching furiously on light-blue lined graph paper with the fountain pens, a manic look in their eyes—adding, dividing—and, at the edge of their peripheral vision but never wholly out of sight, the *other* partners . . . scratching more furiously . . . getting closer, closer, *closer* to the—

"I've got it," announces the Quiet Partner, who wears thick glasses and always gets it first. "Thirty-two point five cents a mile."

"Point seven five," jabs the Danish Partner.

"Not quite. You overcounted downtime."

"Downtime is an opportunity cost."

"Not if you have to incur it anyway, right?"

"What do you mean?" asks the Good Partner.

"In the truck lanes, the quick oil changes and tune-ups, right? Routine maintenance is part of running a truck. So downtime—"

"Has to be net of the routine stuff." The Good Partner nods.

More scratching on the graph paper, then the Danish Partner looks up, scowling. "He's right."

"Of course he's right," says the Good Partner, smiling. "He's always right."

Round 1 to the Quiet Partner.

It is perhaps true that the single distinguishing characteristic shared by all those who make their lives long-term in consulting—as opposed to those, like yourself, who are just passing through on their way to something worse—is their ability to perform very simple calculations *very fast*. Many times you have sat in meetings with, say, three partners, pencils poised, waiting for a simple calculation to perform at *blistering speed*.

You have attended many, many brutal rounds—competitive speed math is the only sport enjoyed by your leadership cadre. It combines all those attributes consultants like to think they possess: all-around intelligence, numerical ability, problem-solving, and a lust for estimation. In fact, as the consultant's rank improves, so does her distance from actual numbers. While associates are not allowed to estimate *anything*, the higher-ups are impatient with precision. Perhaps they have learned something.

Perhaps they have learned that consulting math isn't really math at all.

As business prose is prose for drool-bucket doofoids, so everyday business math is math for blistering bozos. It's math that is an insult to math. Basic to the point of banality: addition (90 percent), subtraction (very rarely), multiplication (in Excel), and division (whole numbers only). It is true that math as complex as any yet invented, and some yet more complex, is practiced by people in business; people on Wall Street with fast machines generating chaos and complexity guiding men with money to burn. Those people are not consultants.

What follows is a brief guide to the quantitative skills required of a top-tier consultant. The guide is brief because— well, because not so very many quantitative skills are required.

Orders of Magnitude—How to compare things that are not really alike

Top-tier consulting requires an easy facility with numbers from all walks of life. Numbers—particularly large, round numbers—are the top-tier consultant's table water. An essential component of any tool kit is an ability to understand *orders of magnitude*, or how things that aren't really alike can be made to seem more alike.

For instance: The population of the United States is about three hundred million. In recent years, Wal-Mart has enjoyed annual sales (mainly in the U.S.) of about $200 billion, making it the largest company by revenues that has ever terrorized the geosphere. It follows that Wal-Mart annually sells over $650 worth of stuff *to every man, woman, and child in the country.* That's a lot of stuff. And it has been estimated that every American generates about one ton of garbage per year, or three hundred million tons of garbage—about ninety-five thousand tons for every Wal-Mart/Sam's Club location. Coincidence?

Addition & Multiplication—How to bill a client (early and often)

Billing of the consultant's time happens like this: Each rank of consultant, from first-year associate (called an "A1") through senior associate ("SA"), principal ("P"), and partners (called "Officers"), has a published hourly rate. A fully billable week is assumed to contain forty working hours. The consultant's hourly rate is simply multiplied by forty to get that consultant's cost for the week. The forty-hour assumption holds no matter how many hours the consultant actually works; whether it's one hundred or twenty, the client is billed for forty hours. Consultants are therefore spared the indignity of lawyers, who must account for their time to the minute and are assessed on their ability to avoid going home.

What's surprising to many new consultants—and clients—is just how astronomically *high* the hourly billing rates are. For instance, a summer associate—a twenty-six-year-old with a couple of marketing classes under her belt—bills out at $100 per hour. Top-flight emergency room physicians bill about $140 per hour. A new associate—now twenty-seven years old with a couple more marketing courses under her belt—charges $225 per hour.

And it only gets worse:

Rank	Hourly Rate
Associate 1	$225
Sr. Associate 1	$415
Principal 1	$495
Entry Partner	$700
Sr. Partner	$865

By comparison, a world-famous attorney—a person such as David Boies, defender of Al Gore in Florida, or Johnny Cochran, defender of O.J. Simpson—has a billing rate somewhere around $500 per hour. So it follows that even a superstar attorney brings less value to a client's table than a first-year principal at some random consulting firm.

There is an important distinction at work here, of course. You can be sure David Boies and Johnny Cochran actually *get* their hourly rate—that is, they personally receive the money and could take it to Tahiti if they chose. On the other hand, you the associate manifestly do *not* get your $225 per hour.

How much do you get? The working ratio is about four to one—that is, you the worker receive in your hand about $55 per hour. Where does the other $170 go? Use your imagination.

This equation can be represented visually as follows:

Partners   **You**

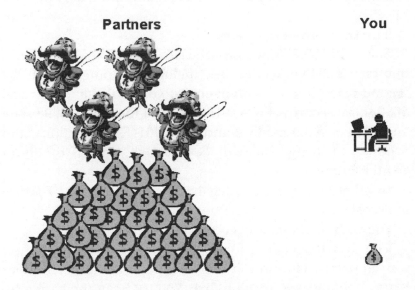

Subtraction—What happens to all that money

You were moving your brother's apartment for the fifth time in four years recently, and he asked you your salary. The mistake you made was that you told him. It felt wrong doing it; it felt wronger after. He was at the time an English teacher at a particularly hairy public school in Bushwick and was battling clinical depression.

"One hundred and fourteen thousand," you said.

"Oh my God." He whistled. "You're set for life."

If only—

Net net, within a few months you are dismayed to learn your brother is boning up for the GMAT. He wants to go to Columbia Business School. This is an illustration of what a business philosopher might call the Fallacy of the Gross.[46]

As a second-year associate at a top-tier firm, you are paid a base salary of $117,000. This amount is payable monthly for the previous month, meaning you gross exactly $9,750 on the last day of each month. This is a highly respectable amount, considering the job on the TV show you left to go to business school paid you exactly $6,000 per month, for each month you worked. B-school seems to have handed you a 63 percent raise!

The key word here is *seems* . . .

Start with $9,750 per month. Now the *subtraction* begins. Subtract: $2,340 in federal tax (including imputed tax on the second-year tuition reimbursement you foolishly deferred), $680 social security/FICA, $160 Federal Medicare, $598 state and city tax, $165 medical and $975 401(K) deductions, and others . . . leaving you with $4,800 per month, or about $57,600 annually.

In other words, entirely legally, *somebody is taking 57 percent of your paycheck every month.* Poor you.

You wish the bewailing could stop—but, but no . . .

The dreaded student loans; there they sit, like a tithe on your impulses. They will sit there forever, or at least ten more years, nibbling at your will to live. You took out the bare minimum, persisting on savings plus $15,000–$20,000 each year,

---

[46]This is the wrongheaded practice of confusing a postgraduate's gross pay (the amount on her paycheck) with the only thing that really matters to that postgraduate: i.e., what she gets to put in the bank.

neglecting your wife's diet and your own addiction to ballet. But you weren't a scholarship baby; you were too freaky and showbiz to get institutional funding. So you resorted to loans heaped upon loans.

You pay them off in two groups—the Sallie Mae–herded federal loans, and a hodgepodge of smaller loans, including two from Columbia University itself, that are managed by somebody else. Each month your bank account is debited by both loan managers and you are denied the enjoyment of these funds. The Sallie Mae debit is for $285, and the other one is for $210—together, they amount to just under $500 monthly, year after year, or over 10 percent of your current net pay.

Grand total, net, after student loans: $4,300 per month.

So it would have been more honest to say to your brother, in response to his question about your salary: "I make fifty-two thousand, whether I need it or not."

This in a city where the average one-bedroom apartment rents for about $30,000 per year.

As the Good Partner likes to say, "That's an awful long way to go for a very short drink."

Final Accounting—The greatest math of all

As an ultimate note, it seems fitting to ask: Who pays for all this? Consultants—top-tier and otherwise—exist. Ergo, clients must exist. Despite abounding skepticism, a recession or two, and sky-high fees, people are still willing to part with real shareholder value for the privilege of securing your help. Who?

The answer contains a kind of existential epiphany, but before we get there let's list, in order, the industries that are the major consumers of strategy consulting services:

1. Information and communications (including Telecom)
2. Financial services

3. Health care
4. Public sector (including the U.S. government)
5. Energy & utilities

Together, these groups account for most of the $22 billion spent on strategy consulting in 2001.[47] A casual observer might conclude that these five industries hired so many consultants because (a) they're more complicated than other industries; and (b) they need more help. Both conclusions are wrong. No industry is inherently more complicated than any other. Dig deeply enough into salmon farming and you uncover a mountain of detail on spawning habits and water temps and trends at least equal in complexity to the memory chip trade. And it turns out these five industries are *not* more helpless—in fact, quite the opposite.

Industries that hire consultants are *the ones who can afford them*—the ones with ample free cash flows to match the ample fees. Consultant-buying companies are the ones that are doing well, making money, building shareholder value, stuffing the piggy bank. Is this because they hire consultants? Probably not—it would be difficult to imagine a pharmaceutical or medical services company so poorly run in the rigged-up U.S. market that it didn't choke on its own spigot of cash. The same goes for telecommunications (until recently). And the U.S. government, whatever it says, is a money machine.

No—the sad fact is, most companies who hire consultants (a) would do fine without them, and (b) have too much green in their sacks. There is a name for a very expensive, dubiously useful item purchased by people of superior means.

That name is: *Luxury.*

---

[47]"Global Strategy Consulting Marketplace" (New York: Kennedy Information, 2002), 71.

Part III

In the Client's Own Godforsaken Town

Part III describes in fervid detail the glamorous daily life of the top-tier management consultant:

1. *Things to do in **Cleveland** when you're dead*

2. *Proper etiquette at dreaded team events, including seemingly **endless dinners***

3. *How to lose your (a) **personality**, and (b) **looks**—yet still be more attractive than your client*

4. *Appropriate ways to handle a client who **hates you***

5. *Paying your own salary by working for the **government***

9

Welcome to the Working Weekend

Good morning!

It is Monday and you have a big week ahead of you. This week is enormous. Its shape is unknown but its size is too clear. A week on the road; a week in consulting, engaged, on the map. You are barely awake, yet your heart is atwitter with shame. The first thing is the bomb. It goes off in a pile of white powder. What time is it, anyway? Does anybody here know what time it is? And the echo . . .

4:30 a.m.

Snooze.

. . . A sound within silence; black and red, a team of surgeons and nurse practitioners holding bowls of ripe fruit. Is there to be a celebration? Maria Kowroski the great ballerina appears arbitrarily, carving careful patterns into the operating theater, her patterns resurrecting garish lamps and . . .

4:39 a.m.

Snooze.

It is not clear when you awake these Monday mornings, but the earliness is so extreme it looks like death. You micturate, rend water on your face. The mirror is a mistake; each day your body retreats from some ideal. You take a bath, which is also dangerous. It's never entirely clear that your wife is asleep. She is halfway there, always halfway there. It used to be a secret set of events, these Monday mornings—padding to the sock drawer, hoping for a blindfolded color match, and out the door without a kiss. But then she said one day, "What you're trying to avoid has happened—I'm already awake. So kiss me good-bye."

The bath is dangerous because it is so wide and deep . . .

4:52 a.m.

What you are trying to avoid has already happened.

You talk to people you work with about travel; there is little you have in common besides a certain rootlessness, and so there is this travel chat. It seems they have a system, as consultants do, and are in possession of two *entirely separate suites of things.* There are those ensembles—the clothes, the shoes, the toiletries and books and electronic equipment—that append their lives. Then there is the separate set of stuff—clothes, shoes, toiletries, stamps, and protein bars—they set aside for rituals like this . . .

Fuck.

5:01 a.m.

The phone rings. A tear falls. There is a country doggerel rhythm to this winter in Long Island City, Queens, ten minutes from Laguardia Airport.

"Hello," you say.

"Is this Marty?"

"Yum."

"This is Allegro Car calling. Your car number five-oh-one is outside *now.*"

"Smmmm."

As you say, your colleagues pack twice to live once. They have their travel bag on call, like diplomats and counterrevolutionaries. Their stated purpose is to organize their trip logistics, cut down on worry time. You know the real reason for compartments, though. They need to separate themselves from themes of loss.

You kiss your wife good-bye. She has never been awake.

The thing you are trying to avoid has already happened.

The cars you ride have skidded down the decimation—the rest of the economy may be in recession, but consulting deserves a better word—have skidded down, so you find yourself inhabiting a Lincoln Continental with a slightly acrid smell. Six months ago it was Boston Car & Limo, a high-end service owned by Warren Buffett's Berkshire Hathaway; its gorgeous black cars never saw more than forty thousand miles before being resold; crisp interiors with GPS guidance and same-day copies of the *Wall Street Journal* in the seat-back pocket, readable with discreet halogen pen lights depending from the soundproof ceiling pads. Riding in a Boston Limo was an excursion into playerhood that is most definitely over. Allegro is your top-tier firm's new "ride of choice," and its idea of service is a year-old copy of *National Geographic* on the slush mat at your feet.

You look through the window at Queens in the winter.

"What way are we going?" you ask the driver, who appears to have advanced bronchitis.

"Airport." He coughs.

"LaGuardia?"

"Yeah."

"How's traffic?"

"How should I know?"

A good point, of course. You decide to stop talking to the driver.

As you say, your colleagues live two lives and pack as such. This, you cannot do. Your life clothes are your work clothes; your living luggage, your consulting tool kit. You have one bag, which you purchased at Wal-Mart in Luddington, Michigan, for $19.95 one time when you were visiting your dad. This lack of compartmentalizeability will someday be your undoing, you know this too.

Suspiciously long for a ten-minute trip, the voyage to the airport ends.

"You have a voucher?" asks the driver.

"What?"

"A voucher? For the ride?"

"I never have a voucher."

"This time you have to."

"The travel people have the charge number. They charge it to the number. I don't need a voucher."

"Yes you do."

"Can you give me one?"

"If I give you one, then you don't have to have one, right?"

This driver—it's like he's been reading Jean-Paul Sartre. If you weren't so sad you'd probe him on this thought.

"How much?"

"For what?" he asks, sucking down a wad of snot.

You have been obsessed with luggage. Particularly, as a cause of pain. Luggage is not about transporting items but about transporting luggage. You think this often—like now, as you stand in line at LaGuardia's Delta terminal in the long line for the "Express Kiosk" for a flight on Northwest Airlines. It would be difficult to design a less wieldy object than the lumpish black steel cubes people wheel through airports worldwide and cram despairingly into overhead compartments. These businessmen and -women on the 6:10 to Chicago—they're the robot elite. Some carry tote bags with their consulting firms' names gladly blazoned: KPMG (a relic now), IBM CONSULTING, PRICEWATERHOUSECOOPERS (also a relic). These are the IT consultants, the implementers. They're something less than you top-tier *management* consultants, of course; they actually know how to do something.

So they wheel their five-ton boxes around for a three-night stay. The boxes are too heavy. They are shaped all wrong. And they look identical, causing problems at bag check.[48] One of your many escape scenarios—all consultants have these,

---

[48]No top-tier consultant has ever *checked* a bag through on a flight voluntarily; they may be often mistaken, but they are not delusional.

though they are never mentioned—one of your more fanciful, is to quit and start a luggage firm. You are convinced there is an unmet need, as the marketers would say, for a lightweight, soft garment bag–style piece of luggage that can accommodate a laptop and papers and gym shoes. You have thought about this a lot, and even made some preliminary sketches in the air. (See below.)

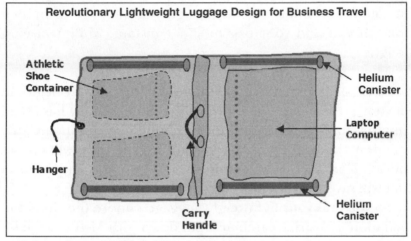

Source: James Meddick, Ltd.

Note the ingenious use of helium in the structural elements, allowing for almost effortless carriage.[49] Conventional luggage is not only too heavy but it actively damages clothing by forcing human-sized garments into a rodent-sized box. Drapage in a garment bag is the solution, reducing wrinkling. In addition, traditional luggage does not accommodate two essentials of the road warrior's entourage: her company-issue IBM ThinkPad T23 laptop computer and her running shoes. She will never use the latter, but they are psychologically necessary. Your design says: *Problem solved.*

[49]This idea originated with the cartoonist Jim Meddick, creator of the syndicated comic strip *Monty* (www.unitedmedia.com/comics/monty).

Until you gain the nerve to strike out on your own and really live this luggage dream, it is a point of pride with you to travel with only a single bag. No computer case, satchel, backpack, or parcel. Nothing but your garment bag, cleverly packed to contain all consulting trip essentials. Each week, you try to make the bag weigh less. You put it on your bathroom scale and trim the ounces off. Last week you discovered you could get by with only two pairs of fresh underwear, saving almost an ounce. It's as though you want the combined total of you and your bag to stay constant, while you gain weight.

The thing you are avoiding is happening now.

The Northwest kiosk asks you if your bag has ever been out of your possession, and if anybody you don't know has asked you to transport something for her. You know this: If anybody you don't know asks you to carry any luggage, you will say no. In fact, if anybody you *do* know asks you to carry any luggage, you will say no. It is simply too heavy.

So you and your lightweight luggage endure the ritual humiliation of a strip search and pat down with M-16s at the security checkpoint, and you're heading for your plane.

You run into someone you know from the firm, heading someplace else. You always run into people you know at LaGuardia at 6:00 a.m. A bomb now would eliminate half the consultants based in New York.

"Hey, Jon," you say.

"Whauopsouauoa?"

He looks upset, very upset; Jon is not a morning person.

You, however, are.

"You know what I was thinking?" you chirp as the two of you head for the Coffee Beanery concession next to the McDonald's franchise.

"Houwsinosea?"

"Yeah—I was thinking, you know those military guys by the pat-down area there? Those guys with the machine guns? It's kind of ironic that the entire purpose of them wearing army camouflage is so they *do* stand out, right? It's like the opposite of what they were designed for."

Jon says, "Hwatpoinseauan?"

"I don't know," you say as you pick up your first enormous flavored coffee today. "I don't know what my point is, exactly."

Jon tries to smile—he really does. Then he's gone, to Baltimore, ironically enough, to consult for the U.S. Department of Defense.

Flights are all alike and differ only in the width of their delays.

You land in Chicago and the transformation is complete. It starts with musings on the state of luggage in airspace, continues through encounters with those transients that walk across your work, and ends as the wheels of your Boeing 737 kiss the concrete cancers of Illinois. Your wife is still asleep, and that is now her life, like a chicken in a plastic bubble at your back. You are a consultant.

My watch reads 9:14 a.m.

Debarking from an aircraft is an exercise in mind control. Many of the flights you take are on smaller aircraft, like the Embraer 170, which has three tiny seats per row split by a comical aisle. The great vexation, however, is the small plane's business-friendly allowance of "gate checked" bags— that is, bags that are stowed below and await your hurried businesswoman self directly outside the aircraft door upon deplaning. This service is indeed a luxury, until the plane decides to land. The platform approaches and docks with the plane's door. The door opens. And then—you wait.

You wait.

These "gate checked" bags, of course, require removal from the cargo hold *before* any passenger is allowed to depart the plane—otherwise, how could these bags be waiting planeside when you leave, as promised?

Evolution has improved the landing process to the point where the long (optional) wait in the baggage claim area for an unlucky few has become a long, mandatory wait within sight of the gate *for an entire planeload of people.*

This is a good time to practice your Zen circular breathing. Four counts in, hold four; four counts out. No air for four.

No air.

Four.

There was a time when trips were not routine. You went home from college on a plane and the process seemed elaborate and queer. It was something you prepared for, like a prom. Since journeys have become a rule, you make the effort to *decrease* your preparations—indeed, all mental and physical energies expended—to just above absolute zero. Your motions are minimalist; your thoughts somehow fanciful, not serious. Helium luggage? In any other context this might seem silly . . .

It is not for the first time you wish you were a poet.

You prefer Hertz to Avis for no particular reason. Consultants, like most frequent travelers, are utter loyalists. Contrary to popular belief, there is no reward for this loyalty outside the realm of dreams.[50] However, there you have it: Hertz. You get on the Hertz bus, crowd in amid the pack of well-heeled refugees. All of them look older than their years, it seems. Including you.

The driver stands in the front of the bus and shouts back, "Is anyone a Gold member?"

"Yes," answers the bus.

"Yes," you say.

It seems that every single person on the bus is a Hertz Gold Club member. It's hard to feel special as a Gold Clubber anymore. In fact, the only way to be truly unique in the eyes of Hertz is *not* to be a member of the Gold Club.

The bus guy starts up front. "Name?"

"Goldman. G-O-L-D-M-A-N."

---

[50]You will have more to say on this critical point later.

The Hertz guy, who is sloppy and a little loud, pecks the letters one by one into his device. This takes a minute. Then he takes a step sideways. "Name?"

"Hirschorn."

"Harts-what?"

"Hirschorn."

"With an *L*?"

"*H-I-R-S-C-H-*"

"Whoa—hold up. It's W—"

"*H . . . !*"

One time, after fifteen minutes of such didgeridoo, you asked another Hertz guy why he didn't just drive you all to the rental place and let you get into your cars. "Well," he said, "we're just trying to save some time."

"How so?"

He thought about this some, then took a step sideways. "Next?"

Hertz is a division of the Ford Motor Company, so it offers only Ford cars, including Volvos and Land Rovers (both owned by Ford). From your point of view, however, they have only one car: the Taurus. And it comes in only one color: matador red. You have never been given anything else. You suspect because there is nothing else to give.

"Hi there," you say to the Hertz lady, who, like Jon, is distressed.

"Last name?"

You tell her. She taps on her ancient IBM PC. "Declining insurance?"

"Yes."

"Want fuel option?"

"No, thanks."

"You've got a Ford Taurus, number one-ten out that door."

"I was wondering—"

"Huh?"

"Could I get a different car?"

"What's wrong with that one?"

"Nothing. I was just wondering—do you have something else? Like a Volvo?"

"Not since Christmas, I don't think."

She taps and taps, you suspect just random letters. She shakes her head.

"We had a Silver Frost. Naw. Sorry."

This sounds intriguing—a new type of Ford. Perhaps experimental. "What's a Silver Frost? Is that an SUV?"

"Naw. It's a car."

"Is it new?"

She looks at you like you're old and strange, which might not be so far from true.

"It's a Taurus," she says. "A silver Taurus."

"I thought they only came in red."

"They do come in red."

You find the fleet of crimson Tauri awaiting you—the mechanical bulls for the bullshit artists of the century. Yours doesn't have even a helpful map of the area inserted into your card paper contract, but you don't particularly feel like reentering into a discussion with the Hertz lady. It is 10:27 a.m. and you have been en route for five hours already.

Your wife, the musician, still sleeps.

This is day one of the new engagement—and it occurs to you now that the engagement is not actually in Chicago. You are in the Chicago airport, driving past the Hertz checkpoint, turning left toward a major highway, tooling past a locked shut Wendy's in your Matador Red Ford Taurus, and you suddenly realize you have less than no idea where you are supposed to be going.

It is always thus, in week one.

The crisis has begun.

The client is located in [Sadtown], Illinois, and is a large company involved in the manufacture, distribution, and selling of tires for cars and trucks. [Sadtown] is not really that close to Chicago, and by the time you've raised the job manager on the cell phone and extracted directions to the city, become lost, raised someone else on a different cell phone, and whittled your directional errors into a sense that you're on the right track, it's almost noon. And while it is understood that consultants from out of town arrive late on Monday morning it is supposed to still be Monday *morning* when they arrive. Some combat the risk of late arrival by flying in Sunday night, but you would really rather die.

This part of Akron or Cuyahoga Falls or wherever you are appears to have been designed not merely *for* but *by* your client. There is a [Client] Avenue, of course, but also a [Client] Library, a [Client] Test Track, a [Client] Veterans of Foreign Wars Center, a [Client] Road and [Client] Mews, a [Client] Auditorium, a [Client] Wellness Center and [Client] Playground, as well as the inevitable, majestic [Client] Museum of Rubber. And like St. Petersburg, Russia, the entire burg appears to have been erected in a day. By the same design firm using the same truckload of red bricks. Everything is red brick; not so red, as times have turned south for your client; times turned south some decades ago, actually, when the U.S. lost its ability to mass-produce commodities economically; and this southness is reflected in the tenor of the brick, which has descended now into a kind of brackish slimy gray with specks of red. The sky is wet like crime. Your radio can pick up nothing, because it doesn't work or plausibly because there is just nothing to pick up in [Sadtown].

You keep it on. Static is the soundtrack of this film.

You're about to drive and dial again when up ahead you see a large gray dome and a flag welcoming you to [Client] World Headquarters. There is a visitors parking, patrolled by two fat women wearing yellow. Their smiles are wide, in unison, as you power down your window.

"Hi there," they shout.

"Howdy."

"You a consultant?"

"How could you tell?"

"The car, for one."

"Of course. Where can I park?"

"You park wherever you can find your car."

"Great."

You take the ticket and think: What a strange response. Not *Wherever you can find a spot* or *Wherever you want to* but *Wherever you can find your car.* There's something deep here too, you think . . . until you see what they mean.

This parking lot is entirely outdoors, a single massive lot snaking around and enveloping the dismal [Client] Community Center. And once you press past the monster trucks of the actual visitors seeking community within the center—once past these evil machines that could crush a child, you find yourself adrift in a crimson tide of Matador Red Ford Tauri. Dozens and dozens and dozens of them. Consulting chariots, awaiting instructions.

It is difficult to feel special, in business.

You enter the headquarters soaked to the bone. A cloud opened up as you crossed under it and dumped a load on you, then stopped. A surreal weather experience. You wonder if there is a [Client] store for new shirts, and if they have the [Client] logo. You have never, ever been wetter.

The security guy behind the headquarters reception desk does not appear to notice. Wet people must show up all the time in here. He hands you a pen and a pass and takes your picture "for the record." What is so important about preserving this moment is not clear. Perhaps he wants to blow up your deep dark circles and your shivering ratlike face and laugh and laugh behind your back.

"Go in there," he says. "No—over there."

He points you toward not the actual front door where people mope into and out of the headquarters but a smaller door, concealed behind a rack of dust-caked promotional pamphlets.

"That there," he says with the shyest little hint of smirk, "is for people like you all."

"Me all?"

"Yassuh."

"What kind of people is that?"

"I'm making some crazy guess," he observes. "But I'm to believe that you are a consultant."

"Uh-huh."

"That door is for you."

It is 12:16 p.m. You have been in transit to this moment for almost eight hours. A full day's work for some; for you, it feels like. Time to turn around and call it a job.

You get buzzed through the door and you push.

"What I need to make perfectly clear here is that *we are late.* We are *behind.* The clock is ticking on this piece of work and we had better start meeting the deliverables. There is a client senior team meeting in *two days.* I need your analysis—all of them to be *done* at that time. We're not gathering data here for anything—we're *done* gathering data, by my schedule, and we're putting together the decks for this senior team in *two days.* Which means I've got to see something *tonight*—and we finalize *tomorrow night.* Is there any part of this you're not clear on, because I need to know? We need to meet these timings, and I'm telling you *we are already behind.*"

Already behind—and you just walked in the door.

The team is gathered in a small and airless meeting room around a table. There are seven of you in the room—an operations partner, a principal from Cleveland, an SA you talked to on the phone once, two associates,[51] and a statistician, a job title available only in the Cleveland office due to its high volume of quantitative operations-type work. The only person you've met before is the principal, an obese and impressive young man who pounds Diet Mountain Dews and chews his

[51]Including you.

fingernails into bloody putrid stumps.[52] The seventh person is the speaker, an ancient *senior* senior partner from the firm's prehistory, recalled from glorious retirement because he "owned" the relationship with this particular midwestern client. You are wondering if there is any particular reason he is in such a foul frame, or if this is the consequence of age and ownership.

He continues: "Are we all clear what we need to do here? 'Cause if there're any problems we need to state them now or we're going to be in trouble with this client. They're operating on a compressed time frame, so we have to also, right? Okay?"

There is an extended moment here.

Then the principal, bless him, decides to speak. His name is Jeff. The senior's name is Jack.

"Now, Jack," says Jeff, "I understand the sense of time pressure here. But do we think it's realistic we get a draft to you by tonight? I mean, we just got here a couple hours ago. I don't even know where the men's room is, right? We don't have connections for the computers, we don't know the clients yet. Now I'm guessing there's a lot of data we're going to have to be sifting through, but we don't have any of it yet. It's difficult to see our value add for tonight."

"Exactly," says Jack, not missing a step. "That's what I'm saying—*we are really behind.*"

Jack breaks up the meeting a few minutes later having granted a concession to Jeff. He doesn't need to see the first draft before 11:00 p.m. There is a review meeting scheduled for midnight. By the time that breaks up, you will have been

[52]His knowledge of trivia limns a vast lonely childhood spent in the company only of a high IQ and a set of the *World Book Encyclopedia*; he is well known for being able to recite the longitude and latitude of any world capital, as well as "Strange Facts" about most U.S. cities. For instance, he told you that [Sadtown] contains the Largest Rubber Band Ball in the world, somewhere, and suffers the highest per capita rate of prostate cancer in North America.

(marginally) awake for twenty-four hours, and your ability to reason will have descended down to the level of a cabbage's. Even by consulting standards, this is a punishing first day.

On-site Rule #1: You Are *Always* Behind.

The team has been given three small cubicles outside a copy room with a high-speed copier going *huncka-huncka-huncka* nonstop 24/7. It must be copying the résumés of the entire employee population, over and over again, as they search for escape. Three cubicles you have—and even your limited math skills come in handy.

"Where are you sitting?" you ask Jeff.

"Where you are."

"So where's Davo sitting, then?"

"Ditto."

"So there's three cubicles *total* for us now?"

"Yes, sir."

"And we have two partners?"

"Jack's sitting somewhere else. They gave him his old office back."

"So we have one partner?"

"Yes, sir."

This is bad—a partner never shares a cubicle. Certainly not with a form of lower rank. So his presence demotes your space grant down to two cubes for five people. These are not large cubes.

"When do we get more space?"

"How about never?"

"Never?"

"Do you see any vending machines around here? I need a Diet Mountain Dew."

*   *   *

On your way to the men's room later you soak in the ambience of [Client]. This is the pre-Christmas season, and many companies choose to enter into the spirit of the time by putting up a green plastic tree in their headquarters entrance, say, or hanging a few discreet wreaths. More distressed firms tape up paper snowflakes in their cafeterias. Holiday parties can occur, even in this deep Republican recession.

But [Client] is relentless in its unwillingness to bend to convention. As you wend through long corridors of 1950s-era carpeting and employees, it might as well be midsummer. There is no holiday here. A couple days later you ask one of the secretaries what's up with that, and she says, "They canceled Christmas this year."

Even Jim Carrey couldn't cancel Christmas.

You cannot find the men's room, no matter where you wend. Could they have canceled comfort?

By now you are so lost you are convinced you are in another building. The headquarters has no windows; that is, there are windows, but none of them are visible to you. It's as though there is another, better building *wrapped around* the building you are in—and the wraparound building is where they have Christmas and men's rooms, vending machines and (come to think of it) lunch. This is the building you want; somehow, by walking and walking and walking, you will get there.

You're underground, perhaps. Large tires are stacked against the walls—racing tires, and tractor tires. You'd heard this company had an inventory problem, but you had no idea it was as bad as this: excess product stored all over headquarters, gathering dust. The employees you see wear white shirts and gray skins, frowning at the calendar place mats on their blocky desks. They look up as you pass, terrified.

You cannot ask them where the men's room is because they might burst into tears.

You are now in an orange concrete tunnel sloping downward . . . a marble on this floor would roll quite fast. Up ahead there is a room with a light, brighter than the others. It spills onto the rust-soaked carpet. Faint sounds of words are somewhere near you now. They're soughing from this room. You come to it and stop and look inside.

Jack is in there, putting down the phone.

He sees you.

"You lost?" he asks. There is no high school play pause before Jack's lines of dialogue; he's right on top of it.

"No," you say, then, "Yes."

"What's your name again?"

"Marty."

"Come in here, Marty. Sit down a second."

This you do. What else can you do?

"Did you get the point of what I was saying earlier?"

"In the meeting? Yes."

"Did the other guys get it? Is there—I'm wondering, is there a sense of urgency in there?"

"We just got here."

"Of course—of course you did."

You are wondering what is going on here. Jack has been written off as an asshole by now, yet here he is . . .

He looks at the phone, takes an audible breath.

"You know, I'm retired."

"Uh-huh."

"My wife is not well. We moved—we moved—we moved . . ."

Jack takes another audible breath and you cannot believe you are going to see him cry in front of you, now, like this.

"I'm sorry. How long have you been at [the firm]?"

"A year, almost two years."

"You're an associate?"

"Uh-huh."

"You seem older. How old are you?"

You tell him, and he seems a bit cheered. He recovers fast—this Jack.

"Okay. I see. Okay, then."

He nods, and you stand up, since this appears to be what is supposed to occur.

"Thanks, Marty."

You step into the hallway, out of the light, and then turn back. "Can I ask you something, Jack?"

"Yep."

"Is there a men's room around here?"

"You see that door?" He indicates a gray steel door directly across from this office. "Through there, up the stairs, and"— he looks at his watch—"you'll find them all in line. The cafeteria's closing."

Upstairs, you find some confirmation of the rumor that Jack is never wrong in matters of fact. The team is scattered in the cafeteria, final customers before the early midwestern closing time. You even find a men's room. Jeff is in there, washing his hands with a kind of frightening intensity.

"Hey, Jeff," you say while springing a leak.

"Where were you?"

"Looking for this place."

"Okay."

He dries his hands and leaves without another word.

The cafeteria itself is dismal and delinquent. The lettuce in the salad bar hangs like a tongue. The dessert cabinet is only tapioca pudding, crusty on top, and red Jell-O. All the soda pop is private label, no-name brands like Mr. Depp in scratched-up cans. The Special Today is SLOPPY JOES. Thankfully, they are out of them. Anyway, you are not so hungry anymore.

And there you are, the team, lined up with your Mr. Depps and little bags of Doritos.

You do not talk. This is entirely by design. There are subtle rules of client-site behavior, and you know them all as instinct now; they are simply what you do.

On-site Rule #2: Do Not Make Group Appearances.

This is one in a series of guidelines related to a phenomenon consultants call optics. You spend your working life in
someone else's hell; you can safely assume they are watching.
Every moment at a client site is another moment in a dish of
petri. Even private team meetings in quiet corners of a warehouse at 5:30 p.m., long after everyone you're working for has
split for home—even these have been known to be observed,
on the fly, by workaholic key executives strolling past on their
way out the door. *Let's peek in on the incredibly high-priced hot-
shots—let's see if they're earning their money.*

This is why the consultant *never* brings his complimentary
USA Today from the hotel to the workroom. This is why the
consultant *never* puts her feet up on a desk, any desk, even at
3:30 in the morning, or takes off her shoes, or rolls up her
sleeves, or calls home . . .

Earning their money . . .

Optics dictate that on-site engagement pods *never* ever,
ever:

1. Walk down public hallways in groups larger than
   three;
2. Linger outside elevators together;
3. Leave at the same time; and, especially,
4. Eat lunch together in the cafeteria.

This last one has destroyed careers. Now, let's see why.

Imagine you are a key executive at an ailing firm and you
have been sweet-talked into hiring Consulting Firm X to take
a look at things. It's a small team, says the partner—no more
than three or four top-tier experts, plus herself. In and out in
a few months or so, problem solved. You say, "Okay. We'll give
it a shot."

Meanwhile, the partner and his buddy have wandered
down the hall, sweet-talked some other key executive—this
one in operations, say—that, sure, they're on the case down
the hall with a high-level strategy team, and *now is the time* to

take a hard look at that inventory problem in Iowa, and those money-losing plants down South, and it just plain *makes sense* to bring in a small team of crackerjack consultants to kick the tires . . . since you're here anyway . . . nothing much, maybe, oh, three or four of your best people and a couple supervisors to make sure they're totally in tune with you, the client, and . . .

. . . and meanwhile, down the hall, the partner's other buddy is sweet-talking some beleaguered sap—this one in human resources, or finance—and this person's hearing: "We're already doing a high-level strategy revamp and an operations rethink for you guys—now, doesn't it *just make sense* to take advantage of this golden moment to peel back the onion on the resource allocation piece . . . no big deal, just a smallish team, say, three or four of our very best people and me, of course, to keep them honest . . . couple months, in and out, problem solved . . ."

. . . and meanwhile, down the hall . . .

Now imagine you are the VP of Business Development, and you've got your top-tier consultants working day and night, but, hey, it's only a couple months and it's a small team . . . and now you're hungry, and you hit the cafeteria for a plateful of those delicious sloppy joes they have up there . . . and you grab a tapioca and a Mr. Depp or two and wander into the seating area, looking for a friend . . . surveying the throngs of middle-aged, sloppy Joes raging about Nascar . . . and you see . . .

Actually, you cannot *believe* what you see.

There, hiding in the corner, a group that manifestly does not fit. They're youngish, okay looking, glasses, some smiles, passing through, whispering conspiratorially—there's got to be twenty or more them, laughing . . . obviously, they're consultants. You set down your tray and start counting. One, two . . . *there's twenty-six of them!* Jesus Christ—at those billing rates? That's all of next quarter's net income—GONE! What in holy fuck is going on . . . ?

You don't feel like sloppy joes anymore, do you?

You kind of feel more like taking a cold hard look at this consulting cluster fuck occurring in your anal cavity.

For this reason, consultants do not sit in groups of more than three in public spaces.[53]

And so the team cubicles become the team cubicle—the partner and the principal have decided their high-level conspiratorial day-long phone calls require them to labor without benefit of company. They each take a cube, leaving the four junior team members to squeeze into a six-by-six-foot space.

"Do you need that phone line?" you ask the statistician, a bone-thin Irani named Baloo.

"Just a second," she says.

"How long is a second?"

"Like a minute."

"How long is a minute?"

"Where's the vending machine?" asks the SA, Davo.

"Are there any more phone lines?" you say to no one.

"Know what?" says Davo. "I'm going to find some Coca-Cola."

"Good-bye," says Baloo.

"Where's Martha?"

"She's doing work."

Doing work—you look at your watch, a B-school graduation present. It's 4:17 p.m. You are exhausted. You have been going for twelve hours straight and have done absolutely nothing for no one.

At some point you extract your lengthy legs from behind the steel desk corner they are wedged behind, smack them to retrieve some circulation, bounce on the balls of your feet, and kind of fall backward against a nearby wall. The team has

---

[53]Some partners have been known to ban sit-down cafeteria meals altogether; usually, you find it safer to eat lunch in your cubicle while reading *USA Today* online.

dispersed to find more phone lines—you need them for your critical 24/7 Internet access[54]—and you are alone.

Well, not quite.

You rub your closed eyelids with your thumbs, digging out the eye-jam in your ducts. You see real stars. You had a seventh grade teacher, Mr. Price, who said rubbing your eyelids is like banging a brick on your nose. Maybe you could use a brick right now.

When you open your eyes someone is staring at you.

You startle, then get embarrassed. This person sits in the cubicle directly next to yours; he has been so utterly quiet you honestly did not know he was there. Mentally, you run through things you all have been saying . . .

"Hi," he says shyly.

"Have we been loud?"

"A little bit."

"God, I'm sorry. I didn't know you were there. I'll talk to them—"

"It's okay. It gets kind of quiet in here anyway. You guys consultants?"

"Uh-huh."

He's maybe forty, pudgy, badly dressed, like an engineer or an off-track betting fan. He wears an undershirt and a mustache. His cubicle is tidy in a way you find soothing and there are reams—phalanxes—cornucopiae of little color photographs of children and babies who look like him.

You can't help saying, "You got a lot of kids."

"Just two." Such a warm look comes over him then.

"They look just like you."

"They're my wife's from another marriage."

"Oh," you say.

He kind of smiles at this.

"I'm Geraldo," he says.

---

[54]Why this is critical no one has determined; you think that while serving precious little work-related purpose, the nonstop Internet connection is like the lonely man's television set, always turned on low in the other room, simulating human company.

"Sorry about your talk show career."

"I know," he says, "but we move on."

You have many limitations as a consultant, foremost among
them your sense of limitations. But one thing you can do is
revel in the pointless superficial temporary interaction of the
office space. You are an absolute master of the forty-second
relationship. As we will see, this skill is your secret arsenal.

Clients clear out early, of course—how early depends upon
their time zone. We are one country, in business. So while
Manhattan media companies can open up shop around 9:30
a.m. and are deserted again around 6:00 p.m., workplaces in
the Midwest are time-shifted two hours. They'll kick into gear
just after 7:00 a.m. and by 4.30 p.m. everybody's gone.
Michigan companies will schedule *meetings* at 7:00 a.m. and
think nothing of it. It's a culture of the early riser. So now it's
6:34 p.m. and the hallways are quiet; the elevators still; vacu-
ums abound, sucking up the silence.

The copier takes a breather from its *huncka huncka-huncka*.

And the data has started to arrive.

Davo has found an empty conference room behind a pile
of truck tires, and you are having a junior team meeting.
Davo, Baloo, yourself, and Martha, the other associate.

There is a cardboard box on the table in front of Davo as
you walk into the conference room. He upends it, dramati-
cally, and a river of CDs pours out. There's probably twenty or
thirty of them, sliding across the table top.

"This," he says, "is the first of it."

"What is it?" asks Baloo, who is exceedingly linear.

"The data dump. The *first* data dump. I've been told there
are many, many more to come."

"What's on there?" you ask.

Davo pulls a grimy dot-matrix-printed sheet of paper from
the bottom of the box and scans it carefully. "Inventory data,
historical inventory data. Inventory by channel and by outlet.

Two years of inventory going up to . . . shit, I don't know. Maybe June."

"That's not going to help us much," you say.

"Of course it isn't going to help us," says Davo. "That's why we got it right away."

"What do we need?" asks Baloo.

"We need it for right *now*—for *today*."

Martha has red hair and is brand new, so she lacks a certain ease in the team setting. But she proves to be quite practical. "What is this project about?" she asks.

You all turn to Davo.

"What are we doing here? Good question. Meanwhile . . ." he divides the CDs into three equal piles and shoves them across the table at their new owners.

"What we need to do is go through all of these and understand exactly what is on them," he says. "Don't go by the labels, because they're wrong. They're written over. In a couple hours we should have another box."

"Where are you getting these from?" you ask.

"I don't know," says Davo. "There's some guy here, an SAS expert, he's pulling all this stuff for us off the mainframe. They still have a mainframe, believe it or not. They still use *tapes* somewhere. There's this guy and he's burning these for us."

"He's still here?"

"I believe so."

"Can we ask him what he's pulling off the mainframe?"

"If we can find him."

"Who's his boss?"

"The client. But he's home now, we can't call him at home."

"So there's a guy here—we don't know who he is, we don't know what he's doing, what he's told to do. He's running all these data dumps for us and we don't know what they are?"

"That's about the size of it."

"It'd be great if we could find this guy," says Baloo, warily eyeing her stack of CDs.

The four of you return to your cubicle in a foul mood. There is nothing more pitiless than inching through trillions of ions of data looking for a ray of light.

But you're powering up your CD-ROM for a good eight hours' beating when you hear a sound that stops you cold.

A quiet . . . insistent . . . *click click click tap bang click tap thwuck* . . . the keystrokes of a piss-poor typist working hard nearby.

You wedge yourself out, step over Martha, and exit the cube.

Geraldo is working at something, typing with three or four fingers max, peering at an unhealthy distance into his CRT.

"Can I ask you something, Geraldo?"

"Okay."

"Do you know SAS?"

"Uh-huh."

"Are you pulling data right now?"

"Yep."

"Does this data happen by any chance to be going onto CD-ROMs?"

You get your answer as Geraldo pushes the latch button on his CD burner and a disc pops out.

"Huh," he says.

"Do you know who these CDs are for?"

He looks at you now, for the first time.

"You guys."

> On-site Rule #3: Be Nice to *Everyone*.

Analysis is at heart simply filing. You take a mass of information, sift through it, and divide it into groups with similar relevant attributes. "When a poet's mind is perfectly equipped for its work," said T. S. Eliot, "it is constantly amalgamating disparate experience." The good consultant is in this way an artist, although his best insights tend to be about trucking routes and tariffs. And the simplest categorical division is the Rule of Two. Take any mound of data. Divide it into two and *only two* different groups. What are those groups? This exercise can reveal the truth.

For instance: **Engagements** and **Consultants**. These are the raw material. Dump every single **Engagement** at every single top-tier firm into a truth machine that divides them into two and only two different groups. What are the groups? Do the same with **Consultants**. What are the groups?

The groups are

Engagements:
1. Data dumps
2. Huh?

Consultants:
1. Marriott points
2. Starwood points

These categories follow the Barbara Minto/McKinsey framework they call MECE—Mutually Exclusive Collectively Exhaustive—which means, simply, the categories are totally different and together they include everybody. Now, you will have more to say about the Marriott/Starwood insight later, but the Data dumps/Huh? discrimination is on point.

Here is a MECE-friendly description of the only two Week Ones a top-tier consultant can experience:

Type 1—Data dumps.

❏ You arrive in Mendocino riding herd on a new summer associate named Jormugandr, who is a dolt. His enthusiasm comes out in mouth spray. He's under the mistaken impression the team has been asked to "hold down expenses," so he imposes upon you to drive him everywhere. The client is a good-sized manufacturer of plastic brackets for trailer curtains, and also has an interest in motion picture finance. It owns three actual factories in the U.S. and at least four in Mexico, or maybe Belize—even it is not quite sure. Jormugandr and you sit down with your team leader, Wotan, engineer-turned-consultant. The meeting is spent drawing graphs on lined paper and ignoring your anger. The halls of this HQ seem surely empty, as though you are missing a better meeting. And as you search floors one through three for a working electrical outlet a forklift motors down the hall, beladen with boxes . . . cartons and reams of brown cardboard boxes extending through the fluorescing ceiling . . . and it's odd, says Wotan, that there's a forklift in the hall but all you can think is: *Oh no.* The forklift stops and dumps the boxes, burying Jormugandr. You open one and find parcels and truckloads of paper and data discs—printouts of eight-point numbers in bewildering columns with no heading, page numbers, or punctuation. As the forklift leaves, another one arrives—with larger boxes. "Here ya go," chortles the driver, Bifrost. "You all *consultants* enjoy the *information* you requested!" You think you understand why he's enjoying this . . . as Jormugandr starts to spit up blood . . .

Type 2—Huh?

❑ No sound in Duquesne but the screams of true silence. Uneventful travel in a prophylactic nap. Flawless team launch as the all-U.S. partner, Luacharma'n, delivered a eulogy to greatness. You wish you shared her boosterism but you are in a spring flu. The partner leaves you in a vast room alone with a seasoned IT SA, Bhrogan, and another associate, a gifted supply chain analyst and fantasy baseball statistician, Cluricaun. Luacharma'n's high heels *posha-posha* down the hall and into greater triumph. Meanwhile, you can't help but turn with Cluricaun to your technically inspired thought leader. "So," you say, "what does this company do?" "Not sure," admits Bhrogan sheepishly, "something in government?" "They don't make curtain brackets? No?" asks Cluricaun . . . two hours later, you have progressed into watching Bhrogan scratching boxes with blue Magic Marker onto a printable white board, then erasing them . . . an hour later you decide to work through dinner . . . at 9:00 or 10:00 at night, the white board has three empty boxes on it. Bhrogan has rolled up her sleeves. She stares through the windowless wall at the bold night beyond . . . so much is shared in silence you wonder why anyone talks . . . "Is this place maybe nonprofit?" you ask. "We need a strategy," observes Bhrogan. "We need . . ."

Of these two—and only two—possibilities, it is hard to say which is preferable. Day one you have either (1) nothing but information, or (2) nothing but questions. Neither gets you any closer to the truth.

Despite your precision with Geraldo, it is still a long night. It's not that you don't get to leave and spend some quality sack time on your Sheraton/Westin Heavenly Bed—you do. It's just that the time occurs from 6:00 to 6:45 a.m. and your Heavenly Bed has chosen to be extra hot. You shave with your backup razor and hack up your puss. The clothes you inhabit smell brackish now. Your deodorant is gone but not forgotten. You dead-walk to the Matador Red Ford Taurus and can't open the door. *Jesus Christ!* you think—*this God-awful Michigan workmanship!*

At some point it occurs to you that you are trying to get into the wrong Taurus.

The second day begins thereafter, much as other days begin. You pull into the consultants' lot and park your Taurus next to all the other ones . . . a line of red matadors, ready for the bull . . .

You run into Martha and Baloo in the parking lot, emerging from the Matador Red Ford Taurus they are sharing. Women are better at sharing.

"Good morning," says Baloo.

"Good," you whisper, but it comes out like "God."

The team cubicle appears to be your final stop; the client's admin drops by at dawn to assert this sad fact.

"We don't have a lot of room," she says. "You guys are okay here?"

"Of course," you say.

"It's great," says Baloo.

You are not okay, nor is it great. But making requests at too junior a level in too early a time frame is discouraged.

"I wonder," you ask the admin, "is the cafeteria open this early?"

"Oh gosh, you might have missed it totally."

"Missed it how?"

"It closes in a minute."

You look at your watch; it's 7:29 a.m.

"It *closes* at seven-thirty? Are you serious?"

"You betcha."

Of course, you don't have breakfast. You get a Snickers and a Mr. Depp and settle in with a pile of discs and a big stack of paper reports. Nothing is labeled. They might as well be random numbers.

Davo, being more intelligent, has found himself a personal space in a hallway near a stack of Nascar tires, insulated both in space and sound. Despite being two-thirds female, your cube is beginning to odorize; but Davo drops by looking fresh, pressed, rested, and relieved.

"Great news," he barks, resting his chin on the cube wall— a decapitated head in motion.

"Yeah?" says Martha, who is not a morning person.

"I had a meeting with the client guy. I know what we're here for."

You wander the rusting mazes of [Sadtown] HQ searching for an abandoned conference room; Baloo whispers, "I heard they're going bankrupt."

"Who is?" you ask her, and think now *Who isn't?*

"These guys."

"Shhh," interrupts Davo, drawing a finger across his pale throat like a knife.

There is no discussion of the client at the client site. There is no gestation, gossip, dissection, or interpretation of its business based upon information sources seen, read, or heard about by speakerphone. There is no use of speakerphone. There is no animated conversation at the client site, period; no loud talk or character-type noise effects such as chortles, grunts, groans, wild laughter, or screams. All cries of despair are internal, all sobbing alone.

No interesting chatter on the depravity of business or of popular culture is allowed, unless there is a poster for, say, a Bruce Willis movie framed in gilt in the client's office, signed by Bruce himself with a wild cherry lipstick: "Keep on Truckin', Love, Bruno!"—in which case there is permitted a single comment to the extent you admire Mr. Willis and are awed by those who've met him.

Unsolicited opinions are a one-way ticket to a counsel out. Sacking is the payment for clear points of view. Remember whole swaths of the U.S.A. are populated by right-wing extremists with pinheaded views on scientific principles such as evolution, global warming, and the Pac-10 conference; these people are your clients and are not open to persuasion.

But never mind. No war talk, peace talk, tax talk, or talk show talk. No blather about Ireland, North Korea, southern Canada. No moments when frustration escalates, the rage appears upon the surface of your blood and you *thwack!* the team room table—say, *"What an ASSHOLE!"* No. No assholes. No whats. No frustration, escalation, genetics . . . no rage.

A calm complacent demeanor with the slight hint of a smile is best. Glasses are to be encouraged, though not with square or ovoid rims. Earrings are acceptable only in females, and only in partner females at that. Tiny earrings. Pants must be Brooks Brothers gray in wool or cotton blends, depending on the season. Large-breasted females must conceal their large breasts in loose fabric. Shirts do not bear logos, even little men with polo mallets; even alligators on a Saturday when all the clients are abed. There is likewise no sense in constructing a style for which you will be remembered. You will never be remembered.

There is not a single famous consultant on the face of the earth.

No reactions. Your client says, "This work is *shit*! You are a first-class *loser*!"—your nostrils do not twitch. *A calm complacent demeanor with the slight hint of a smile* . . . "What don't you like about it?" you say almost happily. "How can we squeeze more hours out of the day and guess more often about your vague hopes and dreams and give to you something that doesn't make you want to have a meeting?"

"God, we should have gone with McKinsey . . ."

No mention of McKinsey, or BCG, Bain, AT Kearney, Deloitte, BearingPoint, Accenture, IBM Consulting, Monitor, Whiziwig, and whatever other enemies lie in the scrublands, awaiting your failure. To hear you talk to the client, there is no competition. It's one-way propaganda of a hopeful kind.

No phone calls. No cell phone calls from home. No cell phones turned on, even during lunch breaks. No lunch breaks. No food procured by any means other than stealth-quiet raids on the vending machines. Don't call your mother to talk. No check-ins with friends on the sly to set up something for Friday night when you're back in the city. No friends. No Fridays. No back in the city. Stare at the phone

but don't use it. Stop sending warm e-mails and they will all
stop responding.

No unnecessarily loud taps on the keyboard. These are the
signs of an amateur. No room-level conversations—the very
best senior partners are quiet folks, almost whisperers, the
kind of men and women you have to lean into to understand.
This spills over into private life, this silence of the mind . . .

No mind. No silence.

No no.

You find a conference room that appears to have been
warped in from the Ike age. The walls were advertised on late-
night TV in the seventies. A risqué calendar from Ollie's Auto
Mall dates from two years back. Two years ago this company
was on life support; by now, the Black Maria is in sight.

"Okay," says Davo, "here's the thing."

You sit in this room—you, Martha, Baloo, Davo, and Jeff.
Jack has not been seen yet.

"I talked to the client. I caught him when he got in at six.
We had a good discussion about what he wants from us, how
we can help. And it's like this. They have too many tires.
They're all over the place—in the warehouses they own, in
outlets they own, in retail outlets they just supply to . . . in the
factory. They're piled up in the factory, piles and piles. They
have all this inventory and it's a problem."

"Why is it a problem?" asks Baloo.

"I'll get to that—but now, basically what the deal is is they
don't really know where these tires are. They don't have a
clue. They don't know how many there are or where they are.
Their IT stuff is old and unreliable, the info they get from the
outlets is incomplete. So they can't trust the outlets are re-
porting real sales levels. But they need us to find the tires and
count them."

"Why is inventory a problem?" re-asks Baloo.

"I'll get to that—what we need to do—"

"We have to go around the country, counting tires, right?" asks Martha, who appears to lack a sense of humor.

"No," says Jeff, "we'll use their data. They have *a lot* of data."

"But it isn't labeled," you point out.

"We've got to label it."

"It's just numbers. Numbers and numbers in rows," you insist.

"We've got to get them labeled."

"Did it occur to anybody these numbers might be random?"

"They're not random."

"How do you know?"

"For Christ's sake, look for patterns. Look *behind* the numbers at the message that's there . . ."

Baloo loses patience with this philosophizing—"Can I ask a stupid question?"

"Yep," says Davo.

"Why do they have so much inventory?"

"They make too much stuff."

"Why?"

"They run these factories full blast, all year long. It doesn't matter."

"Why?"

"That's what they do—make tires, right? What else are they going to do?"

"What if nobody buys them?"

"Then," says a gruff voice swinging open the conference room door, "you have got a problem."

It's Jack. He comes in.

"You all know what you're doing?" he asks.

There's a tactical silence.

"Good," he snorts. "Because we are already *incredibly behind schedule, right?*"

*   *   *

The next day—it might be Wednesday—even Jack concedes the team's efforts have been adequate. Intrepid professionals, you have met the descriptions of your jobs. Each of you has spent your sixty nonstop working hours vigorously performing your time-honored duties, which vary by rank. (See the box below.)

Critical Tasks for Consulting Pod Members

Rank	Job Description	Key Action
Associate	Pecking feverishly at IBM ThinkPad	Typing
Sr. Associate	Reminding everyone about deadlines	Annoying
Principal	Talking furtively on the phone	Whispering
Partner	Holding forth at long, long meetings	Hectoring

You have not actually made any progress at all toward solving the client's "problem," whatever it is—but you certainly have been diligent. So Jack decides to present to you his own form of reward. This particular "reward," as we shall see, is in fact no reward at all, except perhaps to Jack. But the inspiration may be a kind one. This much is possible.

What is to be the team's reward for accomplishing nothing with great application?

Two words that shoot a hard shard of terror into the glands of anyone who has escaped their sentence in consulting . . . two words that conjure up a reef of memories so demanding, so entirely *unsupportable* that they reduce a grown woman to her knees with hands clasped tight and chest susurrating in dry heaves . . . two words so freighted with despair they drive large-headed men to throw their spines back, openmouthed, a deep scream surfacing, a rumble at first—speeding north-ward to splatter on the aluminum craftwork overhead . . . pleading, *No—for the love of all that's HOLY—NOOO!*

These two words are: Team Dinner.

So it's around about 8:15 p.m. on Wednesday night and the odor in the associate cube has become quite sweet with Skittles wrappers . . . and Jeff gets off one of his quiet calls and peaks over your shared cube partition and says, "You guys want to have a team dinner?"

The answer, of course, is *NO.*

Nobody ever wants a team dinner. You haven't slept in three straight days. You are not hungry; you are filled with Skittles and sheer crap. Your stomach hurts, your mind hurts, you want to crash and call your wife in privacy and watch the news. The last thing anybody wants is a team dinner and yet . . .

"Great," says Baloo.

"Okay," says Martha.

You say, "Uh."

Jeff glares, then remembers himself and perks up. "All right," he says. "We'll go at nine."

Team Dinners are held at good restaurants and charged to the client. But goodness in product and service varies widely from coast to coast, and in between. Your suspicion is that world-class comforts are about as endemic to [Sadtown] as are wide-open lesbians.

You are right.

Jeff selects a target, recommended by Jack. Jack in turn dredged it out of some half-remembered engagement with this same client twenty years before. The restaurant's name is O'Neal's and Jack is delighted to find it still exists.

"They'll remember me," he asserts. "I used to go there all the time."

Old people can be charming in their childishness.

Because nobody wants to go to a team dinner, they always start late. Very late. The stated start time is simply a target and appears to be set about one hour prior to reality.

9:00 p.m.—associates are typing, principal is whispering.

9:25 p.m.—associates are typing, senior associate drops by to remind about a deadline.

9:47 p.m.—associates check e-mail, senior associate drops by and says, "Okay?"

9:52 p.m.—you all head out to the Taurus parking lot to locate your cars.

As you cross the road toward the [Client] Museum of Rubber, you see them—the line of Matador Red Ford Tauri, awaiting orders. There are seven of you and six of them. You all take out your Hertz key chains and push the unlock button. And simultaneously, six Tauri unlock and light up—come to life.

There is no way to tell which one belongs to whom.

No problem—you have a secret backup plan. On occasions like this you quickly press the trunk-open button and head for the car with the open trunk. In fact, the trunk-open button is a far better locator than the unlock button—the trunk makes an audible noise when it opens, and its swift motion is visible from many yards away. The blare-horn button is embarrassing. In the daytime in crowded conditions unlock alone rarely works; you can't see the lights going on, and there is no noise. So more often than not, you'll shoot open the trunk to find your car.

You press the trunk-open button and your trunk flies open.

Simultaneously, the other five Tauri trunks pop up.

O'Neal's is not hard to find, unfortunately. It is on Montgomery Street in downtown [Sadtown]. Parking is more than easy; there is so much space around back you wonder if it might be closed. But no, it isn't.

"This place is great," Jack spouts with gusto as you walk toward the small front door. "The ribs—they're unbelievable."

Only partners can eat ribs.

Inside, the restaurant is a combination of a Denny's and a welfare office. It is very dark and warrened, with low ceilings and walls plastered with posters of boxing or wrestling matches; the floor requires some diligence, sloping up and down and sideways at bad times. Why are the ceilings so low? It's like this old inn in Rhinebeck you went to one time that was headquarters for George Washington and his troops in the eighteenth century, when people were shorter, much shorter . . . but the brown vinyl walls and the Wal-Mart chandelier don't seem to speak of historical monuments . . .

"Can I get your coats, gentlemen," asks the waiter.

"No," everybody says.

Keeping your coats is tactic number two for getting out of the team dinner early.[55]

The table is round and the place mats are plastic; your water glass makes you wonder, so you do not touch it. And you are a massive consumer of water. A few other tables are occupied—young kids on dates, on a second or third bottle of Robert Mondavi. The waitress, when she comes, is out of it.

"You guys want a drink?"

"You know what?" asks Jeff. "Can we see the wine list?"

"You're already seeing it."

You look around the table—under things. You can't find a wine list.

"I don't think we got it," says Jeff.

"Oh, you did."

"Do you see it?"

"Yeah—it's right there." She points to the menu Jeff is holding in his hands.

"This," he says, as he no doubt would say to one of his children back in Cleveland, "is the menu."

"Uh-huh," she says, and leaves it at that.

In the silence that follows, Jack emerges from a reverie; he

[55]Tactic number one, of course, is to make sure you bring your own Taurus.

flips the menu over and behold—"There it is!" he proclaims. "It's on the back of the menu."

You all take a look.

There are a dozen or so bottles of wine mentioned, plus things like a Kahlúa Kahuna and a King Kong Kahlúa—O'Neal's appears to have some kind of kickback deal going with Kahlúa. All team dinners start this way—you get the wine list and the principal ponders it knowingly. A senior associate might chip in an observation or a wine-related anecdote. No associate speaks; no associate knows, or pretends to know, anything about wine.[56] At this point, Jeff doesn't seem too happy with the selection, but for some reason Jack is in his element—as though a personal song is zinging through his brain, making him smile.

"Let's just get the Mondavi," Jeff says after some considerable while.

It's after 10:00 p.m. now and you can't believe how *terrible* everybody looks. Martha's eyes are closing, and Baloo appears to have a sinus issue: can't stop sneezing. *Choo! Choooaoohchch! Chooagohkoaicjokqz!*

You stop saying "Bless you."

From the pondering of the wine list to the ordering of the meal, the team dinner can be quite peaceful. There is very little talk. People are tired and topics are restricted; if there is any excuse *not* to yap—*I'm looking at the menu for thirty minutes in case I missed a nuance*—it is taken.

Very quiet.

You order. You all order chicken or beef. O'Neal's does not give the vibe of being a safe place to get fish. You are like people on a transatlantic flight and your options are kept binary. Chicken or beef. Fight or flight. Eat or be eaten.

[56]Every Thursday night from 6:00 to 9:00 p.m. Columbia Business School held a happy hour well known among the graduate schools for being the most debauched, rowdiest, and off the hook; Brooklyn Lager sent reps from the factory to fire-hose refill after refill into the snouts of thirsty preprofessionals; no wine was ever served.

As the waitress walks off you notice a panty line visible under her tightish black dress in the dim light of dinner. She appears to be wearing a thong. Two rolls of fat push past it like the lips of a trout.

Now the ritual begins, like machinery. Jeff looks over at Jack, who stops humming to himself. Jack knows his role now—knows it better than anyone.

"When were you here before?" Jeff asks him.

The first question postordering always goes to the highest-ranking partner. This is the way that it is.

"Hmmm . . ." thinks Jack. "I guess it was—maybe ten years ago. It was when [Retired Client President] was here. We went to business school together, so we'd been back here a lot. Our firm was all over [Client] at one time. We did so much work for them—supply chain, working capital, logistics. We did all their trucking routes. There was a huge piece on optimizing trade promotions—in fact, the whole trade promotions thing started here."

Trade promotions—or cutting deals with stores to try harder to sell your stuff—is one of the few real specialties your top-tier firm has. It is very statistics-heavy work. Like most midwestern consultants, Jack was once an engineer.

"We were here last year, weren't we?" prompts Jeff.

"I think so. Last year or the year before. It was . . . it was . . . difficult . . ."

Nobody probes this point. Team dinners are not about difficulty.

"So," says Davo, also to Jack, "you live in Florida now?"

"Yes," he says, remembering himself. "We moved to the beach about two months ago."

"That recent, huh?"

"Oh yeah. I was in Cleveland my whole career. I had retired—they brought me back. The old man's still good for something, right?"

Nobody laughs. Team dinners are not about laughter.

The Robert Mondavi merlot arrives and you all partake,

except Jeff, who doesn't drink. Whether this is because he doesn't drink or because he used to drink too much is a question you cannot answer . . .

. . . and some minutes later, Jack plays his part by commencing the lecture portion of the evening. After a start, all team dinners turn into a lecture from the highest-ranking partner, which often takes the form of an instructive fable or anecdote.

"That reminds me," Jack says, cradling his lean gray face in the crux of his right-hand forefingers. "We were on some island some time out in—in, I don't remember. There were—we landed on this private airstrip and we got off the plane there, and there was no building or anything, just this green tent and this little guy standing down there in a—in a, like a hat. And he greets us when we get down off the plane—this is the emperor of this island, whatever it is. He tell us this, 'I am the emperor of this island.'"

Jack lightly chuckles to himself, a cue you are to find this amusing. So you all join him.

"And we get into this—this Jeep he has and drives himself. And we're driving, and he says, 'On this island, the emperor has to drive himself. We have seen better times.' And Pablo—who was the lead on this job, I was just coming along—he turns to the guy and says, 'That's why we're here.'"

You see Jeff reach for the Mondavi bottle, then stop himself.

"Anyway," Jack continues, "the client has this factory on the far end of the island, and the emperor gets lost—and, but that's another thing. We get to this factory and it's eight in the morning. Now I know the shift is supposed to start at seven, but it's empty. There's maybe one guy in there doing something. It's a canning factory—they put fish into cans and label them. We find the foreman and we say, 'Where is everybody?' and he says—he looks kind of sad at this—he says, 'Island people very lazy.'"

You're hoping Jack isn't one of those old-timers who missed the '60s and still makes racist jibes.

He stretches his body out now, reaching up, up—he's a very tall man, Jack. Like an elongated, slightly shambly James Coburn.

"This poor guy—he tried everything to try to get these people to come in on time. He moved the start time up an hour, but they were coming in two hours late instead of one. It didn't even work one day. He starting firing the really late ones but it didn't matter—he had to hire them back 'cause it's a small island and there's nobody else. What can he do?"

"Did it matter when they started work?" asks Baloo. This story of lazy island people seems to offend her, though she cannot say so.

"Only 'cause they left early too," he says.

"That's a problem." Jeff nods.

"So you know what he did?" Jack says.

"No," you all say, wondering where the dinner is.

"You—he—heh heh *hohaoh*—he, these island guys had two things." Jack snuffles. "They were lazy . . . and they were very religious. Always dancing around and praying to whatever. So this foreman decides to hold a prayer service at seven on the dot every morning. Fifteen minutes dancing around praying. Not a single late start after that."

"Unbelievable," says Jeff.

Baloo seems about to say something—but dinner arrives. Salad, appetizer, main course—they make no distinction at O'Neal's. All arrive in a cornucopia of wet butter. You are happy to see the food until it is actually on the table in front of your face. There is some orange peel grating–looking sauce on the chicken. Jack doesn't miss a beat—he dives right in.

"Hasn't changed at all," he says approvingly. "I've been eating this for *years*."

You wonder if perhaps they were saving this actual chicken

for him for years. What are you missing? Has consulting so warped you that you cannot eat real food anymore?

One time, after a particularly odious team dinner top-heavy in its partner-to-other ratio, you and another associate plotted an informal chart based upon personal observation. (See below.)

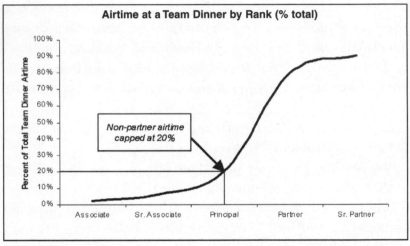

Source: Author analysis.

As this figure shows, while principal time is capped at about 20 percent of total team dinner addressable airtime, partner airtime has a *floor* of 75–78 percent of total. The most junior green-bean partner, promoted last week, who hasn't even gone through partner training camp down in the Caribbean—that partner faces an astonishing ramp-up in her expected contribution to team dinner blather of four times what she's used to. Imagine. While some associates at first find it galling they're not allowed a peep beyond "I agree" or "That's so funny"; in fact, examined right, it's a real relief. Because the horrible truth about the team dinner airtime figure is that it's *nonnegotiable—for every rank*. Has there ever been a tired partner who maybe didn't feel like lecturing, re-

galing, or reminiscing at a team dinner all night long? You
suspect perhaps there has been—but no matter. That burden
is not yours, not yet.

Also, note the touching adherence to medieval constructs
of rank order and hierarchy. It may be true, as some have
said, that consulting firms are the *opposite of bureaucracies*—
that is, they are team- and task-oriented living organisms with
little infrastructure to support a body of pure actors.
Compared to other forms of business, consultancies do seem
to waste less time in intercube meetings, paperwork, and pro-
cedure. But what is team dinner if not a form of pointless
meeting? It has all the characteristics of the bureaucratic
mechanism: It is (1) meaningless, (2) demoralizing, and (3)
mandatory. And the so-called flat-form meritocracy so bela-
bored by McKinsey—this in reality masks a rigid, pitiless *system
of caste* unseen outside Delhi since 1951.[57]

Tonight you have said precious little, and are about to say
less.

As mealtime unwinds, and Jack has put those religious fa-
natic islanders to bed, Jeff seizes a lull to make a tactical ma-
neuver. In retrospect, it appears brilliant. At this point Baloo
is slow-burning (she's young) . . . Martha has a saintly sick
smile on her quivering lips . . . Davo looks like a terrified man
in a coma . . . you are feeling warm butter reflux shooting up
your throat . . . Jack's humming something sad . . . there's
real potential for—

Not for disaster. A team dinner is never interesting enough
to bomb.

—But it has real potential here to induce a lethargy so profound in its participants it endangers those around them on
the road back home.

---

[57]Airtime percents are in aggregate—that is, all partners *together* must account for 80 percent of blather, at minimum; within each band there can be varying degrees of contribution as, for instance, a team dinner unlucky enough to contain two partners might see
one of them stepping up with 50 percent and the other with 30 percent.

So to avoid baking some new road pizzas, Jeff says, "Who gets the points tonight?"

"They're mine!" barks Martha in her first and final contribution to the night's discourse.

"No—I'm the most junior—that's the tradition," opines Baloo.

"I believe the tradition is, it's the most junior *from the farthest office*," notes Davo.

"You made that up," says Jeff.

"I would not—"

Jack abruptly stops humming. "You know who has *great* points is the Ritz."

You know for a fact the Ritz has *no* points—that's their point about points, actually. But the observation Jack is making is more profound.

Tentatively, Jeff echoes your thought: "I didn't think they gave points."

"Oh no, not those kinds," says Jack—

And there is a palpable lift in the collective stream of consciousness as Davo, Martha, yourself, even Baloo elevate by midges in your slick vinyl chairs and come alive, if only for a moment as it seems . . . it begins actually to seem . . . maybe you are going to hear *something you didn't know about points* . . .

"They're not explicit about it," Jack explains. "But they keep track in their system of repeats and they know *exactly* how loyal you are."

"Better believe it." Jeff nods like a Methodist echo chorus.

"And they ramp it up faster than Hyatt or definitely Marriott."

"Marriott is the worst," choruses Jeff.

"What's so bad about them?" asks Baloo.

"Oh, what isn't?"

And so on . . . and on . . . what you are talking about, of course, are loyalty programs at national hotel chains. Hotels, airlines, car renters, credit cards, everyone offers frequent travelers such as yourselves so-called rewards for repeat business; and you will have more say about these loyalty programs in their place. For now the issue is merely this: There is no topic of conversation more galvanizing, powerful, and useful among groups of top-tier management consultants than the accoutrements of travel—hotel facilities, American v. United, Hertz v. Avis, points and (now) top secret points . . .

Galvanizing, common-ground, and—this is absolutely critical—*noncontroversial.*

About one hour later—you don't want to look at your watch—you find yourself popping the trunk on your Matador Red Ford Taurus in the back parking lot of O'Neal's. You are standing next to a very quiet Martha; you suspect that she shares your aversion to night, that she is at heart a morning person. But that would be a guess.

"There's a restaurant in New York called O'Neal's," you say to her.

"Oh, I know. Across from Lincoln Center. I thought it closed."

"Really?"

"City Ballet dancers used to go there. There's a mural from the seventies—Peter Martins is in it. Balanchine used to go there and eat at the bar."

"How do you know this?"

"I was a ballet dancer."

At this moment Martha—a woman you have barely noticed in your life and was worried about making ten seconds' worth of conversation with in a parking lot in [Sadtown], Illinois—steps forward, takes a first position with convincing port de bras, pliés—and executes a perfect double pirouette.

10

Things to Do in Cleveland
When You're Dead

By the time you get to the Marriott, your little Taurus clock reads 12:47. You will have to arise at 6:30, fresh and ready to party again. Where is the point in a team dinner, exactly?

That which you are trying to avoid has already occurred.

So much time is spent in hotels they are better called hometels. In time they become not a home away from home but a home away. Hometels for business travel are newer and more replete than those you recall from your moments in publishing and television, when road tripping meant Motel 6 and Days Inn and gut runs to Arby's. There are high-speed lines for Internet access and two short double beds, with a king unavailable. To you this bed configuration makes no sense—you don't know anyone who shares a room in these hotels . . . have never even walked past a room so superoccupied . . . yet every one of them has two crampy double beds with one all empty . . . and then what you think, in the spirit of your new occupation, is: McKinsey ran an algorithm for them demonstrating slightly higher revenue potential for the double bed strategy . . .

Like dogs, hometels all have their own thing called personality. The Ritz-Carlton in Dearborn is a purebred akita: beautiful, attentive, aloof. You arrive there in the morning and are handed a water bottle and towel, for no reason.

"Welcome back, sir," they say.

You have never been there before.

The Westin is a Siberian husky: all glamour, no participation. Sheratons are the golden retrievers of Hometelville: They demand attention. "Do you know the Sheraton Service Promise?" they bark when you check in, order dinner, pick up your dry cleaning, take a crap in your bathroom. "Are you *aware* of the Sheraton Service Promise?"

One time, very late at night, you checked in to a Sheraton in Parsippany, New Jersey: "Have you been here before?"

"Yes."

In fact, you have been staying at this particular hometel for four months and always check in with the same older, leather-faced woman who asks you every week if you've been there before. You are a very memorable man, evidently.

"Yes."

"Are you aware of the Sheraton Service Promise?"

"Jesus, yes."

"How many nights are you with us?"

"Three. Can I ask you a question?"

"Okay."

"Why do you do that Sheraton promise thing?"

"It's our promise to you that we'll—"

"No—I know that. What I mean is—I mean, did the company say you have to say that? Is it required?"

She doesn't know what to say here. "It's our promise to you that—"

"I know—I know—whose idea was the promise?"

"I don't know."

"Is there a Mister Sheraton? You didn't always have this promise—"

"One or two keys, sir?"—she is starting to look alarmed. But you are not: You are simply not a night person, and you are genuinely interested in understanding this promise. It's written on a large blue banner affixed to the wall behind reception, but it is too late to read.

"What happens if you break the promise?"
"One key, all right?"
"I mean—are there repercussions?"

The Sheraton Service Promise, late of song and story, was announced on September 6, 2002, from Sheraton HQs in Toronto and White Plains, New York. The culmination of a $1 billion effort to revamp the chain, the promise reads thus:

> If you're not satisfied, we're not satisfied. Sheraton's Service Promise ensures you'll have a great stay, or we'll make it up to you with an instant discount, points for our rewards program or even money back. All you have to do is tell us.

The chain has even put a price tag on your feelings.
Minor discomfort = "an apology plus a $15 value or 500 Starwood Preferred Guest Points"
Major discomfort = "an apology plus a $25–$75 value" (paid with credit, gift certificate, or points)
So: You are given a 10 percent discount on your *next* stay at a hotel that has already offended you. This is presumptuous. Or you get points which, as well shall see in a moment, are actually worth *less* than nothing.
You feel dissatisfied—very dissatisfied. Your discomforts in hometels are legion, but none of these has anything to do with the hometel itself; they are existential, perhaps congenital. There is only one aspect of the Sheraton *itself* that brings discomfort: the Sheraton Service Promise.
It annoys you, it really does.
You would like to complain but the "reward" is simply a slight enticement to return and hear *even* more about the Sheraton Service Promise—an enticement that means nothing to those who, like yourself, don't pay for the hotel room anyway.

Your promise to the Sheraton became: "I will never stay here again."

So the Marriott is your hometel of choice, the humble black lab with its hard nylon bone. The selection of hotel chain is not trivial. Top-tier consulting teams tend to stay at the same hotel, congregating in the lobby around 7:45 a.m. for the drive to the client site. This car pooling is done not to save money, exactly, but because *not driving* is a signal of rank, and the senior principals and partners must be driven; they generally do not rent cars. Associates rent cars. Partners *have* cars. Limos get them at airports and take them to lunch. And in the mornings, they ask the team to meet them in the lobby . . .

So the Marriott.

The Marriott does things "the Marriott Way," as it calls it—but this is somehow less offensive.

> Pride in the knowledge that our customers can count on Marriott's unique blend of quality, consistency, personalized service and recognition almost anywhere they travel in the world or whichever Marriott brand they choose.

You might quibble with "unique," since every hometel room is absolutely identical, but you cannot quibble with this: Marriott staff don't pummel you senseless with a nonstop litany of "Are you aware of the Marriott Way, sir?"

Your way is: Stay out of my way.

You open the door to your room. Tonight, you remember the number: 518. Fifth floor, halfway down the hall. Many times you cannot remember your room. Why would you? Which week is it anyway? Numbers are not written on the card keys, of course; so you spend your time flashing ID at the front desk and asking, "What room am I in, again?"

Don't try your card key in a door unless you are sure it is yours; they are deactivated by insertion into the wrong room.

You put down your [firm] backpack, a relic of new hire orientation, and stand quietly.

Breathe out.

Breathe in, counting, counting . . .

You are asleep on your feet, and even the effort of unlacing your shoes seems too monstrous. So you fall onto the double bed. Your jacket is still on; your feet are on the coverlet, toes down. Your mouth buried in pillow. The eyes close and . . .

Shit!

Your breath stinks. You haven't called your wife. You haven't set the wake-up call.

Hometel life consists of a series of strategies for managing torpor. The body cannot be trusted. Ritual is salvation, autopilot redemption. Your strong need for sleep must be shunted into appropriate channels for treatment. Over the months you have observed the following:

Top Five Torpor Management Mistakes Made by Consultants Late at Night

Mistake	Consequence
Use in-room digital alarm clock	"Wake" to music—hah!
Turn on heating unit	Warm cozy feeling—bad!
Close window shades	No blaring a.m. sunlight—bad!
Don't call wife	No wife
Don't gargle/brush teeth/ splash face	Awakened by own stench
Order an in-room movie	See only seven minutes . . .

Kicking off your shoes, you call your wife. She is online, as she often is. The room is very cold—that is good. You set the wake-up call, open the shades, drink some water, and lie down.

Every part of you says: *Go to sleep.*

So that is what you do.

You're asleep. You have no issues with insomnia; rather, with its opposite. And your dreams have become more *productive* . . . less whimsical than during your artist days. Back then you often thought of yourself as a big-knuckled monkey swinging from tree to tree, terrified to fall. Now, having fallen, you dream of going to the gym. This is literally true. You dream about being in health clubs and running around tracks, cutting into weight stacks and pumping metal till your corpuscles bounce. You dream about heaving large palettes of reps in a muscle-tee while women watch obliquely.

Freud called the dream "the fulfillment of a wish," and you wish he were wrong.

You dream about being healthy. You dream about becoming attractive again, as you were as a poet and a miserable younger man.

And these dreams are the closest you ever get to the gym.

Those who don't know think this life may be glamorous.

6:30 a.m. Thursday.

Delighted to have had you with us. *"The weather in [Sadtown] this morning is mild and debris,"* says the automated or prerecorded vocal wake-up unit. At least that's what it sounds like. You never quite put these early-a.m. phone sets up to your ear. There is drool on your ear; your eyes are gummed shut. What town is this? What is the debris?

. . . stumbling to micturate in the flash-frozen light . . .

. . . you have an early-morning erection, a common phenomenon among young men, but then why do *you* have one? . . . plus there is no purpose to erections on business trips and especially on top-tier management consulting business trips. What's going to happen—sex? With whom? With what preamble? Why?

There is a piece of white paper, folded up, on the carpet by the front door. Somebody slipped it in during the night. You pick it up and look at it.

This is not unexpected, this paper—something any other industry might call a bill or an invoice becomes in the euphemistic parlance of the hometel a "guest folio." The folio wherein they put a work of art, just for you. And it is a creative act, charging so much in so many ways for so little. Teams of bullshit artists must have worked around the clock devising secret ways for you to rack up pain. You used to be surprised it was possible to commit so many folio-able acts in a mere three nights—but it is. Oh, it is.

And there is no argument for room service: none. It is hideously expensive, tepid, long-winded, chilly—you wait eight hours for the privilege of having an asshole barge into your room with his palm sticking out, lifting the silver cover off a mound of crap like it's worth something. You've had room service chicken that broke pieces off your teeth; $30.00 New York strip steak that gnawed at your digestive tract, demanding to be released . . . and it's not just that a piece of fruit costs $6.95, two-minute "jumbo" shrimp $9.50, or an invisible sliver of double devil chocolate cake $4.95 . . . no, what really eats at you is that there's an automatic 19 percent service charge added to each and every item and still *the guy wants a tip*. Are you being small? Perhaps. And perhaps a few tunes on the radio might help to dull the pain. What could be simpler—more basic? Free airwaves for a free people. Most hometel rooms come equipped with something brown that does indeed look like a radio: knobs, dials, the letters *F* and *M* printed in white somewhere . . . but when you go to turn it on, well . . . noth-

ing. Static. You move the tuning knob up, down, sideways—
nothing. On AM you can sometimes detect—depending
upon where you are standing—the faint religious tones of a
fundamentalist song-and-rant man, or maybe it's live Nascar
racing, hard to tell.

There is no more consistent phenomenon in U.S. hometel
life than that the radio *does not work*. And why?

It turns out there *is* a reason, and it has to do with your TV.
Turn it on (you can't listen to the radio, what else can you
do?) . . . turn it on, press the green menu button, scroll
around and you will find an option called "Radio Interactive,"
which proffers up "stations" such as "Urban NiteClub"
(Technotronic) and "Alternative Alley" (Cracker) . . . and
these "stations" in turn play for you a selection of music in
your chosen genre for the low, low price of $9.95 (plus tax)
for two glorious hours. Plus, should you be particularly taken
with any of the selections, there is the helpful little "Buy CD"
button at the bottom of the screen.

Once you stumble on this loathsome "service" you cannot
help but look at your dysfunctional little dream machine
radio/alarm as a deliberate act of sabotage on the part of the
Marriott.

You commit another act of sabotage upon your early-
morning face. It is called shaving. Somehow, you can never
quite match the motion to the surface when you're on the
road; there is always blood spillage and hard feelings. Often
you will simply forget your own razor; you use the "complimentary" Marriott razors, available totally free of charge at
the front desk, and these little blue plastic items are perhaps
the cheapest solid matter on the planet; their purpose seems
to be to seek out and destroy your dignity.

But no matter. Today you have remembered your home
razor. You shower . . . and shower . . . and shower . . . does the
day have to begin? Does it really?

Since you don't really unpack, you don't really pack. That's the symmetry.

6:54 a.m.

7:07 a.m.

Shoes, shirt, and service. Scan the room, the bathroom. Ninety percent of items left behind in hotel rooms are left in the bathroom. Ninety percent of hotel sheets test positive for semen. Everything related to hometel life is 90 percent, including the joylessness. This bathroom is empty but for your memories. You close the door, leaving the room key inside. Your memories are gone now. There is, of course, a *USA Today* in wait under your feet. You take pleasure, each day, in stepping over it.

You are waiting for the elevator.

Next to you is a man much like yourself—white, face flecked with dry scabs from a Marriott razor, garment bag (minus helium) in hand. You smile at one another but do not speak. To speak would be the collision of matter and antimatter—an explosion of sameness. You are not special. He is not special. It is a world of sad white men avoiding contact.

You pass the front desk silently. You do not check out—you never check out. Although they do not say it, hotels do not particularly want you to check out. They know when you're leaving; they don't need to know that you've left.

You are outside.

You are in your Taurus, driving.

At the office, your cramped cubi-kennel has become a storage medium for female luggage.[58] This makes for close quarters. Martha is late and seems, when she does arrive, kind of out of it.

Baloo takes a chance and says, "Are you okay?"

---

[58]Women travel with approximately one point four times as much *stuff*, by weight, as men; the reason for this is unknown, but is said to be related to shoes.

Martha looks as if she is going to cry but says nothing. She nods.

Meanwhile, Davo is standing with his back against the wall beside your cubi-kennel, cell phone pressed tight to his ear and jaw muscle, talking in no uncertain terms to his girl-friend/boyfriend/unknown. Normally discreet, he is out of line this morning.

"Are you getting tested?" he whispers in the kind of whisper that is actually more audible in a closed environment than a room tone voice.

"What are you telling me—that you don't care what I think?"

"Is there something you're not—is there something I'm missing here . . . ?"

"We should talk about this later."

"I totally disagree with that and you're being—I can't believe how selfish you're being but we have to talk about this later."

Then: "Good-bye."

Then, twenty seconds later: "Good-bye."

Then silence.

A few minutes later we are gathered in the big tire confer-ence room for a meeting. Davo is in a foul mood. Jeff is sup-posedly "meeting the client," but he may be asleep. Jack is not present. Martha is moping.

"We got some bad news last night," Davo announces. "There was some pushback from the senior team and they want to see those inventory numbers cut a different way."

"What way?" asks Baloo.

"That's the thing. They're not sure. But they do know they have to be recut."

"Recut how?"

"Not sure. I'm just telling you what they told me. 'Recut the numbers.' So let's look at this and figure it out."

"I'm sorry," you say, not sorry at all, "but is there a deadline associated with this? A deliverable?"

"What do you think?"

"My guess is yes, there is."

"Your guess would be correct."

"And . . . ?"

"Jack called me this morning *very early*—and he let me know he wants something by three this afternoon. We're going to meet after that to go over it."

This is very bad news, for very obvious reasons.

"Shit," says Martha, emerging from her mope in a rage, "I have a six o'clock flight. I have to be out of here by four-thirty."

"I don't know what to say," says Davo, "but change the flight."

Then back at the cubi-kennel, to be recutting the numbers.

Recutting is an ambiguous word, and there is no direction, so you make a strategic decision. You step into the next cubicle and ask, "Say, Geraldo, did you take a look at that deck from last night?"

"The one you guys did? On the inventory stuff?"

"Yeah."

"I saw it."

"What did you think?"

"I'd—personally, I'd recut it."

"Okay. That's interesting."

You use this phrase a lot: *That's interesting*, or *Interesting*. What it really means is: *I don't know what else to say*.

So you wait.

"Well, I'd try rolling up the skews.[59] You guys had too many. Roll them into tire families and cut the inventory by stores."

---

[59] *Skew* is consumer product world shorthand for SKU or Shop Keeping Units, which are numerical designations for products, with each product—no matter how minutely differentiated (e.g., two-ounce instead of four-ounce size)—getting its own distinct number. A skew is the most precise way to tell products apart.

"How would you do the stores?"

"Company-owned, franchisees, and other."

"Three groups?"

"Three groups."

"How would you roll the skews up?"

"Personally? I would use a roll-up table I developed and happen to have on my PC right now."

The snake of a smile emerges from the cool depths of Geraldo's self.

"I imagine," he says, "you guys might like to take a look at my table?"

It used to bother you—the fact that highly paid you, marching in to save the day, knew absolutely nothing about the companies into which you marched to save the day. That any guy sitting in any cubicle on any floor knew infinitely more. This used to bother you—but now it does not, not at all. If you knew that much you'd have to change places with the guy in the cubicle.

"Yeah," you say. "Uh-huh."

11:34 a.m. Thursday.

Numbers are recut, deck complete; Martha friendly toward you, her deliverer, since it turns out she absolutely *has* to make that flight at six o'clock or her husband will probably leave her (you don't ask). Jack finally appears to bark a bit and retreat to whisper on the phone for hours. Top secret deals, or something other.

And you do something you've never done before . . . something so egregious and wrong that it enters the realm of pure treason: You ask Geraldo to lunch, as a friend.

He accepts.

So you're in the lunchroom, you and Geraldo, gnawing on some rubber chicken curry pasta or something, and it turns out that Geraldo has quite an interest in consulting. Quite a touching interest.

"How much do you guys make?"

"Gosh," you say. "We do okay."

"I don't mean you—you don't make anything. But what about, like, Jack? What's he take in yearly, you think?"

"I'm not sure. He's pretty up there."

"Like a million? Over a million?"

"Could be like that. I'm not really sure." In truth, you have no idea what partners make. You don't really care. Does this mean you're in consulting for the wrong reasons? Perhaps.

Geraldo reveals he has the soul—if not the tact—of a top-tier consultant when he broaches his next topic of the day.

"So," he probes, "what kind of points do you rack up in a year?"

"What, you mean hotel points? Airline points?"

"Whatever—I heard you guys take all your vacations on points. You have so many points you're always upgraded—first-class this, first-class that. Business in the air and the suites and all that."

"Well, I guess I have a lot of points. They're not really so great."

This *stuns* Geraldo—

"Not so great? But everything is *free*—you don't have to pay for it. It's totally *free.* You can go around the world and . . . and stay for *free* wherever . . . go to Hawaii. You know how much I paid for my last vacation . . . ?"

"It's not like that," you say, feeling a little bit bad about it, too. "It's not so great."

"What? Why?"

"It's like an illusion."

"An illusion?"

"Yeah—it's like a phony thing. It's not real."

"But it's *free.*"

"Yes, it's free. But it isn't real."

The Myth of Points

Loyalty points, frequent flier points, awards programs, status-gathering mechanisms, elite clubs and corporate memberships, redemption, tiers of service, automatic upgrades and upgrades fought for and denied, first-tier and second-tier reward rosters, and free selection matrices and dreams of ultimate leisure—these are the primary topics of discourse among top-tier management consultants, worldwide.

They told you at recruiting events: "You get to keep your points." At the time it alone seemed like a good enough reason to *take a look*. You may not be home much but you get *free vacations in exotic lands* . . . you can repair your marriage, or start a new one.

And it is true—you travel for business, are reimbursed by the client, break more or less even . . . and any and all loyalty points thereby accumulated go to you personally. This arrangement seems too good to be true. Is it?

There was an associate who worked with you on one of your engagements who was more obsessed than most with his points. He loved airlines, knew every quirk of status systems. He booked flights with extra legs—taking ten hours or more to travel from Washington, DC, to Chicago—simply to earn top status. And when he finally got there, you asked him: "Was it worth it?"

"I got a Christmas present from the airline," he said.

"What was it?"

"A bathrobe."

"What else?"

"That's it."

"Was it a nice bathrobe?"

"A little itchy. I can't really wear it."

"What color?"

"It has the airline logo on it."

"How much did it cost you?"

"Like twenty thousand dollars . . ."

As your wife, a wry folk musician who hates the open road, likes to point out: "Life is not a destination, it's a gurney."

You travel a lot; you travel all the time. Every week you're picking up a Taurus, riding in a plane. The points accumulate like silent magic. After six months or so you think: What have I won? You look into Hertz. As a proud number one Club Gold member—there is no Silver membership—you have been earning points for months. Each dollar spent gets you a point. In your city, an average rental day is about $75, so your typical four-day rental gets you around three hundred points *every week*.

So it's been six months and you've got what seems to you a truly impressive seventy-two-hundred points under your belt. You imagine a Jaguar or a Volvo; you imagine a month of free rides coast to coast, you and your proud wife clutching mittens. You imagine wrong. It turns out that Hertz attended the Ebeneezer School of Generosity. One free rental day costs twelve hundred points and a free rental week costs eighty-five-hundred. In other words, you have to rent a full-size Matador Red Ford Taurus four days per week for *twenty-eight continuous weeks* to earn the privilege of *just one free weekly rental* . . . oh, and number one Club Gold membership costs you $50 per year. The gifts are a form of myth, and the rewards a paid-for object lesson. You're guessing Hertz makes quite a tidy profit on this "give-away" . . . and so much for your proud wife and her willing mittens . . .

You called Hertz one day, to claim an award. You called the number one Club Gold hot line. This happened:
"Number one Club Gold hot line, how can I help you?"
"I would like to redeem some points."
"What now?"
"I'd like to redeem points."
"What kind of points?"
"I have number one points and I'd like to get a free rental. How do I do that?"
"A free rental. Ah." [*Long pause.*] "You still there?"
"Yes."
"How can I help you?"
"I'd like to redeem points for a free rental. How do I do it?"

"Yes, we can do that." [*Long pause.*] "Hello?"

"How do I get my free rental?"

"I said we can do that."

"How?"

"You need a coupon."

"Where do I get the coupon?"

"We can send it to you."

"Okay, then, I need to get a coupon."

"We mail you the coupon and you have to give it when you get to the Gold counter."

"Okay. How do I get the coupon?"

"We mail it to you."

"Can I request one?"

"You can request it online."

(Actually, you tried this; it did not at the time appear to be possible.)

"Can I request it from you?"

"From me?"

"Yes. *Can you send me a coupon?*"

"I'm not authorized to do that, I don't think."

"Are you kidding me? You can't send it? You're the hot line—"

"The what now?"

"You are the *redemption hot line*—it says so right on my statement."

"Right. But we can't send you a coupon." [*Long pause; some noises you can't quite make out*] "Sir?"

"Yeah?"

"We can send you a coupon."

"I thought so."

"What's your name . . . ?"

Four weeks later, you did indeed receive your free off-peak week rental coupon. You never used it, however; it was not possible for you to find an off-peak week to your liking. You never knew it before, but apparently you are not quite the individual maverick you fancy yourself to be: All your dreams of travel occur precisely when everybody else's do.

The coupon still sits in your closet at home. It's on top of your stack of weight-lifting magazines.

The End

So you're talking to Geraldo—not reciting all of the above, but trying to convey, in a moment, the flavor of your revelations. He is not buying it.

"I don't know," he says, "you must be doing something wrong."

"Clearly."

"I mean, everybody loves those points."

"That's why they're worth nothing—because everybody loves them."

"That's depressing."

"Tell me about it."

You sit there a moment, feeling the silence. It is then that you make a truly terrible mistake: You take out your pen.

"I figured out something," you say, and start to write on a napkin. "Take something like Continental EasyPass—you need about fifty thousand miles to get a free round-trip. Say you go from New York to L.A., round trip that's about five thousand give or take. So you need ten round-trips from New York to L.A. to get a free round-trip."

"Huh . . ."

"Without much early notice, it's like six hundred dollars per trip, or six thousand for the ten of them. So you're paying six thousand dollars for a free gift. And that's the general rule—at least for the places like Continental where they actually *do* occasionally give away stuff. Some points things are totally illusion, but some are not—and the general rule seems to be buy ten, get one identical thing free. It's like when you go to a coffee shop, with the punch card. But it only works with worthless things—like coffee and airplane seats. Buy ten worthless things at full price, get the eleventh on the house."

"Uh-huh . . ."

Geraldo is still staring at your pen, the one you've been using to illustrate your insight. He's not staring but *staring*—glaring. Then he looks up, and something has changed, changed utterly.

"I better get back."

He stands and walks off toward the tray-dumping area. You sit there, bewildered.

Bewildered, that is, until you glance down at the pen in your hand.

It is a blue ballpoint pen with a gold tip and it says: RITZ-CARLTON.

On-site Rule #4: Do Not Flaunt the 20 Percent.

That is—20 percent is the standard amount added on top of professional fees for travel and other expenses. This amount can be considerable. For a new associate, 20 percent of a week's billing rates is about $2,000, which should amply cover airfare, hotel, dry cleaning, team dinners, and a few twelve-minute adult films, plus the radio. But for a partner, assigned 50 percent to the job, expense reimbursement comes in at around $5,000 per week. That's a lot of sushi.

These expenses, more than the fees, are what rile clients. They do not like to subsidize a lifestyle they perceive to be lavish. You have torn away the tawdry veils concealing this lie, you hope, yet the image persists: highly paid consultant, living high on the broken backs of the working poor.

To diffuse this ticking time bomb, you are advised not to "flaunt" your expenses. Don't mention your hotels by name. Don't talk about "limo services," but refer often to "cabs" or "carpooling." Never say "team dinner"—well, you'd never do that anyway, for other reasons—and don't bring these up. They are boondoogles pure and simple and fine wines and cognacs of the world should not be dwelt upon the morning after. Don't ever say you have a "refundable" airline ticket that you bought "at the last minute"—and never, ever mention the words "business class" or "fully reclining seats." It is better to talk about "three-week advance booking" and "unbelievable discounts"—advisable to go on about "crummy bargain air-lines" and "no peanuts."

And never use a Ritz-Carlton pen to draw on a napkin in the employee cafeteria at the client site while having lunch with a client personnel.

2:17 p.m.

The day wanes, the end draws nigh.

Your meeting with Jack produced an "action item" for you consisting of a meeting with a relatively high-ranking client named Barbara. You don't know her, nor do you know why they are sending you and Davo specifically to this meeting. Nor do you know what the meeting is about.

Negotiating the hall tires on the way to meeting with Barbara, you ask Davo, "So, what is this meeting about?"

"I don't know. Inventory?"

"Didn't Jack tell you?"

"He doesn't know."

"Why did he send us to this? What about Baloo? Martha?"

"Apparently this Barbara has a problem with women."

"A what now?"

"She doesn't like women. Last time we were here—Jack told me this—Barbara had an issue with some of the women and it got to be a problem."

"What kind of a problem?"

"Not sure. Anyway, Jack says she's much better with men. So we're going."

"Why couldn't Jack take the meeting?"

"Jack hates her."

"Oh."

The meeting was everything, and more. You and Davo are made to wait for twenty minutes, and you don't talk much. You can hear the client's shrill voice etching through the door. Her secretary has abandoned her desk and left a half-full coffee cup, a half-eaten oatmeal scotchie. And

Barbara's sharp laugh is followed by: "*Why* did you do that . . . ?"

When she finally appears, opening her own door to you, Barbara is not laughing. No one emerges; she must have been talking on the phone.

"Come in," she says without apology, nodding you in like puppies.

She sits, and you sit, and you look at each other. You're not sure what she sees, but she does not like it. What you see is a tiny little person and a very small head and large glasses; a kid-sized executive with an enormous Chagall print on the wall right behind her. There is horse-riding paraphernalia all around—pictures of horses, plastic horses for kids, even some newspaper clippings and ribbons.

"How long have you guys been here?"

"Oh, it's no problem," says Davo, "just a couple minutes—"

"No—I meant here at [Client]?"

"Oh. Just a week or—"

"What kind of progress have you made?"

"Well," says Davo, sort of rattled by her rat-a-tat. "Um . . . we've been—"

"Listen, I'll be honest with you. I don't like consultants. They're always putting together arrows and little boxes and recycling stuff we give them anyway. But"—here she names the main client, the CFO, who is friendly with Jack from way back—"thought you could help, and he outranks me."

You're both nodding. You, in fact, are taking notes. You're always taking notes that you will never look at again. It is a method of distancing yourself from the unpleasantness around you, and it's common. You have noticed that the tenser the meeting, the more frenzied is the note taking—all around. When the partner breaks out the notepad, that is a sign the meeting has become a disaster.

"So," she says, tilting back in her large leather chair, "how are you going to help us?"

"Well—" says Davo.

"I've been here for twenty years now," she continues. "And there have been a lot of consultants. A lot of them. It was always like I said—they'd look at our data, tell it right back to us, packaged up pretty. Then they'd make some 'recommendation' that didn't make any sense for our business and they'd leave. Two years later, we'd get a different bunch come in—they'd look at our data, make some noise, run around . . . nothing ever changed."

"Sometimes," says Davo, "it can take some time to—"

"McKinsey was the best," she says, "but even they didn't help us. Not compared to their fees. They were wearing suits—how come you guys don't wear suits?"

"It's the dress code," you say.

"Suits are a bad idea—it was making the guys here feel like they're being disliked. Maybe they were, I don't know. But they seemed real smart and had no background at all in this business. You guys know tires?"

"Well . . ." starts Davo.

"No," you say.

"I thought so. And you think you can sit here and tell us what to do? You see the absurdity of that? You see where I'm coming off of here . . . ?"

You're thinking: If you were so good at running your business, missy, you wouldn't be on the brink of Chapter 11 and on chronic deathwatch while the whole country laughs at you behind your back.

And she goes on . . . it's not offensive so much as it is incredibly boring; she doesn't want an answer, she wants an audience; she wants to ventilate. You let her.

In a few minutes, after she's decompressed, Davo lets the silence linger. Then he takes a step he seems to have taken before; something you can learn from and admire. A step toward rapprochement . . .

"You know," he says softly, "I see what you're saying. A lot of people are kind of skeptical about consultants, and for good reason. Because we come in with such big teams there're going to be people on the team who are not experts in the particular industry—"

She makes an explosive sound—like *qjklasjklwchsh-shshshchklskj!*—and chokes it down.

"But if you think about it, we have a lot of expertise we can tap into. We have a company full of experts in the area, people like yourself who know this industry like—really well. How could we top that? What we are good at is doing the heavy lifting—you know, the grunt work of breaking down the problem, finding the data, sorting through it, packaging that up. We're not gonna tell anybody how to run her business—especially not one like this one, tires, it's too complicated"—

You think: It would be difficult to find a business less complicated than tires. But no matter.

—"so all we can do is run some analyses for you, put together some graphs, and so on. You can make whatever conclusions there are. It's like we're here to help you make your decisions, if that makes sense."

"Uh-huh."

"But we can only really do what you ask us to. You guys are paying a lot of money for us—we need to make sure you're getting what you need."

"Uh-huh."

"So," he says—lowering his voice, leaning forward, toward her—"please let us know how we can help."

"How what now?"

"You may not need us right now—but let us know if you do."

She considers Davo's enticement. "Can I ask you something?"

"Sure."

"What's your background?"

"I'm a chemical engineer."

"I mean, what clients have you worked with before?"

"Mainly in the automotive industry, auto parts and service, some consumer—"

"No, I mean *who were the clients*? Ford? GM? Hyundai?"

"I can't say."

"Have you worked for our competitors?"

"I can't say."

"Why not?"

"It's confidentiality. We never talk about who we work for, not by name."

"I never understood that. Everybody has consultants running around—it's not like there's a stigma."

This is always the implication: that clients don't want anyone to know they have a problem serious enough to require the services of a top-tier consultant.[60]

"It's . . ."—here Davo hesitates. You get the impression he's never really thought about this question before. "Uh . . ."

"You know why? I'll tell you—and don't take this the wrong way, okay?"

Oh shit, you think. And after all that progress with the "let us know how we can help."

"Like I said, I've seen a lot of consultants sitting in that seat there," she continues. "They're all the same—we worked for a major this company, a superbig that company and the other. No names, of course. It's kind of like if you fill out a résumé but you don't have to put down where you worked or what you did—or, or even *when* it was. You know why you guys do that?"

"Confidentiality—"

"Yeah, yeah. I kind of think it's because *you're making it up.* Maybe not all of them—but it's a lot easier to seem like a big deal when you don't have to give specifics. See what I mean?"

Davo doesn't know what to say to her. He really doesn't.

A few minutes later, she has made her point and seems quite happy to let you go.

Her door closes behind you. The secretary's doughnut is still half finished, like the final meal on the ghost ship *Andrea*

---

[60]This logic is belied by the reality of consulting economics—as we saw in Part II, it is for the most part only companies with money to burn who can hire consultants, so having a pack of fresh McKinseyites scurrying through your halls, far from being a sign of impending doom, simply means you have a lot of extra money lying around; this is the opposite of a problem.

Doria. You are beginning to believe this godforsaken rubber company will indeed be in bankrupty by next year and another great era of American manufacturing will stop.

"That," says Davo, walking next to you down the hall back to the team room, "was truly weird."[61]

On-site Rule #5: Cultivate Your Mystery.

When you first got to your top-tier firm, at your new hire orientation, there was a lecture given by a partner you have long forgotten. The topic was "Maintaining Client Confidentiality." This forgotten partner laid down the ground rules for your new profession, rules (she said) that had been put into place shortly after World War II and were inviolate.

These rules were

1. Do not mention your client's name to *anyone* outside the firm, including your wife, your mother and father, cousins distant and close, best friends and mentors, and gurus and father confessors—"Not even," she joked, "the pope."

Consultant

---

[61]"At one of the most profitable, elite law firms in the United States, I started to pose my questions, asking 'What percent of your clients would you put in the category of "I like these people?"' The room broke into laughter, as if the question was absurd. It became clear that many professionals do not expect to like their clients." (David H. Maister, *True Professionalism: The Courage to Care About Your People, Your Clients, and Your Career* [New York: Simon & Schuster, 1997], 25. This book was given to all entering associates at your top-tier firm, put on a shelf, and forgotten.)

2. Tell your spouse/SO (a) the general industry/business, and (b) the nearest large city—and that's *it*.

3. *Never* talk about the client or its problems in public, on the tarmac, in planes, in restaurants—never *ever* talk about them in elevators of any size or shape—in the gym, on your cell phone in a crowd of yahoos pushing onto the Metro North train to Larchmont.

4. Do not tell one client employee what another client employee—even at the same firm, on the same floor, in the same department, in the adjoining cubicle—told you or showed you.

5. Don't even think about mentioning to one client that your top-tier firm has any other clients.

6. If pressed, admit your top-tier firm may in the past have had some other clients—and that these clients in addition to being worldwide household names are among the most successful companies ever.

7. Smile and nod a lot . . . offer very little personal information . . . stay strong.

The tradition of total secrecy has been endemic to the top-tier consulting business since the beginning. For years after the firm was founded, Bain consultants had no business cards—and not because they couldn't afford them. McKinsey consultants are referred to even in some internal documents only by a first name and an initial, like recovering sexaholics. To your knowledge BCG has never publicly admitted to having a single client. McKinsey occasionally acknowledges only those, such as Swissair and Johnson & Johnson, for whom it has toiled in large numbers over many, many years, and who are succeeding. To this day Monitor has never aired the name of its single biggest (some say only) client—AT&T.

Now for a contest. One of the following real quoted passages was written by an unemployed liar in the pages of a half-baked women's magazine; the other by a highly respected, far beyond top-tier management consulting eminence in the archives of a preeminent management journal. Which is which?

> Passage 1: "Carlos, 32, is chiseled and has the taut dancer's body women respond to. 'I don't think about my looks a lot,' he says. 'Still, it really bothers me when a woman says "You're handsome" straight out. It's not only embarrassing, it makes me think, Is that the only thing she cares about?'"

> Passage 2: "In many of the companies I work with, hundreds and sometimes thousands of people get involved in crafting strategy. . . . In one company, the idea for a multimillion-dollar opportunity came from a twenty-something secretary. In another company, some of the best ideas about the organization's core competencies came from a forklift operator."

Okay, not so difficult. But as the author of Passage 1—which appeared in the pages of *Cosmopolitan* in June 1999, to your eternal shame—you can now admit an uneasy truth: Sorry, ladies, but *there is no Carlos!* You made him up. Fabricated. You had finished the piece, turned it in, and your editor said: "We need a quote here, something sexual and Latin, you know. Make the guy named Carlos or Antonio or something—those guys know women."

"I know women."

"Not like those Latin guys—it's a different league."

"I don't know anyone named Carlos."

"Then make him up."

Now, this editor might deny this assertion, but you were there. And so you made Carlos up, put words in his mouth and thought, What's the harm? You cashed the $1,500 check and moved on . . .

As for Passage 2,[62] you would never go so far as to assert its much-admired author, Gary Hamel, capable of misrepresentation, lying, quote fabrication, fictionalizing, mendacity, or even simple laziness. But it is a very common practice to pepper business books and articles with case studies and references to walletfuls of unnamed "clients" running around unspecified "large manufacturing companies" and "midsize professional services businesses" with a "global footprint." Such characters are useful because they hint at vast shadow networks of power and place the author at the dead center of the storms of influence—and they are totally uncheckable. When you worked briefly at *Forbes* in the early 1990s you realized there is nothing less truthful than the public face of management. Except, perhaps, the public utterances of management consultants.

It is as though a man were to stand in front of you and say, "I have a rather large penis." Can you prove him wrong?

It is this collision of puffery with puffery that makes consulting for the U.S. government so entertaining.

About a year after you joined the firm, you were sent to work for a division of the U.S. intelligence services known as the MPO, for Maryland Procurement Office. At first this name does not excite you. It seems you will be sent to some warehouse to count staples and order office supplies; in fact, you try to wriggle out of the assignment. But your power has, and had, its limits; it had, and has, nothing but.

It turned out MPO is the old-style alias for the National Security Agency, or the NSA. As opposed to the CIA, which is legally enjoined from spying on U.S. citizens and focuses its activities upon gathering worthless "intelligence" on foreign countries, mainly from paid-off sources in the field and un-

[62]From Gary Hamel, "Strategy As Revolution," *Harvard Business Review* 69 (August 1996).

dercover operations, the NSA is a high-tech global informa-
tion-gathering posse. The NSA is the nation's eavesdroppers,
wiretappers, encrypters, decoders, and database protectors.
The agency, commissioned in the 1950s, underwrote most
modern electronic cryptography and is in charge of defending the classified computer networks from outside (or inside)
attack. And it is out of the closet—there is a big sign on the
highway south of Baltimore that says NATIONAL SECURITY
AGENCY, NEXT EXIT and a National Museum of Cryptography
just outside Linthicum, Maryland, that has a large and well-
stocked gift shop.

So you found yourself, during three hot summer months,
earning full commercial consulting wages from a branch of
the NSA known as the IAD—Information Assurance Direct-
orate. There is no arm of human endeavor more besotted by
acronyms than the U.S. intelligence services. Like consult-
ingspeak, acronymitis is the tribe's way of putting up signs
outside their tree house reading KEEP OUT and MEN AT WORK.[63]

You showed up in a nondescript office park in Linthicum,
Maryland, within sight of the decrepit IAD office park, and
you entered a windowless office. This was your home for the
next three months. Clean-cut, heavy right-wingers with no
discernible work task dropped by from time to time, poked
their heads in, nodded, said something about the heat, a
barbecue, buying a car at CarMax or an auto mall, and then
they left.

And that first week there was a meeting where you learned
something about secrets.

What the meeting was about . . . it was related to scheduling meetings or discussions over the coming months.
Something about the SPIRNET, which is the computer net-

---

[63]Once you had a meeting in the FANX at the V43 division of the IAD with the TD in
charge of ST&E for the SNS computer network guard. The topic was streamlining the
SABI process of the DITSCAP and the DODI 8540, which dealt with interoperability issues. The TD expressed concern that the SSAA template effort was not compatible with
the GIAP and would be disapproved by the OSD and the CINCs.

work for the defense community containing information classified as secret. There is a top secret classification, of course,
but most working military information—battle plans, weather
reports, satellite imagery—is merely secret.[64]

The meeting took place in a government-issue conference
room in Maryland. Folding chairs and very long, slightly
wobbly brown tables with thin legs. A collection of military
types from all branches and civilians, many of whom—this
being a hot day, this being the U.S. government—were wearing Hawaiian shirts and shorts. There is no dress code for
civilians; there is no code but to be out of shape, out of sorts,
and dull.

You all faced frontward, though there was no speaker and
no presentation. Thirty-odd people, facing forward, talking
to the backs of people's heads or the air in front of them.

After a while, somebody took it upon themselves to say,
"Let's get started."

Somebody else had to courage to say, "What's this meeting
about?"

Somebody else: "Shouldn't we wait?"

"Who for?"

A very large man in a colorful shirt with various Caribbean
islands named upon it said, "I think we all know everybody
here. Except for *you*."

He pointed directly at *you*. You felt like a Cuban, or something.

"Yes—my name is [your name]. I work for [your top-tier
firm]. We're working with Holly over at the IAD on an information assurance strategy."

"Do you have clearance?"

---

[64]Top secret information, mainly relevant to the intelligence agencies and their clients,
is confined to a network called the JWICS. There are rumored to be other, even more secret, networks, and these rumors are no doubt true. As for what is actually on these networks, you can quote an air force major you asked early on during the engagement: "It's
all a lot of crap."

You were afraid of this question. "Well—no. But I was told it was okay for this meeting."

"Not even secret?"

Like information, people are categorized as unclassified, secret, and top secret. You were undeniably unclassified.

"No."

Heads turned, necks craned, sclerotic crania contorted until thirty-some pairs of eyes were blearing at you—the man who was unclassified! How could such a thing be? Unclassified was hardly worth the effort of getting out of bed in the morning. Unclassified was an affront to all that is holy. Unclassified was an affront to this . . . very . . . meeting.

"I'm not sure I'm comfortable—"

Somebody sitting up front interrupted, "It's okay. This is only a scheduling meeting."

"But we might say something—"

"I'm pretty sure it's okay."

"I could leave," you offered, envisioning a nice cool drive back to the office park.

"You might want to—"

"No, really," said your defender, who was a hard-looking woman in the light blue colors of the air force. "What is the purpose of this meeting?"

"You're right," said someone, "it's to schedule the next meetings."

"I don't think schedules can be classified."

"Depends what the schedule's about," said someone.

And then they're off—discussing their absolute favorite topic: secrecy. They were all top secret. Everyone is top secret. Aldrich Ames was top secret. Robert Hanssen was top secret. That's why they could betray the U.S. so spectacularly for so long. The screening system does not work—it's worthless, in fact. Lie detectors and grilling sessions with clock punchers have no value. There is no internal watchdog; nobody is watching anything. Nothing about the system works, except perhaps the check to make sure you are a U.S. citizen. But the feeling of being top secret is so . . . so . . . apparently, so delicious . . .

You started to put away your notebook, recap your pen, as random voices were saying—

"Yeah, schedules definitely can be classified."

"We haven't even made a schedule yet."

"But we're going to. That's why we're here."

"How can a schedule be secret?"

"It's secret if we say it's secret."

"But it doesn't have any secrets—"

"I'm just telling you about policy."

"A schedule is just a bunch of dates."

"Dates and topics—"

"Whatever—there's no secrets in a bunch of topics."

"There could be."

"I'm just saying, you know, let's not take that chance."

By this time you were at the door, your computer bag slung over your shoulder, your cell phone in your pocket.

You opened your mouth but said nothing.

And then you left.

5:42 p.m. Thursday.

Good-bye!

As your wife pointed out once, consulting is a job where you work *very hard* for three and one-half days. And then—not work. Travel, talking in the office, sitting at your desk looking wistfully out the window at the MetLife Building getting scrubbed by rock-hard jets of heavy water . . . your three and one-half days are over, over . . .

There is satisfaction in your parting, which happens in fits; those living farthest from the client site check out first, as early as 4:00 or 4:30 p.m. Your flight is under two hours, so your window is not quite so wide; your unwritten departure time is after 5:30 or so. Each departure from the team room—first Martha, then Baloo, then Jeff and Jack together (Jack never drives)—is like two fingers parting, a balloon set free. You get your own cubicle for five minutes as you pack up.

Something you often forget is your power cord, so you roll it up now. No power cord makes working on this "secret project" over the weekend rather difficult. So you're rolling the black IBM ThinkPad T23 power cord up when . . .

"Hey," says a voice behind you.

You look up—and it's Geraldo. He's wearing a dark blue shirt with [Client] sewn in white thread over the left breast pocket. It's kind of a sharp shirt.

"Hey."

"You guys heading out?"

"Yeah."

"You always leave on Thursday, huh?"

"Yeah—otherwise we wouldn't get any office life. We'd never see anybody at the firm."

"So you're in New York on Friday?"

"Yep."

You stand up—you're really kind of in a hurry now. The plane, the traffic, the car return—all will take time. Geraldo, too, is taking time.

"I'd like to go to New York," he says.

"You've never been there?"

"Nope. Never been out of Illinois much. My mom moved to California."

Bags up, jacket on—you're ready to go, but Geraldo intervenes. You look at your watch, nakedly.

"You're in a hurry." He notices.

"You here next week?"

"Well—that's what I wanted to say. I—I'm leaving [Client]. This is my last day."

"What?"

"I want to work outdoors. I'm not an inside kind of guy."

"Walk with me to the elevator?" You're pushing past him now, moving down the corridor, though he is not following.

"That's okay, man. I just . . ."

You stop and look directly into his eyes, as a dominant dog or a mother would do. And you wait.

He says, "You can't help this company, can you?"

"No."

"Nobody can. Nobody can."

You chew on that for a moment, approaching the elevators, realizing they don't work, looking for an unlocked staircase and a way out of this treacherous debilitated place.

Four hours later a black Allegro limousine pulls up outside your apartment in Queens. Your cell phone is off. It is 2217 in military time, and you are all in military time right now. The lights are on upstairs, and downstairs where the landlady lives. Her name is Olga and she is a fourth grade teacher born in Serbia. She lives with a seventeen-year-old daughter so absurdly beautiful you actually make an effort to avoid her.

"You have a voucher?" asks the driver.

"I don't need one."

"You need a voucher."

"Not really."

You open the door and get out. The air is some version of wet, like a dog's nose.

There is a dog at the top of the stairs as you climb them. There is a wife attached to the dog with a brown leather cord.

Part IV

Analyze This:
A Minute History of
Classic Consulting Texts

Part IV presents a welcome final chapter in this seemingly endless litany of woe, with these tips:

1. *How to summarize any business book in just a **single word***

2. *The tiniest version ever of the **greatest all-time consulting book**, Michael Porter's* Competitive Strategy

3. *Mercifully **brief descriptions** of every other great consulting classic—all three of them*

4. *How to turn vague feelings into actual **money***

5. *A strangely unsatisfying **ending***

11

Strategy Is
a Contact Sport

Whenever anything is being accomplished, it is
being done, I have learned, by a monomaniac with
a mission.

—PETER DRUCKER

You have always believed all books about business could be
summarized in a few sentences, and you often wish that they
were. It would save you the trouble of having to wade through
them and then summarize them free for the people.

For instance, take the most famous consulting book there
is—the book that is credited with legitimizing academic consulting, giving top-tier management advice-mongering a
patina of Harvardesque credibility. That book is, of course,
Michael Porter's *Competitive Strategy: Techniques for Analyzing
Industries and Competitors*. Porter was, and remains, a professor
at Harvard Business School, and he published his landmark
framework in 1980, two years before *In Search of Excellence*. It
was to be a grand decade for McHarvard . . .

Competitive Strategy introduced a simple—some might say,
butt-obvious—way of looking at any industry and figuring out
why some companies were making a go of it and others were

just wilting by the side of the road, looking stupid. He pointed out that companies are either low-cost providers or they are differentiated and can charge more. To make the low-cost idea work you had to be certain *your* costs were lower, as the Japanese were beginning at the time to demonstrate with admirable zest. To make the differentiation ploy work you had to have something special. Companies lacking either were said to be "stuck in the middle" and, implicitly, doomed.

Unless they called in the consultants to (a) cut their costs, or (b) jack their differentiation.

Porter also identified the so-called five forces that worked their magic in any industry; these were the currents that determined how *attractive* the industry was to investors, and explained why the winners were winning and the also-rans were gaggling back in the chicken shack.

No consultant uses the forces in her daily work, of course; and no consultant applies them to any actual analysis. You've never encountered a situation where they helped you to understand anything, even during business school, where the standard cases are all written by Porter's alma mater and some indeed by Porter himself. Perhaps this is so because Porter's wisdom has seeped into the fabric of the nation's moneymakers and integrated with their pulse. Who knows?

But it is important for a top-tier management consultant to know what the five forces are. It is not important to have read *Competitive Strategy;* reading of any nature is discouraged by the top tier; however, you have read it and, as you said, it is your notion to take this bullet and now summarize the work for the people.[65]

You are the people.

One-word summary of *Competitive Strategy*: "Differentiation."

---

[65]Speaking of footnotes, you can't help but notice that many of Porter's specific company examples cited in *Competitive Strategy* appear to come from *Forbes* and, especially, *Business Week* during a few months of the year 1977 (generally August–December); perhaps, during those recessionary times, Harvard rationed Porter's access to magazines.

Ten-word summary of *Competitive Strategy*: "Power of buyers and sellers. Entry barriers. Substitutes. Industry rationality."

There they are—did you see them? The five forces, in the form of a ten-word summary!

Again, for the challenged, Porter's five forces:

1. Barriers to entry—or, why pharmaceutical companies are so f——ing rich (answer: patents).
2. Substitutes—are you special? Oh yeah?
3. Power of buyers—is Wal-Mart your biggest customer? Uh-oh.
4. Power of sellers—when you bargain with them, do they just laugh?
5. Industry rationality—is everybody crazy, or just Crazy Eddie?

Now you don't have to read the book.

Another book you don't have to read is this one—*House of Lies: How Management Consultants Steal Your Watch and Then Tell You the Time*. It is absolutely critical that you buy a copy or two, of course, just to have around the house, like a quilted blanket or a nice warm puppy. But mucking your way through all the blather may not be necessary. That is why it occurs to you—the writer *you*, not the nonreader *you*—to provide another *Competitive Strategy*-like summary of *Lies* for the people. The hoards. The throngs in their thongs with their bongs.

There was a time when you wanted to be a poet.

Essentially bone-lazy, you look for a substitute to the tedious chore of rereading your own rantings—and you find, to your joy, there is one. Microsoft Word 2000 includes a feature called "AutoSummarize,"[66] which, according to Microsoft's own voluminous documentation, "identifies the key points in a document for you to share with others or quickly scan." Perfect!

[66]The fourth item down on the Tools menu.

The feature gives you the option of cutting the text down to 25 percent of its full length—hardly a help, in this case—or trimming even further . . . down to five hundred words, even one hundred words (less than 1 percent of the original). You decide brevity is the soul of sloth and choose the latter.

The results *exactly as they are generated by Microsoft Word 2000's AutoSummarize* are presented in the box following.

**Microsoft Word 2000 [9.0.4402 SR-1] AutoSummary
of *House of Lies* (Up to Here)
in One Hundred Words or Less**

"Have you guys worked together?"
Value a company?   Working.

Never used consultants
Number of McKinsey consultants in 1999:
     10,000
Home Depot's consultant is **McKinsey**.
     The team.

Consultant's Panic Buttons

2.   The Consultant's Dictionary

     "Right."
     "Right—"
     "Right—"
"Right."
"Right."
"Right."
"Left, right?"
"Right—"
Core values

Core Values. Right?
"[Your top-tier firm's name.]"
1.   Client Service
McKinsey's four core values, paraphrased:
1.   Client Service

$$Value = Money$$

"Right? Right?"
"Right now?"
Those people are not consultants.
Consultants—top-tier and otherwise—exist. "Name?"
"Name?"
     "Never?"
"You guys consultants?"
     "The client."   ***Consultants:***
          (1) Marriott points
          (2) Starwood points
"Airline points?"
     "Right."
     I work for [your top-tier firm].

Although missing much of your style and élan, this summary gets across something—the essence, perhaps, that which is beyond words and so cannot be summarized in words. Eccentric spacing, the eclectic dialogue—"Name?" "Name?" "Never?"—the indentations sensical perhaps only to a Dadaist or a small child . . . the relentless emphasis on core values and client service . . . no, you must admit, your skepticism has melted away and you are sold. AutoSummarize *gets you* in a way only your mother has before (and sometimes you wonder about her).

Value = Money . . . ?

Even your cynicism comes through. *Only* your cynicism comes through. Wait a minute. Is this the book that came out of you? Is that what you are up to? Now that you think about it, AutoSummarize has *shamed* you . . . it is as though you are being mocked by a bug-ridden slab of code.[67]

This is business cruelty.

This is business poetry.

[67]In its defense, Microsoft admits "AutoSummarize works best on well-structured documents such as reports, articles, and scientific papers." Although you believe this book to be nothing if not a scientific paper, it does perhaps have an . . . original structure.

12

Tinybizbooks—A $48.99 Value ($68.44 Canadian)

Business books," a wise healer and sage once said, "are boring. They are bloated compendiums of half-baked ideas committed in fourth grade prose. Their purpose is to transform a commonsense concept or two into a consulting career through the catalyst of hollow jargon."

Process theorists would point out that the consulting career is the *end state* toward which the business book is directed—that is, the book is a *process* or *node*, not an end in itself. Which is perhaps why they never seem to end. How many times do you suspect the creeping onset of senility as you turn the page of a well-regarded B-book and think, I've read this book before—but then you haven't. It's just that the book is freeze-dried, reprocessed essence of B-book . . . it is a line extension, not a book; a collection of words, not a meeting of the minds; a contract deliverable, not a poem in prose.

Silence is the legitimate greeting for such works of commerce. And silence is their farewell song.

With some exceptions. These are the so-called classics—the books that sold millions and became influential and turned their ex-McKinsey authors into personal cottage industries. These are the "must-reads" that nobody you know has ever read. Perhaps they are a previous generation's wisdom; perhaps people simply like to have them on the shelf, knowingly nodding, like a T-shirt stenciled *au courant*.

You decide to read them. There are only three; it's not a large chore. The three titles are, of course, *In Search of Excellence*, *Reengineering the Corporation*, and *Built to Last*. And it turns out the first and third of them are actually the same book—far-ranging studies of "excellent/visionary" U.S. companies and what it is they do differently. They appeared at the beginning of long run-ups in the market (1982 and 1994) and were conducted during the darkness before the dawn, so their tone is messianic in its hopefulness. "People feel inspired by the very notion of building an enduring, great company," write the authors of *Built to Last*. And so they do. *Reengineering* took a different tack, injecting some Germanic fatalism into American business by suggesting nothing less than wholesale "revolution" (guided by the author's consulting firm) to restructure their companies; many, rightly, saw it as an invitation to dismissal so bleak its words might as well have been written on pink slips.

Nonetheless, they are what they are: American consulting classics, written by and for consultants or those who employ them. And no discussion of early-century top-tier management consulting would be complete without a free synopsis of these works. Therefore:

In Search of Excellence:
Lessons from America's Best-Run Companies

Thomas J. Peters and Robert H. Waterman Jr.
(New York: Warner Books, 1982)

Consulting Pedigree: Began as an internal McKinsey study when the authors worked at the firm, the best-selling book (three million copies) by McKinseyites ever. (Peters started his own consulting firm; Waterman stayed at McKinsey.)

Core Values: "Good management practice today is not resident only in Japan."

1-word summary: "Open."

10-word summary: "Spartan settings, open doors, fewer walls, fewer offices. Less layering."

100-word summary: "Conventional business leads to obsession with cost, not quality. People are not very rational; we desperately need meaning in our lives. Actions speak louder than words. Top companies . . . experiment more, encourage more tries. A bias for getting things done. High degree of informal communication. Organizational fluidity. Excellent companies *really are* close to their customers. Service obsession. Quality with quixotic zeal. Better listeners. Radical decentralization and autonomy. Treat people as adults. Intense rah-rah. Spartan settings, open doors, fewer walls, and fewer offices. More qualitative statements of corporate purpose. Pursue diversification yet stick close to their knitting. Small is almost beautiful."

Reengineering the Corporation: A Manifesto for Business Revolution

Michael Hammer and James Champy
(New York: HarperBusiness, 1993)

On the Cover: "May well be the best-written, most well-reasoned business book for the managerial masses since *In Search of Excellence.*" —John Byrne, *Business Week*

Consulting Pedigree: Cambridge-based CSC Index became the most profitable boutique consulting firm in the U.S. in the early- and mid-1990s due solely to its "reengineering" service offering.

Core Values: "We believe that . . . the difference between winning companies and losers is that winning companies know how to do their work better."

1-word summary: "Re-creating."

10-word summary: "If . . . re-creating this company today . . . what would it look like?"

100-word summary: "If I were re-creating this company today, given what I know and given current technology, what would it look like? Companies today consist of functional silos, or stovepipes, vertical structures built on narrow pieces of the process. Reengineering . . . start[s] with the needs of the process customer and work[s] backwards from there. Many formerly distinct jobs or tasks are integrated and compressed into one. Eliminating handoffs means doing away with the errors, delays, and rework that they engender. [Also, get rid of] 'standardization.' Segment your customers. Get suppliers to do your work. Outsource. Make an operational 'vision statement' focused on customers."

Built to Last: Successful Habits of Visionary Companies

James C. Collins and Jerry I. Porras
(New York: HarperBusiness, 1994)

On the Cover: "*Built to Last* . . . is one of the most eye-opening business studies since *In Search of Excellence.*" —*USA Today*

Consulting Pedigree: Collins is a McKinsey alumnus who met Porras while teaching at Stanford's business school; he runs his own consulting firm based in Colorado and earns some $3 million per year in speaking fees.

Core Values: "The only truly reliable source of stability is a strong inner core."

1-word summary: "Goals."

10-word summary: "Big hairy audacious goals, cultlike cultures, more demanding home-grown management."

100-word summary: "Building a visionary company absolutely does not require either a great idea or a great and charismatic leader. Shift from seeing the company as a vehicle for the products it makes to seeing the products as a vehicle for the company. [There is no] specific ideological content essential. Highly ideological and highly progressive at the same time. Big hairy audacious goals—tangible, energizing and highly risky. Cultlike cultures—pervasive mythology of 'heroic deeds.' Corporate songs. Try a lot of stuff and keep what works—unplanned progress. Promote from within to preserve the core.[68] Good enough never is—relentless self-improvement. More demanding."

Great books inspire thought, and so you start to think: Wouldn't it be great to write a great book? Wouldn't it be wonderful to have a best-selling compendium of truisms sit atop the curricula of, say, all the B-schools that rejected your application while you sleep with the comely wives of their deans and . . . no, that would not be great. But the book—the book—that's the idea . . .

Your next book—*In Search of Last!*—is more than just an exercise in hitting the shift-1 key, that is, the "!". Don't care what critics think. It is an honest attempt to do what every ambitious entrepreneur and serious student of business is supposed to do: make money. Lots of money. Millions. Not Euros, not dinars or lire or francs—but dollars, baby—millions and millions of dollars, so you can finally do what you've been wanting to do but somehow can't afford. What that is you have no idea, but heck—give you the money and you'll figure it out. Honest!

But seriously. There appear to be seven immutable laws of business, and they are outlined on page 222 in "The Ultimate Business Book." These laws hold true through the decades, so there is no reason to believe they will be entirely outmoded by 2006—twelve years after *Built to Last* and right around a clear moment of need. Every twelve years, apparently, the average American business manager decides to buy a book—and you fully intend to meet that decision with a product.

One full of truth, or something.

---

[68]". . . across *seventeen hundred years* of combined history in the visionary companies, we found only *four* individual cases of an outsider coming directly into the role of chief executive" (*Built to Last*, 173).

The Ultimate Business Book
or, Why *In Search of Excellence* and *Built to Last* Are
Actually the Same Work,
Plus a Preview of the Best-selling B-book of 2006—
In Search of Last!

Concept	1982 *In Search of Excellence* calls it . . .	1994 *Built to Last* calls it . . .	2006 *In Search of Last!* calls it . . .
• Don't just stand there, do something	• Bias for Action	• Try a Lot of Stuff and Keep What Works	• JUST DO IT!
• The customer is never happy —even when she's smiling	• Close to the Customer	• Good Enough Never Is	• KEEP ON KEEPIN' ON!
• "Keep your feet on the ground, and keep reaching for the stars!"— Kasey Casem	• Autonomy & Entrepreneur-ship • Simultaneous Loose-Tight Properties	• Big Hairy Audacious Goals	• AIM HIGH!
• You have to drink your own Kool-Aid	• Productivity Through People	• Cultlike Cultures	• GET YOUR GROOVE ON!
• Business is about more than just making money— honest	• Hands-on, Value-driven	• More Than Profits	• KEEP IT REAL!
• You are what you are; it is what it is	• Stick to the Knitting	• Preserve the Core, Stimulate Progress	• EYES ON THE PRIZE!
• Nurture your winners and beware of bloat	• Simple Form, Lean Staff	• Home-grown Management	• GROW YOUR OWN!

Outline of *In Search of Last!* by Martin Kihn—the best-selling business book of 2006:

Ch. 1 *"Just Do It!"*: No business ever got mojo by sitting on the couch watching life go by. The only way to seize the day is with your two hands and a map. So what if you don't have any idea what you're supposed to do? Who invented "supposed" anyway? Some Greek philosopher? You did! As they say in the program, only you can help you—so be you and help you.

Ch. 2 *"Keep on Keepin' On!"*: It turns out the nuns and priests were right: Everything you do is wrong. Whatever you do or make—it just isn't cutting it! Sorry. People don't like you, yet. Sure, they're falling over themselves to write you get-well cards, but that's because they're sneaky little bastards who are sleeping with your wife. Do not listen to them! Are you hearing me? Helloooooo . . . You *are* not good enough, you *were* not good enough, you *will not be* good enough . . . not ever. But don't give up.

Ch. 3 *"Aim High!"*: That doesn't mean you shouldn't bang your head against the concrete wall of dreams and bark your shins on the doorjamb of hope. That doesn't mean your notions and leaps don't deserve to be leg-upped out of their cat boxes, if only for the weekend. Be alive, be free, be afraid . . . oh, wait, no, don't be afraid. Forget that. That's the voices talking. Don't listen to the voices.

Ch. 4 *"Get Your Groove On!"*: Listen to this: Ommmmmm. Ommmmmmm-a-a-a-a-a-oommmmmmmhhhhh . . . sound familiar? Well, it shouldn't. It's just some letters on a page, not a sound at all. You've got to think of your company as a festive little toga party amid a larger whole, a dark and mysterious body teeming with waterborne amphibious life forms from the rim of Planet Delta Phi. Wear a white sheet and be brief. Jump for joy and let her go . . . okay, an old joke, but you get the point, don't you? Remember, it ain't a "cult" if nobody gets arraigned!

Ch. 5 "Keep It Real!": There is more to life than just punching the clock, jumping the gun, looping the loops in the parking lot outside the deli; there is more, much more down here than walking the walk, toeing the line, dotting the i's and marking the mark. There is infinitely largely more than there seems when you're ambling the road, ankling the pact, or lining the drawer. There is. What?

Ch. 6 "Eyes on the Prize!": People ask you what they should do with their lives. You get this question a lot. "What should I do with my life?" As if there were an answer to such a vague and open-ended question. As if there could ever be an answer to such a meaningless pretentious line of words. "What does it matter?" you want to reply. "What do I care? They say everybody can do something *really* well but I'm not so sure. I have yet to see anybody I work with do anything *really* well, even once."

Ch. 7 "Grow Your Own!": As a nation we are morphing into a grotesque pendulous gelatinous cake of soap; we are inevitably becoming a residue of the kumquat and vapors we ingest. Soon there will be nothing to show of ourselves but a closet full of empty smocks and a notebook full of lies. Can such a state of torpor feed itself forever? Of course it can. Just leave some room for dessert.

You are drifting now from your real purpose. This began as a paean to truth and evolved in a state of real rage. But now the soft curtains of months have been closing, muffling up the sound, shorting the paean. What was so clear and honest has devolved into impressionistic streams of thought. Perhaps this is the truth. Perhaps this is the ending you deserve.

13

Case Study—Reengineering for Nonengineers

Y ou a *consultant?"*

You arrive one day in your Matador Red Ford Taurus ill-prepared for danger. But there is danger in the parking lots and the parking lots are not marked, and they have secret identities. One is for the engineers on their missions of safety. The other—vastly larger and in front—is for the suits. Everybody drives a car from a single manufacturer, a customer and a semibankrupt.

The third parking lot is around the side, is full, and is for you.

This is a company in the Midwest that makes parts for automobiles. It does not make the whole automobile and it never has. Its humbler mission is to outfit the car, truck, or van with a good set of form-fitting headlights, brake lights, front and rear bumpers, gas tanks, fluid tanks, emergency brakes, instrument panels, and CD player/radios. This company is quite large and sells its array of parts mainly to one of the big three U.S. automakers, but also to others.

This company is in serious trouble.

Nobody knows why, but it is. Management blames the unions; union members blame the management; engineers blame the systems people; IT turns around and blames the software vendors. It is hard to hear in its headquarters build-

ing at times for the cacophony of blame ricocheting off its re-
inforced concrete walls.

"You a *consultant?*"

After you have dwelled long enough to earn a space you
make the long walk to the long, low building that reminds
you of dental office clusters in your suburban Midwest grow-
up town. The building is brown with kelly green shrubbery. A
highway houghs across the way and the sun spits down.

The young woman with the firearm behind the circular
greet desk takes you in quite quickly: "You a *consultant?*"

"Yeah."

"Who you here for?"

Now—this, you don't know. They didn't tell you who the
client was, or where you were to go. It's the same old story, so
it won't detain us here.

Except to linger for a moment in the lobby—there is a life-
size mock-up of a large American-type car. Except it is missing
many things. Wheels for one. And brakes. And a windshield—
any windows, in fact—and a body and doors and seats. It has
see-through Plexiglas to "stand in" for these missing parts . . .
it's like a skeletal car, with vivid brake fluid lines and a gorgeous off-black ten-gallon gasoline tank—gorgeous! A desic-
cated car-thing like what might be left in a desert to die after
a terrible war.

"Where's the rest of it?" you ask a woman with a cafeteria
tray and one Pop-Tart walking past, and she says nothing to
you.

You're in your home state now—Michigan, where you grew
up, went to high school, kept your virginity, started to drink—
you're in Michigan, and you find yourself quite bold with
strangers. They remind you of someone.

"You look like a *consultant,*" says your new client, bobbing
her head.

You are disappointed she is plain, but she's a woman. Her
office has a view of the engineers' parking lot. Turns out she

was an engineer, a mechanical engineer, which in your experience means she is good with her hands. Probably fixes her own car.

She's skinny and blonde and sounds like a Michigander. She will all but end your career, though you don't know it yet.

"I'm Marty," you say. "I'm from [your top-tier firm]."

"I know." She smiles. "You look like a consultant."

"What do we look like?"

"Kind of out of place."

You know enough to shut up here.

"So sit down. Tell me what you're gonna do for us. I'm Tina."

"Well," you say, sitting down in her guest chair. The guest chair is at one end of a very long work table; she sits at the other end. You two are like characters from a scene in *Citizen Kane*, peering at one another in the distance.

"Well," you continue, "we are part of a bigger team here, as you know—"

She interrupts, "Where's the other guy?"

"What guy?"

"You said 'we'—so there's another guy somewhere, right? Or not?"

"Well," you say. "I guess not specifically for this part. But there're other people—"

"You're working alone?"

"Of course not. There's—"

"But no one's coming to this meeting, right? Nobody else? Like, backup?"

"No."

"I got confused when you said 'we' before."

"I'm sorry."

"Do you want a doughnut? Did you grow up in Michigan, or Ohio?"

"Michigan, yes. How'd you know?"

"I'm *great* with accents. I can totally tell. What's your city?"

You tell her, then turn down a doughnut. Her assistant,

Tamara, brings in a plate of Krispy Kremes that do not, frankly, appear to be fresh. And Tamara is of the proportionality indicating she is indeed no stranger to doughnuts, and worse. She has a sweet smile. She has a pendant with a little tiny golden Buddha, a fat man, cushioned in her gelatinous boobies.

"Okay," says Tina after the smallest talk in the world, "listen to me. Here's the plan. Get up."

You get up.

"Let's get out of here."

You go to a country club somewhere out in Livonia, or maybe it's Novi. The whole state is foreign to you now, it's been so long. You never went to Livonia, or Novi—or Dearborn, for that matter—when you lived there, except maybe to a mall or on the way someplace better. This is blue-collar Michigan, not your collar.

It is very hot and there is no one playing golf. Maybe because directly across the street there is a large factory that makes doors and trim. It says so on a sign on the small lawn out front. The country club has tried to limit its view of the factory with a line of trees, but the trees aren't doing the job; they're scraggly and kind of runty, maybe from the fumes wafting over from the door and trim factory across the street.

What is trim, exactly?

You scramble to catch up to Tina, who is already through the big wood doors and into the main hallway. Then she's talking to some men, big men, very big men. There are four of them and as you get closer you notice the place has the feel of a church; a medieval cloister, with carved wood detail at the edges of the ceiling and the wall seams and stained-glass windows.

"What're you up to, you bastard!" she says.

"Hey, Teen. I can't kiss you, right?"

"Not unless you want to get fired."

"Or promoted," says one of the others.

"Depends on the kiss," she shoots back. And it's pretty clear she and these big, big guys go way, way back. It's also pretty clear you're not getting introduced, so you hover, then you disengage . . . and then you're wandering around this weird religious country club in blue-collar Michigan feeling disoriented.

The place is filled with enormous men in work shirts with Blackberry pagers, one or two degrees removed from the factory floor. And there's a vibe about them makes you think they might be in sales—it's the volume, the sheer amount of noise, as the big boys work the halls and hidden recesses. Nobody seems to quite meet your eye.

You walk through a door and end up in a quiet garden. It is miraculous, for a moment . . .

"Can I help you, sir?"

"I just wanted to come down and tell you guys what a . . . *great* job I think you all did on twenty-one-twelve. It was a real . . . *difficult* time for all of us and the lines really had to come together. We used fourteen of the plants for this rollout which is the second-biggest—I think—that's ever, that we've ever tried. Isn't that right, Mitch?"

A silence, as you all realize Mitch is not in the room.

"He's doing rework," someone says, and the clerestory erupts in peals of laughter. Every face in the place is convulsed in sheer joy but you, in the back, sucking on a diet Coke. You feel as out of place as a spider on a piece of angel food cake.[69]

"He can rework all he wants," Tina says, standing out in front, "so long as he keeps delivering like he did on twenty-one-twelve."

"Delivering *rework*!"

"Okay," she says. "I can see some of you came here in the

---

[69]Raymond Chandler is rumored to have invented this simile, but you've never managed to locate it.

bar car. But seriously—whether it's number two or whatever, this product launch had a lot of problems and we executed on time. We didn't hold up day one, we didn't let down the customer. Ultimately, that says a lot about us, right? Right?"

"Right," say a few.

"So I've got some slides here I put together about the re-work—"

And the room gets dark.

Car part manufacturing, it turns out, is a difficult business. Think about it. Cars are designed in some other building by some people you barely know (the customer), who then turn around and give you "specs" for parts of this car, which doesn't exist yet. You're supposed to go away and make a bunch of parts which have to (a) fit perfectly, and (b) be ready at exactly the moment they are needed at the big assembly line where the actual car is put together. If you fail in (a) you are worthless and if you fail in (b) you are charged money and make everybody angry.

None of which would be a serious problem except that the customer, apparently, keeps changing her mind. This is extremely common in the car world. Usually because you don't really know what something looks like until you see it in front of you. In three dimensions. So the part is designed and fits and will be ready with some time to spare, and then the powerful president of the powerful client number one gets around to looking at the mock-up of the car and says, "Hmmmmm."

"What?" asks Tina, who will be there if it's one of her projects in the scope.

"Hmmmm hmmmm."

"What?"

"See that brake light?" asks the president.

"Uh-huh."

"Don't like it."

"Uh-huh."

"Could you guys do something—I don't know—something, like, *rounder?*"

So Tina rushes off and has her engineers change everything and—well, of course you see how it won't be round enough, or it's too round . . . and after a few go-rounds, so to speak, well, it doesn't quite fit with the rear fascia[70] assembly, which has to be redesigned . . . but then it doesn't fit into the well in the body itself anymore, which is quite a major change, which, sadly, will affect the design of the electrical system, which is being done by another company which is perfectly happy with their design the way they have it already and . . . well, and then you're looking at being about six months late for the vehicle launch, which won't happen without nice round brake lights anyway, so you pour everything you've got into making this insane deadline . . . and you miss it by, maybe, two days.

And sooner or later you're losing money and calling in the consultants, a big team of them, who charge you $1 million per week to tell you how you can cut costs. It occurs to more than a few people in your ailing company that there is at least one easy way to save, say, $1 million per week.

One of these people is Tina.

"Okay," she says to you over lunch in the cathedral cafeteria, "here's the plan."

She's like your wife—she doesn't eat so much as vigorously rearrange her food on the plate with a fork and then say, "Boy, am I full."

"Here's the plan," she says to you quietly. "I need you to do something for me."

"Okay."

"Have you ever heard of Casanova?"

"He was a lover, Italian—"

"No, it's a software."

[70]What people in the car parts business call a bumper.

You admit your ignorance of this piece of code.

"Good, I need you to be objective about it. Here's what I need you to do, okay?"

And she describes an assignment that seems so utterly ordinary and straightforward you wonder why the air of conspiracy in that religious golfing setting.

"Hierarchical organizations seduce us with psychological rewards like feelings of power and status," someone once wrote in *Harvard Business Review*. "What's more, multilevel hierarchies remain the best available mechanism for doing complex work. It is unrealistic to expect that we will do away with them in the foreseeable future. It seems more sensible to accept the reality that hierarchies are here to stay. . . ."[71]

Tina had done well in the hierarchy of the failing firm. An engineer, like most of the managers, she ran a small plant somewhere in Canada at a young age and got booted up to headquarters, where she became known as the go-to girl for problems, then big problems, and finally—the biggest problem of all—a disaster known as 21–12. It was a parts assembly for a popular truck that had somehow become about twice as expensive as it was contracted to be, so the company was going to lose even more than usual on this one unless it could be gotten under control . . . and it was, thanks to Tina and the big, big men in the church.

And she had been promoted to a level just under VP, and there were no women VPs. There were nine men, and no women. But the thinking was maybe Tina could be the first, if, say, one of these nine men were let go (or died) and she could keep that good mo' going.

Of course she wasn't the only star in this firm of ten thousand. There was a well-regarded marketing guy named Bill

[71]Harold J. Leavitt, "Why Hierarchies Thrive," *Harvard Business Review* (March 2003): 102.

everybody seemed to think a lot about. And there was a slightly younger woman who had rocketed up the ranks in IT and seemed poised to make noise. And so on . . . oh, and the IT woman's name was Kelly van Dyne.

Everybody thought maybe Kelly van Dyne could give Tina a run for her money someday.

On your second day, you meet Jerry. Your work stream is essentially self-directed and independent, although you are managed by a guy in England who checks in on the phone from time to time. Long-distance job management. Now, Jerry is an important person to this story—a critical character with the key role in its unwinding, though, like most critical characters in real life (as opposed to reel life) doesn't look particularly special. They've put you in a cube next to a bunch of engineers with flat-panel screens and Jerry ambles over one day and says, "Hi, I'm Jerry."

Okay. You weren't expecting a Jerry. There's no Jerry on your work plan. Tina never mentioned a Jerry.

"Hi, Jerry."

"I'm a guy you probably need to know."

"Then I'm happy to meet you."

"What do you know about the APDS?"

Jerry, in a thick work shirt, has a graying beard and a shambly manner. He's checking a well-worn PDA as he speaks, poking it so hard with his stylus you think the glass could shatter.

"Nothing, Jerry."

"Then we need to talk."

"You first."

"Well," he says, moving the stacks of paper off the runty swivel chair you have set up in your cube for visitors, "okay then."

Turns out he's an expert—at least he's under the strong impression he's an expert—in product development. More specifically, in documenting product development processes. More more specifically, in documenting product develop-

ment processes relating to the creation of engineered parts
for automobiles and trucks. Each new product, from the most
humble lug nut to the grandest instrument panel assembly,
goes through a process from concept to prototype to testing
to refinement to launch, and companies in general like to
write down this process in excruciating detail and debate the
merits of each step and then rewrite the process and redebate
the merits . . . it's called the STAGE/GATE process (always
capitalized) because there are stages and there are gates, or
hurdles, which allows the bean counters and men in suits to
get their meaty paws on it and stop it in its tracks or, be-
grudgingly, permit it to inch along to the next stage until it
crashes into the hard wall of the next big gate and the bean
counters and men in suits reappear with their paws retracting
looking for a problem . . . or so you hear . . .

"APDS," says Jerry, taking out his wallet, "is a process I put
together from scratch here. It's the [Client] Product
Development System—APDS. Here's a wallet-sized version of
it."

He shows you a card with infinitely tiny text and some slender arrows going to the right.

"It's fully laminated," he points out.

As the days go by, and you're into week two, you find yourself reaching out to Jerry more often than you might have
wanted. But the truth is the [Client] Corporation is a bit of a
labyrinth, or conundrum. First of all it has about twenty building sites spread all over southeastern Michigan and down into
northern Ohio. And everybody's on the same phone system
so you can't tell from the phone number where a person is.
Plus no one's ever there when you call, and certainly not if
you visit. So second of all, the problem is *it's impossible to figure
out what anyone is doing.*

What are their *jobs?*

When you find people, they're sitting somewhere with
someone just chatting. There are meetings where chat gets
done. There may be slides, there may not be. Nobody looks at

them. Meetings are easy to schedule when you can find the schedulee because nobody has any conflicts, not really. It's like a wide-open day on the prowl for obscurity.

You reach out, as you say, to Jerry. And he's happy in his role as spiritual adviser to wandering consultants.

"So tell me, Jerry," you ask him one day in the cafeteria, "what do you know about Casanova?"

He looks up suddenly from his Pop-Tart.

"You know, the software," you prompt.

"I know it."

"Do you like it?"

"I can't say as I've ever really used it."

"How's the rollout going."

"They're just testing it now. Why do you want to know about Casanova?"

"Tina asked me to write up an assessment."

"An *assessment*? What for?"

"I don't know—she's just, she doesn't know anything about it and she wants me to talk to the engineers and the program management people and find out what their opinion of it is."

"That's what she told you? She doesn't know anything about it—"

"Uh-huh."

"Oh."

His Pop-Tart is unfrosted. You've never known anyone to purposely select an unfrosted Pop-Tart when a much tastier frosted version is sitting right beside it on the rack. But Jerry, it turns out, is a bit of a closed comic book. He's also apparently not telling you something.

"What's wrong? What aren't you telling me?" you ask him.

"Nothing."

"Why are people so strange about this Casanova?"

"How strange?"

"Like they're paranoid why I'm asking them about it. They're paranoid why Tina would want to know what people think."

"There's a lot of political bullshit here," says Jerry, "you don't wanna know. Believe me. Plus there's the whole consulting thing—like, why is this consultant in here asking me these questions? You know—"

"Yep."

"Like you're going to lose them their job. Is that why you're here, by the way?"

"What?"

"To fire people?"

You are surprised by this question, coming from Jerry—but then you realize you never really told him why you're there.

"I can't fire anyone."

"Then why are you here?"

"We're supposed to find ways to cut costs but we can't fire people."

"You have to cut costs but you can't let anyone go? So how're you gonna do that—fewer paper clips, fewer team lunches?"

You have no idea what to say here.

"What's your bogey?"

"Seven hundred and fifty million dollars."

He shakes his head, smiling. Then he covers up the remains of his Pop-Tart with a napkin, like a shroud.

"Listen to me," he all but whispers, reminding you of Tina in the golf church with her Casanova. "Do yourself a favor, okay?"

"Okay."

"Show me anything you do on Casanova before you give it to Tina."

"What for?"

"Just trust me, Marty. This is something you should do."

| YOU: | How was it first presented to you? |
| PERSON: | It was totally oversold in the beginning—in its, in its capabilities. The sessions gave the |

impression this tool would be the total answer to everything.

PERSON: . . . and we have to input the exact same info into three places, every week.

YOU: Why three places?

PERSON: Let me put it this way, okay? One of the places is directly tied to the paycheck—it's how we get paid, putting our time in this system. Then Casanova comes along and says, "Oh, and take another thirty minutes and put the exact same stuff in here too 'cause management wants to be able to keep track of exactly what you're doing 'cause—just 'cause." What are you gonna do?

So Tina magically appears in your cube one day during week three and says, "Let's go."

This is what your trainer has told you to say to your Bernese mountain dog, Hola, to distinguish it from "Come on," which is a different command. "Let's go" means move forward; "come on" means come to me.

So you move forward, following Tina down the hall, the stairs, the skeletal remains of the car in the lobby, and out into the cancerous sun. She drives a silver Expedition and it makes her look quite tiny and ridiculous.

"Follow me!" she shouts out the window, as you scour the guest lot for your Matador Red Ford Taurus. You know it's here somewhere . . .

On the road, you listen to a radio station you listened to in high school; it has changed formats, as have you. It's gotten harder.

You pass the Fairlane town center on the right, which when you were a kid seemed huge and kind of cool and this time around feels like a dangerous Dumpster. It's very ghetto and the stores are for shit. The bookstore seems to be making a steady segue out of books and into maps, calendars, and theme versions of Monopoly.

It is very flat, southeastern Michigan, like a warm bath with no perturbations.

Where are you going?

Although you are politically opposed to giant cars and personally drive the smallest automobile in the country, you do appreciate one thing about Tina's Expedition during this particular high-speed rampage through the burbs: It is very easy to see. Even when some lesser cars intervene you can make her out, charging ahead to—

Well, to an office park somewhere in Troy, or Rochester, where Madonna was a baby-sitter many years ago.

She lets you in the building with her pass card and you say, "What are we doing here?"

"Just a meeting."

So you follow her past new cubicles in a large open room space populated by engineering/computer types who look at her with a kind of horror. You suspect this is not because they actually know her but because they don't encounter women very often. There are certainly no women here. You are suddenly very thirsty.

She stops outside a corner office and tells a young guy with a satanic beard-scrub, "Tina's here for Kelly."

"She's inside."

And she is—Kelly van Dyne, the IT woman, the one you've heard so much about, there she is at last! It's always better that these people of mystery and myth are tiny, swallowed up by their big black power chairs. And so she is: a little bitty woman with glasses and a great big smile and short black hair and she stands up, looks right at you, and says, "Who are you?"

Her voice is funny, kind of high, like a cartoon character's.

"This is Marty," interposes Tina. "He's from [your top-tier firm]. He's helping me out."

"Oh."

Kelly sits and so do you and Tina. There is a moment. These two are not friends and not enemies. You kind of feel as though maybe they don't know each other very well.

"So," says Kelly. "You wanted to see me—"

"It's about Casanova," says Tina, to your surprise.

"Uh-huh."

"I wanted to—I think you know I'm having [your top-tier firm] take a look at it, just to get my arms around it."

"I had heard something."

"But I just wanted to—I wanted to let you know what we're up to and see if you had any input, like, from the top down. What we're trying to do is just from a program management point of view, we're trying to understand this thing—and what it's going to do for us, how we can . . . maybe help *shape* the program or get some *clarity* into our headsets about it."

"Let me ask you this," says Kelly, who strikes you as someone who is probably pretty blunt most of the time. "Are you just fact-finding or are you out to kill the project?"

"Well," says Tina, "just fact-finding. Right?"

"I'm asking questions," you say.

"That's fine," says Kelly van Dyne, unimpressed. "We're happy to have a dialogue. It's a really great idea. Maybe we should do a workshop or something. But I'll tell you, what I'm concerned about is—I'm concerned when I hear somebody's going around talking to the engineers and people on the design team, some consultant, and they're not—maybe they're not all as informed as they could be. There's a lot of misinformation out there about Casanova, and maybe we haven't done the best job communicating. But we've been in design mode and . . ."

And so on. Kelly stresses that your sources are unreliable and she would be happy to give you a list of names, which you take away with you, out into the parking lot, where you catch up to Tina, climbing up into her Expedition.

"What did you think of that meeting?" you ask her, genuinely curious.

She smiles at you. "I think she's an elf."

So you call some of the people on Kelly's list and you put together a short deck on Casanova. It is the middle of week three, and you're really beginning to settle in here. The guy in England seems tied up with English car parts problems, so he neglects you. Your client is obviously going places. You get your daily call from Jerry, who says, "I'm coming by in an hour, okay? We'll have lunch."

"How's the low-carb thing going?" Jerry was trying the Atkins diet, which was sweeping through the engineering building like a virus with no discernible effect at all.

"One hour," he says.

You go over to Tina's office but the door is closed. Tamara is reading her Bible, as she likes to do. "She's in there," she says.

"Can I go in?"

"Always."

So you go in. Maybe you should have knocked. Tina is gazing dreamily out the window in a most un-engineer-like way, and for the first and last time you startle her. But she recovers fast.

"What's up? You want a doughnut?"

"I'm trying to avoid the carbs."

"You don't need to do that. I tried Atkins, you know. Me and George [the company president] did it together. I lost like two pounds, but George gained weight. He gained five pounds!"

"I didn't think that was possible."

"It's possible. What's up?"

"I'm almost finished with the Casanova thing. I'll have it for you this afternoon."

"Okay, I'll put together a conference call. We'll get the pro-

gram management people on it. We'll have like a minisum-
mit. You can present."

This was kind of rare—a junior consultant presenting to a
senior client management team.

"Maybe you should do it? I could support you—"

"No way. It would look biased. Just—you can be objective.
Just present the findings to the team as your fact-finding and
that's that, okay?"

In truth, you don't like it and you don't really want to do
it.

At lunch you mention to Jerry that he looks a little skin-
nier. This is a statement that always brightens people's days in
the West, though apparently not in India. In Dearborn, Jerry
says, "You're just saying that."

"No, really. There's a difference."

"Thanks, man." You stop for a moment, probably both
thinking that if you're not careful you're going to end up as
friends or something crazy. It's a nice moment.

There's a TV on, as there always unfortunately is in
American corporate cafeterias, and it's tuned to the channel
where all the bad news is told. This is every channel at this
moment. Either the Supreme Court is sending poor people
to jail for life because they stole a videocassette or the A.G. is
holding people in secret locations for no reason or the whole
country is put into Orange Alert on a whim, to no effect, until
the alert is lifted and it's time to stage a fake "dirty bomb" attack on downtown Seattle. Mind control did not go out with
Mesmer.

"Five men of Middle Eastern descent are wanted today for
questioning by the Department of Homeland Security," says
the TV. "They were seen crossing the border from Canada in
a white van . . ."

You say, "Why does every bad person drive a white van?"

"What?"

"The sniper in DC, these Arab guys, even—what's his name?—Ted Bundy, they all drove a white van."

"The sniper had a station wagon."

"That's my point—everybody thinks they're driving white vans, even when they're not. What is it about that type of car that seems so scary?"

"You never know what's going on in a van."

"Good point."

"There's a lot of open spaces." He pauses. "So what's up with Casanova? How's that going?"

You mention to Jerry that you're just about done with the presentation, should be done later that day, which is a Wednesday.

"Have you showed it to Tina?"

"Not yet."

"If you want I can look over it for you, just for a second set of eyes."

"Okay."

"Just in case there's anything from the process point of view I can add."

"Okay."

"So you'll send it to me today?"

"Yeah."

"Coolio."

A couple hours later you finish up the presentation, and it's nine pages long, and you e-mail it to Jerry with the following note:

> Hi, Jerry—here's the Casanova presentation for Tina. she's going to present to her team in PM [program management, *ed.*] and figure out what to do from there. let me know what you think.

And then, around six or seven, not having much else in the hopper and a little on the tired side you leave for the hometel, which is a Ritz-Carlton. The service there, as you have said, is so good it makes you feel guilty. But it's cheaper than the Hyatt and, gosh, you deserve it, right?

And you sleep.

And you wake up.

And there you are, sitting in your cube, gently typing up another couple slides for the program management training analysis you're working on, when one of your [top-tier firm] colleagues from another building shows up, looking kind of pinched or panicked . . . and then everything slowly falls apart . . .

"Marty," he says, "John Jacobs is looking for you."

John Jacobs is the senior partner overseeing the team in the other building, and you have never even met him.

"Right."

"I'm dead serious. He said to me, 'Are you Marty?' and I said no, and he said, 'I wouldn't want to be him right now'?"

"What? Why?"

You honestly cannot think of a single reason why John Jacobs would have such a thought.

"I don't know, man. I should go"—and he leaves, like a cockroach scattering from a light.

And you wait.

You peer down the hall.

You continue to wait.

John Jacobs is looking for you?

Twenty-one minutes later John Jacobs appears, and his face is red.

"Are you Marty?"

"Uh-huh."

"Come with me."

He walks ahead of you down the corridor, past the drinking fountain and the vending machines. You are surprised to see he is quite young—early forties, maybe—and he wears flashy suspenders like an old-time rich guy. His hair is sandy and he's got a gut; a large kid turned into a big man. He says absolutely nothing.

Walking ahead.

It is now that you notice he is carrying something in his left hand, some papers. And suddenly you realize what this is all about.

He opens the door to a small conference room and holds it for you, nodding you in. There is a videoconferencing unit in the corner of the room and a speakerphone setup in the middle of the table, but both of these are unplugged with their wiring dangling. The door closes and you are alone together, sitting, breathing.

"Did you do this?"

He shows you the papers he is holding.

"Yes."

"What were you thinking?"

"What happened?"

"Answer my question."

This is to be a hostile interrogation.

"Tina asked me to do this. I talked to people and put together a report."

"You put together a report?"

"Yes."

"This one?"

"Yes."

"Who was supposed to see it?"

"I was going to give it to Tina today. Later today." You have no idea why—but you think about your little puppy, Hola; she wouldn't understand this, any of this, nor care at all.

"Then how did I get it?"

"I don't know."

He looks out the window of the conference room at the hallway and the plant, then he gets up and sits down again. He lets out some air, and shrinks.

"Think, Marty. Who did you show this to?"

"Jerry."

"Who's Jerry?"

"He's my main client team member. There's Tina, who's the main client, and she gave me a team—a couple of teams—and Jerry is the one I work with the most closely."

"You sent this to him?"

"Yes."

"Electronically?"

"Yes."

"Why'd you do that?"

"He wanted to—he . . . he asked to see it . . ."

"Is he an expert in this software?"

"Not really."

"So again—Marty, help me here, what's the point of sending an *electronic* copy to this guy? Because he *asked* to see it?"

Somehow your sending the document to Jerry seems like the lamest logic in the world, and you are ashamed. But it is vague shame, which you feel all the time anyway, like a permanently guilty man on the run from a crime so horrible you didn't even commit it.

"I'm sorry."

"Don't be sorry. I'm just having trouble understanding—it's . . . you don't have any idea what happened, do you? Do you?"

"No."

He gets up and sits down again. You wonder if he has hemorrhoids in his anal cavity.

"Kelly van Dyne got a hold of this document—and she was very angry. She sent it all around her team last night and they had an emergency meeting to figure out what was going on. So they pretty much decided we were out to derail this Casanova thing however we could—and she elevated it. She called the VP, who called George Venarchik *at home*." George Venarchik is the president the North American business. There are, as you have said, a few people in an organization with the power to say 'You know, I don't think we need these consultants anymore,' and the consultants disappear. George is equivalent to two or three of these people.

"So I get a message from Venarchik this morning," he continues, "asking me what the *hell* is going on."

"My God."

"Yeah. So I had to talk to him. I'm running around meeting with Kelly—I'm going over after to talk to her team—this is a train wreck, Marty, this is a *very bad situation*—do you get me?"

"My God."

"Kelly van Dyne championed this software. She got Venarchik to go along with it. It's a lot of the reason she got herself promoted. You didn't know any of that?"

"No."

"Jesus Christ."

He stops again and looks kind of sad. Angry people often have a melancholy timbre as their anger ebbs away; it can only be sustained in the young, and the very religious.

"Okay," he says, standing up again. "I need to get out of here."

"What can I do?" you ask hopelessly.

"Don't send out any more documents."

And he leaves the room.

Your nine pages assessing Casanova were not very laudatory. You pointed out that while Casanova was supposed to be able to reduce resources working on nonapproved projects, redeploy them to productive channels, assign people at the beginning of a project, and provide tools for continuity of effort, significant questions remained. For instance, would it be configured to provide the promised functionality, especially since it was to be only partially enabled? What kind of additional burden would the software place on team members in terms of data entry? You pointed out that the software was supposed to adjust resource loads at the first sign of trouble, reduce the number of reports generated, maintain links to

process records, and cut down on performance variation—
but it wasn't clear, even to the people implementing the suite,
how it would define "trouble" or whether the built-in templates were the right ones. Also, it would generate more reports, not less.

You quoted actual people in your assessment. "Casanova
can't do financial tracking and program budgeting." "The re-
porting requirements look onerous." "The templates as they
are now are unusable." "It doesn't look much different from
MS Project." "Nobody knows what the 'Big Picture' looks
like."

In summary: "A persuasive 'business case' for Casanova
does not yet exist."

You are not productive that day. You don't even call your
wife, which is a sign you are taking this very hard.

Sometime in the afternoon you get a call from the guy in
England, who has a sweet voice, really, but has some awfully
bad news to deliver to you. There is something about the way
he says "Hi there, Marty" that fills you with a liquid dread.

"Hello."

After some words you don't later remember he says, "Do
you know they had a meeting about the Casanova situation
today?"

"Who did?"

"The senior team. Jacobs was there. They got Tina on the
phone and they hashed it out. Anyway, the point is—the out-
come is—they're going to have to roll you off the project."

A thousand doves fly out of a very tall tower.

"Okay," you say.

"They're going to need you to go back to New York."

"Okay."

"They need you to do that tonight."

"Oh."

You look at the stuff on your desk. There is a lot of pulp,

reams and reams of paper, mounds of documentation and white binders you have collected from the engineers.

"I'm sorry about this, Marty."

"All right."

You gather up your stuff and leave the building. You will never see Tina or Jerry again. They don't call you or send an e-mail, and you have no idea what ultimately happened with Casanova or the [Client] Company and at this point you don't truly care.

You don't lose your job, but for some reason your hitherto rapid ascent seems to have slowed. There are people around you who say, for a time, it has stopped.

You write this book.

A couple months later you read in the *Wall Street Journal* buried deep in some story about the problems in the U.S. car business how Kelly van Dyne has left the parts company for personal reasons and there is a surprise appointment for VP, a woman.

Her name is, of course, Tina.

Epilogue—or, "Is Consulting for Me?"

One Year Later . . .

I lied—I'm back.

To sum up: I did not lose my job. In fact, my firm reserved a special punishment for me, one more horrible than any I could have imagined as I flew home in tears from the car parts debacle and started to update my résumé. My performance appraisal was launched and the particulars of my conduct in the Midwest thrown up for scrutiny; John Jacobs himself was contacted, spoken to at length. I don't know what was said, but there was more than one occasion when—frustrated by the white-collar recession strangling New York, choking off my chances for escape—I actually (ashamed to say) picked up the phone to call Nosering and Cereal Boy to beg for my old job back.

But my wife stopped me. She tried to be cheerful: "At least," she said, "we don't have any kids."

As I braced for the inevitable "counsel out" and budgeted myself for six months' unemployment, something quite unexpected emerged from the appraisal room.

I was standing outside the door, behind which the partners were mulling me over, and I was waiting for the worst; John

Jacobs appeared at the door, looking gloomy. He shook his head when he saw me, and then came up.

"How you doing?" he asked.

"Okay."

He lifted his right arm and—in a moment of blind panic—I thought he was going to bitch-slap me. But he delivered two soft pats onto my back, *thumph thumph.*

"Congratulations," he said.

"For what?"

My wife and I celebrated my promotion to senior associate with a night out at Sizzler's. My dog was very happy, but she was always happy. Some time later, the phone rang in my new window-free office on a Friday morning and the firm's business school recruiting person said, "Marty, we need you for an event tonight."

"I don't do events."

"That's a problem—we need you to help out. It's a panel at Columbia, just uptown. It's called Is Consulting for Me?"

"I have a problem with events, Jennifer."

"It's on your development matrix. You have to do it or you'll get a ding. You need to Build the Institution more. Come on . . ."

"I'm going to the ballet."

"You're going to Columbia."

So I'm sitting in a large room at the top of the tallest building on the Columbia University campus in Morningside Heights, behind a long table decorated with three microphones, three water pitchers, and three empty notepads and pens. To my right is a partner from Chicago I have never seen before, who is wearing an overripe dark blue suit; to my left is a principal with a high-pitched voice and matching black luggage under his bloodshot eyes. All three of us could use a shave, and an amphetamine.

The room is thronged—packed—festooned with some two hundred eager young people in the business line, looking for work. The economy has turned around a bit, but not quite enough—not enough to wet the creeping dread within this room of future victims. Rumor is McKinsey has picked up its hiring for second-years, and Bain is adding Columbia to its target list. This is not good news for [my top-tier firm]. So recruiting Jennifer has scheduled a series of hard-sell sessions disguised as "forums"—sessions such as this one, tonight, called Is Consulting for Me?

The format is question-and-answer. The three of us represent status (partner), experience (principal), and the real world (me). In the prebrief Jennifer said, "The message is upbeat. The firm is expanding again."

"What if they ask about the layoffs?" I mentioned.

"There weren't any layoffs."

"Yes there were. They were massive."

"We had some bar raising in the regular appraisal process. That's the word, okay?"

I looked at the partner, but he couldn't meet my eyes.

The questions start with the usual softballs from the teacher's pet types—question such as "What's the most rewarding client you've worked for?" and "What's the most satisfying thing about being a management consultant?"

The partner is obligated to answer such questions, which he does with practiced aplomb. "I'd have to say the time I was called in to a major turnaround situation in Canada. . . . " "I think the satisfaction of seeing a client grow and deliver value because of some advice you've given. . . ."

Whatever. I'm in the middle of scanning the crowd, wondering (not for the first time) why so few good-looking people go to business school, when a reddish youngster right up front points directly at me and says, "I have a question for Martin."

"Okay."

"What is the biggest difference between your firm and McKinsey?"

Now, this question I cannot believe. It's like he has pried apart my personal laptop computer and read this "secret book project." How can he ask me such a thing?

But the silence grows, I look at him, he faces me, I look out the window at the lights of the beautiful brownstones on Riverside Drive none of us will ever own. I think. The partner seems about to jump in for me when I say—

"McKinsey is an awesome place. They have a reputation for doing the best work and delivering great client value. Not everything they've done is perfect—but not everything we've done is perfect. That's not what consulting is about. I'd say the biggest difference between us is our mix of clients and the people we have on board. Every firm has a different culture. Get to know some of us, get to know the guys at McKinsey—see who you're comfortable with. Either choice is great. We're not that different, really."

Then I stop. I literally cannot believe what just came out of my mouth—but what was I supposed to say, really? What I actually think?

Later, a woman standing near the door, still wearing a long winter coat, waves a white mitten at me and says, "Do you like being a consultant?"

It's getting later—people are ready to hit the drinks table and schmingle. And the question doesn't seem all that serious to her, more like a good-bye gesture to fill a silence. But what a question. *Do you like being a consultant?*

Do I?

I say, "It's great. There no better way to get to know a range of companies, really see them from the inside. You get exposure to a variety of problems and—a—a variety of business realities you'd never get to see if you worked in industry somewhere. Sure, there's some lifestyle issues; you won't be home all the time. But nothing's perfect, right? It's a great way to learn, spend time with a lot of smart people—put in practice all those things you're learning about here in business school."

"So you'd recommend it?" she persists.

"Of course. Of course I would."

After the Q-and-A, Jennifer seems pleased. "Great job," she tells the three of us.

"I need a drink," says the partner.

"You read my mind," I say.

We are besieged by office seekers, and I can't half believe what I hear myself saying to them ("You really get used to the travel—it's not so bad" "They weren't layoffs, just like raising the bar a little") . . . until, after a while, and a few Amstel Lights, it begins to sound almost natural.

Almost like the truth.

Appendix A

THE COMPLETE CONSULTANT'S DICTIONARY

*Words & Phrases You Need to Know to Talk Like a Top-Tier
Management Consultant*

Consulting Word/Phrase	*p.o.s.*	Definition / Used in a Sentence . . .
add value	*vi*	give the client more than you're getting; what consultants are supposed to do
admin	*n*	administrative assistant; exactly equivalent to, but much more acceptable than, "secretary"
advance	*n*	an invitation to return; usu. after a **pitch**, e.g., "We got an **advance** at the last **liaise**."
afterwork	*n*	work done after the original **engagement** ends, for an additional fee; the ultimate goal of all consulting, really
air cover	*n*	part-time expert; or small team to provide support for real action
architect	*vt*	outline; usu. followed by "the **deck**," as in, "Marty, why don't you go and architect the deck?"

Consulting Word/Phrase	*p.o.s.*	Definition / Used in a Sentence . . .
arms and legs	*n*	people with nothing better to do; similar to **capacity** or **resources**, but usu. of a lower rank, e.g., new associates or **summers**
at the end of the day	*adv*	in reality; not the literal end of the day, which doesn't happen in consulting; usu. prefatory to "I don't really care" or "It doesn't really matter"
baked-in	*adj*	included; used when a client asks a question you forgot to address; e.g., "Those projections are **baked in** to the stick figure on page four."
bake off	*n*	process whereby a sadistic client auditions a number of different top-tier consulting firms for the same **engagement**, only to hire none of them
bandwidth	*n*	attention; usu. used by partners, as in, "I don't have a lot of **bandwidth** for you today, I'm arguing with the decorators."
baseline	*vt*	describe or profile; get to know; e.g., "We need to **baseline** the current salesforce and profile calls."
beachage; beach time	*n*	time between **engagements**; usu. spent pretending to optimize your **knowledgeware**
benchmark	*vt*	compare

Consulting Word/Phrase	p.o.s.	Definition / Used in a Sentence ...
billability	*n*	amount of a consultant's work week that can be billed to a client, expressed as a percent; the ultimate measure of a consultant's worth
bio break	*n*	an extended **process check**, to allow for #2; usu. can only be called by partners over fifty
black factory	*n*	where consultants go when they're doing an open-ended "study" no one will ever read
blessed	*adj*	okayed by a partner
blow up	*vt*	revise heavily, e.g., "I'm going to **blow up** your last page, Marty."
blue sky	*vi*	brainstorm
bogey	*n*	goal
boil the ocean	*v phr*	what associates do when they are not **reinventing the wheel**
bottom line	*n*	profits, net income; never used by consultants, because it is too easy to understand
bounceback; fallback	*n*	**fallback** is the place you go when you're in trouble, to retrench and regroup; **bounceback** is what you try to do after that
brain dump	*n*	process of a person who actually knows something imparting information to a consultant

Consulting Word/Phrase	*p.o.s.*	Definition / Used in a Sentence . . .
bucket, bucketize	*vt*	category; categorize; an early step in the consulting process, right after the **brain dump**
burning platform	*n*	serious business problem; what you try to convince the client they have during a **pitch**
buy-in	*n*	agreement
cactus job	*n*	bad degrading perhaps dull assignment, esp. one beneath perceived **skillset**, e.g., "I've been **on the beach** so long I'm willing to do any **cactus job** they hand me."
cadence	*n*	regular meeting schedule, though with spiritual overtones, e.g., "I thought you and I had a kind of **cadence** on this problem, but I was wrong."
call down	*vt*	fire; or, in the best case, merely reduce to almost nothing; e.g., "The client woke up on Friday and decided to **call down** the team."
cap	*n*	capital
capacity	*n*	days **on the beach**, e.g., "I have **capacity** today"; something most consultants have but none ever admit to having
capital call	*n*	a requirement that partners give their own money to the firm, in times of trouble; usu. used by McKinsey, then denied

Consulting Word/Phrase	*p.o.s.*	Definition / Used in a Sentence . . .
change agent	*n*	consultant, rarely
chunk out	*vt*	do a rough draft
client education	*n*	coercion; applied to clients who are either too stupid and/or too smart to agree with your conclusions
client team	*n*	group of low-level client employees assigned either full- or part-time to impede your progress and fail to gather necessary data
cook	*vt*	finish, e.g., "Go **cook** that spreadsheet, Marty"; not to be confused with falsify, as in "Go cook the books, Marty," at least, not usually
core competency	*n*	thing you can do; *not* "core competence," which is actually grammatical; popularized by Hamel & Champy's *Reengineering the Corporation*
counsel out	*vt*	ax; terminate; fire
craft skills	*n*	the **toolkit** of **core competencies** specific to consulting; slow progress in developing one or more of these is the most common reason given for getting **counseled out**
critical path	*n*	things on a schedule or agenda that really *should* happen, as opposed to everything else

Consulting Word/Phrase	p.o.s.	Definition / Used in a Sentence . . .
crunch mode	n	takes place, e.g., night before **deliverable** is due, in an odoriferous conference room with Japanese food ordered in
data dump	n	same as a **brain dump**, only more numerical
deathmarch	n	an **engagement** that rarely ventures out of the **pain zone**
deck	n	PowerPoint presentation; from the old days when the presentations were on paper with gold edges, resembling a deck of cards
deliverable	n	the **deck**, basically; what you give the client, before the **invoice**
dentists	n	investors
disconnect	n	difference; thing you don't understand
dotted-line	vi	supposedly talks to; informal relationship, e.g., "He reports to maintenance, but he **dotted-lines** to marketing"
drill down	n	analysis, e.g., "This **drill down** is shoddy and putrid."
drill-down	vt	improve, e.g., "We've really got to **drill-down** this **drill down** down more."

Consulting Word/Phrase	*p.o.s.*	Definition / Used in a Sentence . . .
drive	*vt*	make happen
driver	*n*	something that makes something happen
ecosystem	*n*	market; similar to **environmentals**, but not so mysterious
end state vision	*n*	many **bogeys** put together into a **grand unifying theory**
engage	*vt*	talk to, e.g., "Should we **engage** the principal on this **deck**—or just take a **process check**?"
engagement	*n*	project to which you and your **pod** are assigned
environmentals	*n*	things you can't control, like market forces, e.g., "We're afraid **environmentals** might **drive top-line** growth **going forward**."
exposed	*adj*	in trouble, e.g., "If we don't get on a **deathmarch** right away we're gonna be really **exposed** on that Tuesday deliverable."
exposure	*n*	problem; implied it's a potential problem, but it's actual, e.g., "We have **exposure** on that point in the meeting tomorrow." (We're wrong.)
fallback	*n*	*see* **bounceback**

Consulting Word/Phrase	*p.o.s.*	Definition / Used in a Sentence ...
farmer's math	*n*	flawed, quick, in-the-ballpark calculation; usu. accepted as the answer because it is done in public by a partner
feet on the street	*n*	salespeople
FHA	*adj*	made up; comes from, "from Henry's ass," although Henry remains unidentified
five-forty	*n*	changing your mind, changing it back, then changing it again; a combination of doing a **three-sixty** and a **one-eighty**
flavor	*n*	industry, business, example, e.g., "This section is about the pharma sub, but let's make the next one a different **flavor**."
flex	*adj*	flexibility, e.g., "This new software should give you added **flex** in your model."
food fight	*n*	competition, usu. in unclear or transitional markets, e.g., "There's a **food fight** going on the wireless **space** right now."
forcing function	*n*	"This deadline will be a **forcing function** to get him to make up his mind" or "What is their **forcing function** to get them out of this funk?"

Consulting Word/Phrase	*p.o.s.*	Definition / Used in a Sentence ...
game over	*n*	a disaster; usu. applied in the negative, e.g., "It's not **game over** if Marty can't be in the meeting."
gap; gap analysis	*n*	what's missing; trying to find what's missing
going forward	*adv*	in the future
grand unifying theory; GUT	*n*	explanation, e.g., "In a couple weeks we should be able to come up with a **GUT** to explain all these crazy numbers"; from the world of physics, where a **GUT** would theoretically unite gravity, relativity, and quantum mechanics
granularity	*n*	detail, always expressed as a deficit, e.g., "We really need a lot more **granularity** in this **drill down**."
grow	*vt*	increase
hard stop	*n*	time you have to leave for the airport, usu., e.g., "We'd love to answer that question, but Marty has a **hard stop** at three thirty-five."
head end in the sky	*adj*	dreaming; dreamy
hockeystick	*vi*	shoot up really, really fast, e.g., "After the IPO, the stock price really **hockeysticked**." (ca. 1999)
hypothesis	*n*	guess

Consulting Word/Phrase	*p.o.s.*	Definition / Used in a Sentence . . .
incentivize	*vt*	ungrammatical verbalization of the noun **incentive**, as in, to inspire
incrementals; incremental change	*n*	really small changes, over and above baseline trend; incremental change is the opposite of **step change**, which is impossible
invoice	*vt*	bill, always followed by "the client," e.g., "I can't wait till we **invoice** the client."
iterate	*vt*	read; edit, e.g., "Let's **iterate** before you go off and do something crazy."
journeyline	*n*	history, story, e.g., "This résumé has quite a bizarre **journeyline**, Marty."
knock-on	*adj*	additional, e.g., "This reorg is going to have major **knock-on** effects in our ability to sell **afterwork**."
knowledgeware	*n*	ideas, usu. derived from reading *Business Week* or Google News
la-la land	*n*	**la-la mode** that extends beyond six hours . . . to a few months
la-la mode	*n*	state of doing nothing, usually waiting for a **data dump** from the client
learning curve	*n*	process of accumulating information
learnings	*n*	what you get when you study something

Consulting Word/Phrase	*p.o.s.*	Definition / Used in a Sentence . . .
liaise	*vt, n*	meet, meeting; can be used as verb or noun, e.g., "Get Dave on the phone—we've got to **liaise** about the **liaise**."
low-hanging fruit	*n*	simple problems; stuff the client should be smart enough to fix for themselves, but aren't
mag-a-logue	*n*	catalog that is thick, like magazines used to be
moral equivalent	*n*	different business but an analogous idea from partner's one job she can remember
net net	*adv*	equivalent to **at the end of the day**, but easier to say
new alums	*n*	recently fired employees
noodle around	*vi*	think; mull over
off-line	*adj*	never, used during client meetings, e.g., "That's a good idea, Marty, can we talk about it **off-line**?"; equivalent to *shut up*
off the reservation	*adj*	doing creative thinking, not in agreement, usu. applied to clients
on board	*adj*	in agreement; never "get on board"; in consultants' nonconfrontational style, "I'm **on board** with that."
one-eighty	*n*	a total change of heart

Consulting Word/Phrase	p.o.s.	Definition / Used in a Sentence . . .
on receive	*adj*	listening without talking; a safer position for a consultant to be in than **on send**
on send	*adj*	talking without listening; dangerous, unless you are the **air cover**
on the beach	*adj*	not currently able to bill one's time to a client; too much time spent here will turn one into a **new alum**
open the kimono/tent	*vi*	reveal something, e.g., the strategy or the ideas
optics	*n*	how something looks; esp. related to consultants in client workspace trying not to look like they're costing/wasting money by e.g., sitting in a large group at lunch
outside the box	*adj*	used to mean "creative"; currently a cliché meaning "I don't have anything to say right now."
owner	*n*	worker; person responsible for doing a portion of the **work stream**
pain zone	*n*	the product of (a) the number of partners involved in an **engagement** and (b) the inverse of the time until the first **deliverable**
parachutage	*n*	the arrival of a partner into an **engagement** the night before a **deliverable** is due; inevitably **game over** for the **pod** as it proceeds to **deathmarch** into the **pain zone**

Consulting Word/Phrase	p.o.s.	Definition / Used in a Sentence . . .
ping	*vt*	call someone and ask her something
PIOUTA ("pee-yáh-tuh")	*adj*	acronym for "pulled it out of thin air," e.g., "Tomorrow's presentation is gonna be strictly a **PIOUTA** strategy."
pitch	*n*	a desperate plea for work; your turn in the **bake off**
pod	*n*	work team
populate	*vt*	fill up; usu. used with "binder," as in "Don't bother me right now, I'm populating my binder."
positioning	*n*	selling part; to analyst community, to dealership network
pro-act	*vi*	opposite of react, e.g., "We need to **pro-act** to changes in the **environmentals**."
process check	*n*	coffee break, urinary break, or both; not appropriate for defecation
puke/throw up on	*vt*	react negatively, e.g., "Marianne really **threw up on** your deck at the **pulse check** yesterday."
pulse check	*n*	update for client; also a six-month internal firm appraisal after which many associates become **new alums**

Consulting Word/Phrase	*p.o.s.*	Definition / Used in a Sentence . . .
pushback	*n*	a retort, but much more genteel
put a stake in the ground	*vi*	make a statement; actually write down, or say, a **hypothesis**
put up a chinning bar	*vi*	state a **hypothesis** you know is probably wrong; what you do to build up strength before you are ready to **put a stake in the ground**
reach for	*vt*	call or e-mail; usu. in the future tense, as something that will never occur, e.g., "I'll **reach for** you when I'm further up the **learning curve**."
red-face test	*n*	somebody challenges you about something to see if you at least have enough of a clue to talk about it knowledgeably; esp. when applied to an "idea" you've spouted somewhere or a pet project—when challenged, can you defend it?
red light/ green light	*n*	document listing steps in a process, each step accompanied by a green, yellow, or red light; the significance of the lights is unknown
reinvent the wheel	*v phr*	*see* **boil the ocean**
resource	*n*	employee, in the sense of being a commodity
rev	*n*	rewrite, editing revolution, e.g., "Let's get this in tonight so we can get going tomorrow on the next **rev**."

Consulting Word/Phrase	p.o.s.	Definition / Used in a Sentence . . .
robustify; robust	vt	complicated and good-looking, e.g., "This model is **robust** [we can't figure it out but we don't get an error message]"; "We need to **robustify** this graph—it looks like we made it up."
rolling off	vi	leaving an **engagement**, probably to go **on the beach** and then get **counseled out** due to low **billability**
sanity check	n	final look over asking if something makes sense; never changes anything; otherwise known as "common sense"
sat	n	satisfaction
scribe	vi	to take notes; an honor reserved for first-year consultants and summer associates with whom the partner does not want to speak
showstopper	n	very bad thing
skillset	n	abilities and talents; those things that allow you to **add value** with your **tool kit**
socialize	vt	strong-arm, e.g., "I have to **socialize** the client into buying this point of view."
solution	n	product
so what?	n	purpose; every page of the **deck** is supposed to have a **so what?**

Consulting Word/Phrase	*p.o.s.*	Definition / Used in a Sentence ...
space	*n*	business
spike	*n*	special talent, e.g., "We can't hire you here at McKinsey, Marty, you don't have a **spike**."
sporty	*adj*	optimistic, e.g., "twenty-five percent CAGR in the dried milk sector seems really **sporty** to me."
stakeholder	*n*	someone who actually cares about the outcome of the **engagement**, as opposed to the client, who may not
step change	*n*	really big change
straw man	*n*	very rough idea no one really believes in, often not improved upon and presented to the client as final conclusion
stretch target	*n*	difficult-to-achieve goal; usu. a function of low expectations
strong-form	*adj*	possibly true; usu. followed by **hypothesis**, e.g., "Marty needs to learn how to develop **strong-form hypotheses**, or he's going to get **counseled out**."
stuckee	*n*	one who gets stuck with some hideous task no one else wants to do; usu. **client team** member
sub	*n*	subsidiary

Consulting Word/Phrase	*p.o.s.*	Definition / Used in a Sentence . . .
suboptimal	*adj*	loathsome
summer	*n*	intern, e.g., "We have too many **summers** on the team."
swag	*n*	a **wag**, only a smart one
take-aways	*n*	memories; similar to **learnings**, only without any real information
target-rich environment	*n*	an **ecosystem** where there is plenty of **low-hanging fruit**
task	*vt*	assign; usu. followed by "the associate," e.g., "Let's **task** the associate with getting all the ice off our windshields tonight."
thought leader	*n*	a person who is supposed to know something, as opposed to a consultant
thoughtware	*n*	same as **knowledgeware**, only doesn't require reading
three-sixty	*n*	total change of heart (*see* **one-eighty**), followed in short order by a total change of heart back to original position; **net net**, you end up where you started
tool kit	*n*	some combination of knowledge and abilities

Consulting Word/Phrase	p.o.s.	Definition / Used in a Sentence . . .
top-line	vt, n	sales; the money coming into the company, as opposed to the better-known **bottom line**, which is what is left after the company has paid for its consulting services
true north	n	soul, or essence; a term invented by Bain & Co., and understood only by them
turn off the lights	–	close down a project after it's **called down**, e.g., "Jim is going to **turn off the lights** at Lucent."
visibility	n	information, e.g., "I don't really have **visibility** into the financials right now."
visioning	n	scenario building
wag	n	a *w*ild-*a*ssed *g*uess
warm fuzzy	n	true; used like the phrase "good feeling"; doesn't happen very often; used in futuristic, skeptical sense, e.g., "If we can get these numbers to add up, this page will be a **warm fuzzy**."
warm handoff	n	delegation, usu. to client, e.g., "Marty is going to do a warm handoff of all his doodles and stick figures to Marina."
we	n	them, i.e., the client; consultants always refer to the client as "we," presumably to maintain the illusion that they care

Consulting Word/Phrase	*p.o.s.*	Definition / Used in a Sentence . . .
wordsmith	*vt*	make minor edits, e.g., "We need a little **wordsmith** action on this **deck** now."
work streams	*n*	discreet task groups that make up the overall **engagement**; each **work stream** may have two to five people assigned to it
worry bead	*n*	concern, e.g., "That upcoming seat launch is my **worry bead** right now."
write down	*n*	forgiveness of debt; what happens after someone like the Rainmaker sells a $4 million job to a Hollywood character who decides to spend the money on a boat instead

Acknowledgments[72]

The author would like most gratefully to acknowledge the invaluable contributions of the one person who made this book possible: himself. Nobody really believed he would finish it, and certainly nobody believed it would be published. Many people told him he would never get an agent, that there was no market for a book like this, and that he was much too old to dream. They also told him he would never be able to afford an apartment in Manhattan, and they were right. So at times, he found himself in a state of doubt brought on by the negativity of the pissants around him, but he decided to reject the nay-saying and cynicism of his so-called friends and family and press on. Other people are extremely selfish and probably won't read this far, but the author knows whom he has to thank for this effort and he does so now as he lovingly dedicates this book, in its entirety,

To Marty

---

[72]These acknowledgments, while true to their time of writing—when the author was an aging hack with nothing but a pipeful of dreams and a mailbox stuffed with despair—are no longer real: To Marty's surprise, he was rescued from the slush pits by the great Dan Lazar at Writers House; taken on out of more than just pity by Dan's brilliant boss, Simon Lipskar; noticed by the perceptive Dan Ambrosio at Warner Books; championed by the monumental Rick Wolff; and shepherded to the finish line by the eventful Ivan Held, also at Warner. Additionally, his friend Jim Meddick, his long-suffering parents, Ron and Patty, and his delightful wife and companion, respectively, Julia, and Hola the Baby Bernese, deserve love and gratitude.